ROAD
SCHOOL

by
Jim Marousis
Janet DeMars
Kaitlin DeMars Marousis
Jordin DeMars Marousis

ROAD SCHOOL
Published by:

BLUE BIRD PUBLISHING
1739 East Broadway #306
Tempe AZ 85282
(602) 968-4088, (602) 831-6063
FAX (602) 831-1829

© **1995 by Jim Marousis & Janet DeMars**

ISBN 0-933025-36-X $11.95

Cover art by Dave Huebner

Library of Congress Cataloging in Publication Data

Road school / by Jim Marousis ... [et al ...]
        p.   cm.
    ISBN 0-933025-36-X
    1. Home schooling - - United States. 2. Automobile travel - -
United States.   I. Marousis, Jim, 1948-
LC40-R63   1995
649'.68- -dc20   95-11770
                                                     CIP

Dedication

This book is dedicated
to those people who
provided us many days of rest and
shelter during travels:

Marge DeMars (Grandma)
Andy and Laurie Flambouras
Gay Medina
Mel, Jeff and Travis Strub
Larry, Mary, Brianna, Bethany, and Paul Williams

CONTENTS

Photo: Wayne Schmidt

The Road School Family
From left to right: Kaitlin (& Lion), Janet, Jordin (& Sidewalk), Jim

INTRODUCTION

We are embarking upon a journey that we feel well qualified to undertake: we have an aggregate of 21 years of teaching that spans the public to private school spectrum, rural to urban, and the Midwest to Alaska. We have travelled extensively as individuals and as a family, including Europe, Canada, and 35 of our 50 states. But most of all, we have a continual, nagging adventuresome spirit...

But before we share our journey with you, we'll give you a bit of history...

In August of 1991, we moved to Alaska, from Wisconsin, for two reasons. The first was pure adventure. We had travelled Alaska during the summers of 1987 and 1989 and enjoyed the scenery and the attitudes of the people we met. There was the "Last Frontier" mystique as well, and we wanted to experience that firsthand. Secondly, we felt that the school district wherein Jim taught and the girls attended was a stagnant pool, with little hope of any significant sparks of learning. Our girls were bright, achieving and happy there, but we wanted to show them the larger picture of life. We felt that a family adventure (by moving) would stretch us all as we grew and experienced new challenges with each others' support.

Following the job fair in Anchorage in April of 1991, which produced two job offers, we decided to move to Craig, Alaska. In August of that same year, we sold our house in Wisconsin, had a huge garage sale, packed a U-haul and hitched it to our pick-up truck, an extended cab, tied mattresses to the top of the trailer and coolers to the open tailgate (it was too full to shut), said our goodbyes to friends and family, and took the leap, landing 3,500 miles away on Prince of Wales Island in southeast Alaska, where we were in for a very wet fall and winter. October, November, and December brought an aggregate of 100" of rain, but we all adapted, adjusted, and adequately found ways to enjoy the drastic change in our lives.

The school system was full of energetic educators and ample advances in technology (our girls had 30 minutes of computer class, daily, on brand new Macintosh computers), but the social problems of the area permeated the classes. There were too many discipline problems that put teaching and learning on the back burner most days. Jim burned out, while the girls tired of their peers' social behaviors.

It soon became apparent to us that our quest for better education had not been satiated, and we started formulating "Plan Z" (the initial name for "Road School").

The wages in Alaska, especially for Janet, were substantially higher. So with these added wages and the profits of our summer-time ice cream/sub sandwich shop (called Sub Marina), we were able to save what we thought was enough money to sustain us through nine months of travel and road schooling. The desire to do this was kindled years ago when we first were parents, always looking for unique and rewarding experiences for our girls.

Planning began in earnest during January of 1993; financial goals were set, dreams of lands beyond were dreamt, and we began gathering school materials for our soon to be third and fifth grade daughters (Kaitlin 10 yrs., and Jordin 8 yrs.). In addition to travelling and road schooling our daughters, we had an additional agenda of looking for a place to "land" and call home after this year was done.

We opted out of the correspondence school that Alaska provided due to its rigidity and our unknown destinations. Instead, we chose to plan our own curriculum as our daughters would be the ages that Jim has taught for 10 of his 20 years' teaching.

Deciding on the status of our jobs has been difficult. Do we ask for a leave of absence or terminate employment, cutting our throats financially? Will we get hooked on this life and decide one year is not enough? Jim asked for and was granted a leave of absence from his teaching position. Janet did not, and will not ask for a leave, wanting the person who replaces her to be totally committed from the start.

As we begin looking at the maps, we are immediately cognizant of just how much of the U.S. there is to see and explore.

How will we be able to do it all? Rather, how will we be able to do and see enough so that satisfaction and contentment exists within us when we are through?

So with no home to sell, we gave our landlords notice that on September 16 we would be gone....for a long time, with no place that we can call home.

Okay campers, let's see as much as we can, keep an easy pace, stay warm, dry, happy, and try to make the money last.

HAPPY TRAILS!!

PREPARING FOR THE SOJOURN

July 14   **Craig, Alaska**

When I contemplate our travels for next year, I am either resting on the couch, lying in bed, sunning on our deck, listening to music, or sitting at the kitchen table. Numerous spots that are both comfortable and taken for granted. Where will we spend our evenings next year if not on a comfortable couch? How many comforts of home will we (can we) bring with us and how many am I willing to do without? Traveling sounds wonderful, but do the sacrifices? Are they sacrifices if the pleasures out-weigh the discomforts?

But, then, the reason I sat down to write was because of a book I perused on the National Parks of the U.S. They all sound intriguing and beautiful, and I realize that I can't see them all. Not that I didn't know that, but one can always hope. We will need to be selective as we set out and discerning as we travel.

Three out of four letters of inquiry we sent out for information on Mexico have been returned to us without reply. The book from which we acquired addresses was nine years old. (Remember, we are on an island in Alaska.) We have an inter-library system for the state, but it is a timely matter ordering a book from yonder. Imagine an inter-library book travelling the distance of a thousand miles or more. It would be like a Minnesotan requesting a book and having it sent from a Denver, Colorado library.

We have also had the inquiries from Oregon and Arizona returned to us. In fact, of all the letters we sent (10?), half have been returned without a forwarding address. (Maybe I need to order a more recent reference book from Denver?!) (Janet)

July 24

Point of view is everything. For months I've vaguely been aware of President Clinton's push to try to balance the budget. The details escaped me, but just this morning as I was listening to the news on public radio and cutting meat at the Sub Marina, they were talking about the proposed energy tax on gasoline. The Senate had passed a 4.3 cents per gallon tax and the House was pushing for 9 cents on the gallon. Someone in the Senate had been quoted as saying 9 cents would never fly. My ears perked up because gasoline is obviously a major component of our travel budget, but even at 9 cents, a 20-gallon fill-up would only cost $1.80 more. At what point will our country be willing to pick up the tab for our insatiable appetite for natural resources? (Jim)

July 26

Jim and I have the ability to amass various sums of money in relatively short periods of time, but, at present we are "off course" for our fall travels. With a family of four on the road for an entire school year, adequate finances are necessary if we do not want to work during that time. Our projected, and somewhat padded, budget totals $21,000. The biggest uncertainty of our expenses is the option of sleeping accommodations. Do we tent camp, with occasional stops in generic blue roof inns, or do we purchase a pop-up camper that would be pulled along behind? Obviously, these two items create a different total for the budget. Ideally, a used camper would be the route to go. We temporarily have a budget of $4,000 for the camper, if we need to buy a new one.

At present the food budget is possibly out of line because the inflated food prices here on the island distort my prediction for the price of a gallon of milk and anything else we will purchase at grocery stores across America and Mexico. We are paying $4.09 for a gallon of milk, while my Mom in Minnesota is paying $2.89. Bing cherries are $5.00 a pound, in Minnesota they are $1.49. I wonder, "What is the average price of a gallon of milk, a pound of bananas, a box of cereal, or a bottle of dish soap?" Real estate is a rare commodity here on Prince of Wales Island, but then I make it sound like food is also, don't I?

We were recently approved for an individual policy from Blue Cross, *starting on September 1. We had originally budgeted $3,600, but have come in $1,800 UNDER budget because of the meager coverage we have chosen. [Note: When I turn 40, it will increase from $150/month to $168/month.]*

My hands smell! I've been canning my first batch of King Salmon, which was caught by brother/friend, Dave Fisher. Being a native Midwesterner I'm used to green beans, corn and tomatoes. Salmon is a new experience.

This is the continuation of preparing our food cache for the coming travels. Jan and I have been plotting the growth of our savings, and it's going to be nip and tuck with our projected budget. Jan managed to cut $1,800 from our allotment for insurance. That's a major difference. Now the main areas are food and lodging. We're figuring on eating out once in a while, but our daily routine will include breakfast of granola, fruit, pancakes, or eggs, lunch of sandwiches, crackers and cheese, and dinner around a campfire. Keep the cost down and eat healthy, that's the plan.

July 29

Berries are meant to be picked in the rain, at least in southeast Alaska. I just got in from picking huckleberries in the rain for two hours and I'm happy as a clam. You start out dry, ducking the drops, but the berries won't let you get away that easily. Pretty soon you're noticing the weight of a wet jacket and the pull of wet jeans. You look at the berry bag and know that you don't have enough for a batch of jam so you hunker down and keep picking. Pretty soon you are wet to the bone. At this point you have to decide to head in or crash through "the wall." You start to notice how pretty the berries are when they're wet. It really brings out the colors.

And soon they'll be boiling in the pot and the smell of jam will be in the air. Aaaahhhh...!!

August 2

Projected income took a dive this weekend, as the partners (us included) of our sub shop decided to close two weeks earlier than planned. That not only means two weeks less of wages for us and our kids (we're organized as an S-Corp), but it also means a diminished chance of year-end profit. (But as Kaitlin says, as she stands here watching me type, "That means two more weeks of travel.") What first seemed like an attainable budget is beginning to appear impossible. As a last resort, Jim has retirement money in the State of Wisconsin that we will draw out if needed.

As we plan a two week earlier departure, other glitches present themselves. The State of Alaska does not distribute its dividends until the first of October. Originally, we thought we might still be here, but it appears we won't and will have $4,000 less in our pockets as we depart. (It's a psychological matter, not financial.)

Because of the flexibility of my job and the intense amount of hours required for the annual Natural Helpers retreat, I was planning to do two months worth of work in five weeks. With the retreat being one week earlier, I now need to condense two months into one. Will I receive two full paychecks as planned?

I'm now realizing that we will not have the $20,000 needed in our pockets when we leave here; some will trickle in after we are gone, and some may never have our name on it. Personally, the excitement of leaving early outweighs the disappointment of having a tighter budget. Jim and I both have the ability to earn money when needed, and if worse comes to worse, we'll have to work for a while somewhere.

August 6

Ooh, I've got the travelin' fever bad, doctor!!

Two days ago as I was cutting meat at the Sub Marina, writing dates on the bags as I packed the cut meat away, I realized that we're going to close in exactly one month! WOW! I had a real surge of energy that has lasted for two days now. I'm going down later this morning to get some empty boxes so that we can start packing, and I've been looking through our well-worn road atlas, dreaming and planning.

Our full insurance coverage from the school district runs out at the end of this month, so Jan, Kaitlin, Jordin, and I are getting our teeth checked and cleaned. I was in the chair yesterday and the hygenist said, "Boy, you guys are lucky. You won't have to worry about mail or paying bills or anything." Bills always need to be paid. It's just that we'll be on a cash basis for probably

> ## Ooh, I've got the travelin'
> ## fever bad, doctor!!

98% of our daily expenses. We'll be getting mail too, but probably once a month or less; we'll have Dave Fischer, pick up our mail, sort and toss, and then forward it on to us wherever we are.

We'll be moving outside of social forms and institutions that many people in our culture rely on for daily security and continuity. No job, no house payments or rent, no daily mail service. No roof over our head unless we put it there, no couch to flop on at the end of the day, no stereo, TV, or VCR. It will be interesting to see what effect this has on us.

August 7

We are in a beautiful area here on Prince of Wales Island. When we decided to implement Plan Z we said that a goal was to fully explore our environment here during the summer before we took off. Yesterday we hiked up One Duck Mountain; it's one of our favorite spots and the view at the top is majestic. We usually go as far as the shelter at the top, but yesterday we went a little farther and spent some time in the Alpine meadows. A beautiful sunny day.

Today Kaitlin and I started a hike at Crab Creek just outside of town, trying to get to the top of Sunnahae Mountain. We walked a long way but never reached our destination. The road led toward Klawock and then finally doubled back toward Craig, but by then the day had been long enough. It was a nice hike, though. Really nice.

If I had any doubts about the learning opportunities during the coming trip, they were taken care of today! During our walk Kaitlin and I covered many diverse topics. We started by comparing the geological differences between Wisconsin and Prince of Wales Island and how it affected water runoff during a rainstorm. During our lunch break we ate near a small quarry and talked about how the sedimentary rock had formed and had been lifted and twisted by subterranean forces. She understood that the top of the mountain

> **I was in the chair yesterday and the hygenist said, "Boy, you guys are lucky. You won't have to worry about mail or paying bills or anything."**

had actually been the bottom of the ocean. We talked about fossil formation.

Later we talked about how bees aid in pollination. We examined fireweed blossoms to show how the pistil and stamens help to form the seeds, then how the flower matures and dries out to produce a seed pod that splits and allows the silky seeds (very much like miniature milkweed) to spread on the wind.

The highlight of our academic exchanges was in the area of literature. We passed a small gurgling creek hidden in the bushes at the side of the road. She heard it and we stopped to investigate. She said wouldn't that be a great spot for the "Littles"? We talked for half an hour on that tangent: they had a home there under the mossy overhang of the bank, they kept their red rowboat beached on the pebbles by that big mossy rock, and they swam in the pool that was just out of the main current. On hot summer nights they could camp on that cool mossy pad by the swimming hole, and they could weave a swing from long grasses and swing from the overhanging log out into the stream. What a life!

August 14

Well, the education takes another turn! Two days ago we received some travel literature from the state of New Mexico. Whew—it's a lot higher than we thought. Nary a campground below 3,000 feet and average winter high temps in the upper 50's, with lows in the teens to low 30's. Not exactly what we had in mind. Talk about assumptions!

So now we're focusing more on Arizona, southern California or Mexico. A boater who had done a lot of sailing in the Sea of Cortez between mainland Mexico and Baja, came through Craig last week and said that January was beautiful in Baja because of all the wildflowers, which are fed, of course, by the rain. Well, we have no predetermined destination or timetable, so we'll play it by ear and head for the best port (in any storm?)

August 15

What do I think about Plan Z? I think it will be fun. I like the idea of having only two hours of school a day. I think the best thing will be being able to see Charles Barkley play along with Kevin Johnson. (Kaitlin)

I'm excited about PLAN Z a lot. I bet it will be fun. I bet we will hike a lot. My mom and dad are thinking about buying a trailer thingy. (Jordin)

August 16

As I work the window at the Sub Marina I'm always on the lookout for people who have traveled in the Southwest. Today a man came by who had traveled in Baja in January of 1983, and said they only made it halfway down the peninsula, but there was frost on the ground in the morning and the water was always "frigid." Yikes—are we going to have to go to Central America to get warm???

But, then, a little later a guy came in with a Southern Cal sweatshirt. I asked him, and seeming vague, he said the highs were in the 70's in the winter and only down into the 40's at night and very rarely ever froze. That sounds better. I can see myself coming out of the tent, a little stiff from the cold, my breath making little clouds of vapor, but the sun will warm me soon. And I will not be facing a full class of little'uns that day.

I started going through our "school materials" for next year, things that I had thrown together at the end of last year. Kaitlin and Jordin really got excited looking at some of the art projects and AIMS (science and math) activities. Vibrant, interested learners. I hope I still remember how to challenge and motivate kids like that. I hope, I hope...

August 17

Four weeks from last night we will be leaving Craig, embarking on a journey that has a vague itinerary, few limits, and no doubt, many unexpected surprises.

As the date of departure draws near, I look around our small space and feel overwhelmed by the enormity of our possessions. Yet, I know that all we have could fit in the back of our truck and a small trailer. As I begin to pack for the beginning, I wish I had fewer possessions, but know that I have fewer than most middle aged couples with two children. (But what good is that, other than selfish justification?) I don't know any friends who could fit into the living space to which we've become accustomed.

By the time we leave Seattle, we will be the proud owners of TWO storage units. Yes, we will be a bi-geographical, two-storage unit family— one unit in Baraboo, Wisconsin, and one in Seattle, Washington. The storage unit in Baraboo is oozing out the cracks with "stuff" we just needed to keep, but have now lived without for two full years. We will also have "stuff" at Eleanor and Steve's, my Mom's, Gay's, Dave's, and Nancy's.

August 18

Yes! Verification of warmth somewhere in the south! A lady from southern California came to the window today. Of course I took the opportunity to ask about winter temps and she assured me that it did not freeze. That's a start. I'm beginning to regain confidence that we can move around and see the areas that we want to see and still find some sun and warmth.

Dave and I were sitting on the porch tonight after work, coaxing life from a pile of charcoal and he commented that it would be interesting to see what we thought of Alaska after we traveled elsewhere. I've been thinking a lot about it lately, because I suspect we will only be back to visit or to work the Sub Marina. It's physically gorgeous, but the attitude of the people is the main thing that will stick in my mind. I think we share a feeling that we are all living on the edge, in a place that most people would not choose to live because of the climate and lack of amenities. There is an unspoken pride in that, and maybe just a tinge of arrogance. Also, things are done here if they need to be done, seldom for the sake of appearances. I am comfortable with

> **The vast majority of kids come into kindergarten with eager, inquisitive minds and a load of energy and curiosity. By the time they get to sixth grade, much of the joy of learning is gone. So what's wrong with education these days?**

those attitudes. It feels like me. But is this the place where I want my girls to go through puberty and dating??

I did an hour and a half worth of work on our curriculum this morning. I'm beginning to get excited. It will be fun learning together!

August 21

Today is windy and spitting rain. In a few weeks it will undoubtedly be like this most of the time. We dealt with the weather while we lived here, but it will be nice to be able to bid it adieu.

You know, a main driving force in both our move to Alaska and now our move into Plan Z is the quality of education that our girls are receiving. The vast majority of kids come into kindergarten with eager, inquisitive minds and a load of energy and curiosity. By the time they get to sixth grade, much of the joy of learning is gone. So what's wrong with education these days?

Some older people feel that what was good enough for them should work today, but there are some real differences in today's students that contribute to the failure of our educational system. I feel that TV is one main factor. Kids are used to being passively entertained in short (I mean SHORT!!) little sound bytes. By and large they're unwilling or unable to put in a sustained effort to learn or achieve. Work (not to mention the teacher!) must be "entertaining" or it doesn't fly.

The instability of families today is another major factor. Too many kids come to school still looking for nutrition, either of the stomach or the heart. Until they have that foundation, they will not (cannot) be willing learners.

The system itself must share much of the blame, however. Teaching styles and schedules are too often very inflexible. "Teach the moment,"

"Carpe Diem!" We ALL have to study fractions today from 9:00-9:40 and then verbs from 9:42-10:05. I'm a veteran teacher who has tried to do otherwise, but it is difficult, if not downright impossible, with schools set up as they are today. Daily classroom schedules are driven by gym, art, music, physical education, and band schedules. With a class of 25-30 or more it is difficult to have individual student interests and abilities drive your lesson plans, even for a few periods a week, much less the whole time.

When I taught in Wisconsin, we had a levelized reading program (Mary Jayne's brainchild!) that I felt really worked! We had the whole school, grades 1-6, scheduled for reading class at the same time. (The gym teacher was a flexible flier...) Then we had the students go to the room that matched their reading ability rather than their chronological age. Thus, in the fourth grade classroom you might have fourth graders working alongside advanced third graders or even second graders. (We never moved a student down in grade level because of social and psychological impact.) Every student was reading and working at the level that challenged them, instead of some struggling with new words and learning to hate reading, while others sat totally bored with work that they had mastered already. We also had a special class of 10-15 students that were "above" the sixth grade reading level. They did plays, creative writing, and explorations in literature. What fun for all, and the parents and kids loved it!

That will be one of my main interests during the coming year, to explore the questions...what is learning, what is teaching, and how can a school system be designed to keep it all alive?

August 23

Today we went to Ketchikan to have our braces adjusted. The dentist did not have to take Jordin's off but on mine they did. It hurt. And if Jordin does not stop sucking her thumb she will have to have a retainer put in. Bye! (Kaitlin)

August 30

The opening day of school in Craig, and for the first time in 17 years

> **That will be one of my main interests during the coming year, to explore the questions...what is learning, what is teaching, and how can a school system be designed to keep it all alive?**

I was walking to work going away from the local school. (At this time it definitely feels like the right thing.)

While I was walking to the Sub Marina this morning I heard voices coming through the trees. It was a second grade boy who had been in Jordin's class the last 2 years. We had had problems with him physically harassing her—pushing, kicking, tripping, even throwing wood chips and rocks. He and his mother were screaming at each other.

Then I met Lisa Yates and later Randy James, two really nice kids from my last class (my LAST class?), on their way to school with smiles and eager expectant faces. Thus continues the dichotomy of Craig, the Alaska variety.

Just a quick note in the "Ain't Life Funny?" department. Jan's job at COHO (Communities Organized for Health Options) might possibly be developing into a full time spot at $33 G's per annum. The salary on the teaching contract that I returned, unsigned, was about $42,000. With coaching, which I think we'd both enjoy, that would total around $80,000, plus paid insurance and summers off for both of us. The **velvet handcuffs**, as a friend used to say. Jan and I are in agreement that we are not enticed to stay. We'll see what light the future sheds on this crossroad.

As for the near future, Chaco, the largest prehistoric native settlement in the southwestern U.S., seems to be gathering energy in my mind. Gay Medina told us a story about spirits going bump in the night there, and a surveyor that came to Sub Marina told of working there when snowstorms raged everywhere around the area, but none in Chaco itself. Anasazi, the Ancient Ones. Am I ready?

Today all the kids go back to school but I don't! I feel so good. In the morning I felt like I had to go to school (Yuck). But we get to start school too. I bet it will be fun. I get to have my dad for a teacher (yes!) (Jordin)

I am glad that I don't have to go to school today. But now it is only 9:00 and I am bored out of my wits. Now I know why the teachers start school when they do. By the end of the summer the kids are bored and then they start school. I bet to Claire it was the worst day of her life. I say that because they took away the little toy and you cannot play tag on the big toy. And Claire is in the same classroom with the same teacher, Ms. Kathleen. I learned all of that from Conrad. Boy, just thinking about school gives me the creeps. I think PLAN Z will be much more fun. Mom and dad are good teachers. (Kaitlin)

August 31

Tomorrow is the first of September and we leave two weeks from last night. We'll sail through the night (we started our austere budget by not renting a stateroom), sleeping on the sundeck and then reach Prince Rupert two weeks from today.

Our packing is going well. Instead of renting a trailer as originally planned, we are leaving some things (kitchen table and chairs, music system, and 2 rocking chairs) at Gay's house and shipping some cardboard boxes on pallets down to Seattle. That should save a couple of hundred dollars.

Home schooling started yesterday. So far I'm flying by the seat of my pants, but it's going very well! The girls and I are excited about learning. This is the payoff for 19 years of teaching experience in different situations. Next week, after the Sub Marina closes down, I'll have a little more time to plan some units. That will give us a week of "home" schooling before we start "road" schooling. We'll start a science unit on classifying and studying animals, which will give us a real framework for exploring new kinds of wildlife in the different environments that we'll be travelling through.

September 1

Today was a little busier at the Sub Marina, but fishing season is winding down and so is our business. I'm getting anxious to close, finish packing, and hit the road south.

September 2

I can't believe that it is has been one month since I've sat here to type. Well, actually I CAN believe. Since that time, my job has started up again, my Mom came for a three week visit, and we've lost 50 hours of employee-time at the sub shop.

Ah yes, the sub shop. Our business increased this summer, but our profit is far under our expectations, and therefore, we are leaving on Plan Z with approximately $7,000 less than what we had anticipated. That's about 33% of the original budget. I've yet had the feeling that we shouldn't go, but I sure am not as excited as I would be if I had a pocket full of cash. But, we don't and we are leaving.

We've been living in the midst of boxes since my Mom arrived. Mothers always trigger hard work ethics, don't they? Once she arrived, the pace picked up, closets were emptied, the attic cleared out, bedding washed, and boxes were loaded and made ready for a year of storage.

Boxes....boxes....what goes to storage, what comes with us, what to sell, and what we give to P.O.W.E.R. (similar to the Salvation Army). I had all my cook books packed neatly away, legibly marked on both sides of the box, and put away under other boxes. Then, of course, I decided I needed a recipe while my Mom was here. Off come the top boxes, out comes the box, out come the mugs on top, and out comes the cookbook. The rearrangement of the boxes created pressure on another box which contained a "singing" teddy bear, batteries still intact, which began playing Christmas carols many months out of season at 3:00 a.m. I was awakened by the sounds of what appeared to be a singing computer, that electronic sound that grates on the nerves. It was quite soft, but woke me up, and prompted me, of course, to wake Jim up. He immediately rolled over to go back to sleep, deciding very quickly that it was not loud enough to keep him awake. Well, I was persistent enough to keep him awake, and both of us climbed out of bed and began the hunt for the singing teddy bear. I had heard its entire repertoire at least 20 times by the time we found it, the same few Christmas carols over and over again. Boxes...boxes...

I've been reading information on Baja California, and have decided that the climate and cost of living there are appropriate to our meager budget. I hope we find the delicate balance between being frugal and being leeches. I hope we are creative in our daily finances, and not always worried about money. I hope this is a challenge and not the start of a financial disaster. I hope for the best for me and my family, and hope that we are fulfilled when

Plan Z is something we read about in our journals and look at in our photo albums.

Happy Birthday, Mom!

September 3

I'm reading the latest issue of *Teacher* magazine, which came in the mail today. Although I'm pretty well "burned out" (I dislike that term: I should put some time into thinking of a more accurate and descriptive term for the frustration I feel at this point.), I find that I still enjoy reading and thinking about issues concerned with teaching, learning, and children.

Home schooling has been really refreshing for me this week. My children are challenging me to make this year's work interesting and flexible. Reality-based curriculum. I am feeling that I would like to continue my teaching career at the end of this year. Part of my trip will be to explore different possibilities as we travel. It is a noble profession.

We received some bills from our (Sub Marina's) food supplier today. More than we expected, which means that we will be even shorter than we thought when we leave town. Our original budget called for 20 G's, and we'll have about 12. It will test our ingenuity and stamina. I think that family togetherness will be a strong bond once we leave town and get on the road together. We are looking through tourist info and locating free or cheap campsites. We'll sell some dream catchers that we make, maybe play some music for barter, and do Reiki, a hands-on healing process that Jan learned in a workshop with Gay Medina and friends here in Craig. She has signed me up for a workshop in the Tacoma area as we travel through.

I feel that this trip on which we are about to embark is a once-in-a-lifetime experience. Money needs to be acknowledged and dealt with, but hopefully it will not be a drain.

September 4

Two lasts today...the last day of Sub Marina (closing tonight at 9:00, about three hours from now) and baking my last batch of granola. An oven will be hard to come by unless we're visiting friends or family.

Baking granola is such a part of the continuity of my life. We will be giving up old patterns and searching for new ones. This can be a real eye opener, a chance to examine and restructure (or reaffirm) parts of our lives. There will need to be lots of love and understanding to help smooth the rough spots.

I love these ladies that I'm about to gallop away with.

September 5

Yesterday at 3:00, as I was making a shake for a customer at the Sub Marina, I thought to myself, "I've been working too much lately!" But moments later I thought, "I have an hour to go before Whickers come to relieve us, and that is my last hour of work for eight or nine months!" What a strong thought!

Well, that was yesterday and this is today. The first day without a "real" job, but work to do nonetheless. It starts with the immediate and very concrete task of getting boxes ready to ship on a barge which leaves for Seattle in three days. Then comes the more subtle, but all important job of making $12,000 last as long as the $20,000 we had planned to have at this point in time.

Creativity and flexibility will be our main tools. We'll start by staying in a motel only once a week instead of every third night as we had budgeted. That should save $300 a month, at $50 per night. Any free camping we find will save us $10 on the budget. At this point I would like to explore the idea of one day of fasting each week. There would be a saving on the food bill, and with care I could reap physical and spiritual benefits as well. Museums often have one day a week with free or reduced admission. Matinees often cost less than evening performances. It's a job with immediate consequences.

One thing I learned about the girls' schooling is that I can keep the schedule I made up in case any "official" person wants to see it, but in reality the learning is a lot more fluid than Math from 8:00-8:30 solely. Kids are individual learners, even when there are only two in the class. Kaitlin could read most of the day, and although Jordin is reading more and more all the time (up to two hours at a stretch now), she would much rather be doing math, while Kaitlin would be satisfied to skip it altogether.

I wonder where and how the publicized difference in math

achievement between boys and girls happens?

I was loading boxes into the back of our pickup tonight and realized that I was looking forward to another change in life. I'm sure it's due in part to my teaching experience here which was pretty draining, but I think there's more to it than just that. The last time I saw John Holst before he left Craig for his new job in Sitka he said, "I just have to be repotted every now and then." I feel the same way. I get an energy charge from the change of seasons, a new house or job, and definitely from a stretch on the road. When we moved to Alaska I wrote letters to many of my friends, including the 19 year old son of a man I had taught with 12 years ago. The boy wrote back saying that he thought it was pretty neat that a person my age was "leading such a nomadic lifestyle." That gave me a pretty good chuckle.

> **He thought it was pretty neat that a person my age was "leading such a nomadic lifestyle."**

September 6

Labor Day. I moved most of the remainder of our shipping boxes out of the apartment and into the truck. The final layers of cleaning out the nest begin in earnest now. If the ferry schedule holds, we leave one week from tonight at 7:00. Jan is having trouble leaving her job and all the good friends she's made there, especially Gay Medina.

Time is an interesting concept. When I opened the Sub Marina each morning I would get up early and do about 15 minutes of stretching and yoga. It limbered me up and gave me a good start to the day. Now that the shop is closed for the season, I have been doing my yoga more slowly, paying more attention to my breathing. It has put me into another dimension. I'm sure it's taking no more than 4 or 5 extra minutes, but it has given my mind some peace.

Jan gave me a Reiki treatment on my back this morning and for the first 5 minutes it was hard for me to sit still that long. (Our lifestyle is so driven that it seems we must be doing something all the time.) I relaxed into it and really enjoyed it.

Time is an interesting concept.

September 10

Knee deep in boxes for the third time in two years. I'm at the point now of labelling a big box "Misc." and putting all the leftovers in it.

Three quick comments on school. Jan left at 7:00 this morning for her Natural Helpers' Workshop in Thorne Bay. Kaitlin was still sleeping, so I woke her up. She came out of her sleep kicking and contorting her face. As she came fully awake she looked at me and grinned sheepishly. She said she had been dreaming about going to school and thought that was why I was waking her.

I had to go to school to turn in a check, and I took the girls with me. All three of us felt a little like we were behind enemy lines, and were relieved to walk out the door.

In the grocery store I ran into Barb Douville. She said she was thinking about taking her kids out of public school and home schooling them. Raymond (third grade, Jordin's age) was so unhappy because he was doing the same math that he had done in kindergarten. Mass production necessitates a common denominator.

September 11

When we went up to the school, Tammy Demmert asked how the home schooling was. I told her that it was a great experience, and for some reason tossed in that it took us only about two hours a day to cover the material which left beach time for the girls on these last few nice days in Craig. She looked skeptical and Kaitlin picked up on it (this year we've seen her begin to cross the line into adult awareness) and later asked me if I really felt that we were covering the material that they would have gotten in regular schooling. I said yes, and the more I think about it, I'm sure that we are. If you take out the scheduled time for lunch, recesses, phys ed and music classes, and especially all the down time when some students (like both Jordin and Kaitlin) get done before the other kids, and of course the ever-present discipline time and lectures, it would be pretty amazing what the actual "on-task" time would be in a regular classroom. (And this is from a nineteen year veteran of teaching, folks. I know what I'm talking about here.) We have two hours with no interruptions and lots of individual attention. I feel confident that they will get an excellent education this year, with the added bonus of all the travel experiences.

The home schooling experience so far has revived an old interest of mine in starting my own school. I know I could do it and enjoy it while delivering a quality product. I'd keep the numbers low, do academics in the morning and some kind of community service project such as recycling or landscaping in the afternoon. I know how to make connections with people and marshall resources. I'll continue to explore this idea. What would it take financially? Should I teach a couple of years wherever we land after Plan Z to establish my reputation again and get to know the people and resources of both the public school and the community from that angle? Do I have the energy and interest to do this??

A few days ago I was talking to my dad and he asked a very common question. "What about next year when the girls re-enter public school?" (Assuming they will.) Our society is so tied into the "official" way of doing things. Very few people doubt that the girls will learn an immeasurable amount during the coming year, and anyone who knows them will acknowledge that they are at least a year ahead of grade level now in most areas. Still there's doubt about whether "the system" will readmit them. I told my dad that I was keeping track of our work daily on the computer, and that should satisfy any "officials." He said that's fine, but what about when you're travelling? I replied that we had gotten a carrying case for our computer and that we could pull it out at a campsite, plug it into a socket if electricity was available and type away at a picnic table in the middle of the woods. The image was too much. There was a moment of silence.

There are no preconceived boundaries. That as much as anything is what Plan Z is all about.

There will be some ups and downs in this trip. It will be a test to see how we handle them.

September 14

Have you seen the part of the movie where the fort is surrounded and the sweating guy is sitting at the wireless tapping out a message, hoping to get through before they cut the wires? Well, this is it. I'm sitting at the keyboard, typing out the last entry before we unplug the computer and hit the road.

We've spent much of the last two days at Gay's house, brief periods of relaxed company between semi-chaotic rushes of packing. Last night she gave us a brief lesson on speaking Spanish. This morning I got up at 5:45 and took Jan's and Jordin's bikes to POWER (Prince of Wales Emergency Resources), the local used goods store. I had a tender moment as I said goodbye to the little bike that could. Both of our girls learned to ride on that bike, one of the real milestones of childhood, and now they've outgrown it. It will have another life I'm sure.

I think we'll each take two more stabs at Tetris™, the new addictive game on the computer, and that will be the final standings for now on the scoreboard.

The girls have been content and happy the last few days. They're doing their schoolwork, singing Chuck Berry tunes, doing dialogue from the movie "Homeward Bound," and helping us get organized and packed.

Adios, amigos y amigas!!

Two Years In Alaska:

We moved from Wisconsin to Alaska in August of 1991. In 6 days we are leaving for Plan Z.

I have a cat named Tricker. He is black with a white spot on his chest. He is very nice!! Sometimes we play ball with him.

From 1993 to 1994 we are doing Plan Z. For the first month we are heading down the West Coast. I am very excited! Mom and Dad are schooling us. We are living in a tent.

After I am done with school today I am going on the beach. We play boats with driftwood. We also catch rockfish. It is fun!

Home is my favorite place. It is very peaceful. The people that live there are Mom (39), Dad (44), and Jordin (8). And......Buck the Truck (2).

Dave is my pretend Uncle. He asked Mom if she would be his sister. He works at the same place my mom does, C.O.H.O. He has two kids, Jenny (15) and Mike (14).

From 1993 to 1994 we are doing Plan Z. For the first month we are heading down the WestCoast. I am very excited! Mom and Dad are schooling us. We are living in a tent.

They are all nice.

Ms. Kathleen was my teacher for 4th grade. She is a good teacher. She is also my next door neighbor. She has three cats, Boots, Spinnaker, and Gray.

Claire is my best friend. She is mostly Eskimo. She lives out on Port St. Nicholas Road, a logging road. I gave her the nickname Penny. My nickname is Baggy. She has her own dog, named Cleo. She also has a little sister, Tracy. My other friends are Nan, Gay, Cale, and Sarah. They are all nice.

It's fun at the beach by Claire's house. We find multi-colored starfish, fish eggs, and crabs. Sometimes we have crab wrestling matches!

We also go shrimping with Jerry or Nola. The shrimp have golden eyes.

In the two years I have lived in Craig I had three other teachers besides Ms. Kathleen. Ms. Vik, Ms. Unruh, and Mrs. Griffith each had their own room and the rooms were connected. It was fun.

I was also in Gifted and Talented. For the first year I had Mrs. French and the second year I had Mrs. Barlow. Mrs. Barlow also taught pottery in the summer.

In school I went on some fun field trips. Recess kept me busy playing basketball. My science fair project on outer space was interesting.

Two means of transportation from Prince of Wales Island are float planes and the ferry. The float plane costs more, but the ferry goes slower. So it's a tradeoff. We are taking the ferry from Hollis to Prince Rupert to start our trip.

Three other places to go on the island are Sandy Beach, Sugar Point, and Ballpark Beach. I enjoy wading at all three. (Kaitlin)

I got to meet lots of people. We moved from Wisconsin to Craig in August of 1991. In a week we are leaving for PLAN Z!!!!!!!

I have a friend named Shona. She is a lot of fun to play with. I like to play with her because she has a kitten of her own. Darcie is a lot of fun too because she has a lot of fun. At her house we mostly play with Minnie her dog. I have another friend who has two dogs. Her name is Gay. We get to take care of her dogs for two days. Some other friends I have are Dave, Christina Hamilton, Nola, Terry, Jenny, Tricker, Mike, Cale, Sarah, Melanie, and Nan.

On Plan Z we get to camp in a tent. We get to travel in Bucky. We have to leave Tricker our cat. IT IS VERY SAD!!!!!!! He is very fun to play with. I love him!!

At home I love to dance. Kaitlin loves to read and draw. Mom loves the computer. Dad loves his guitar. I'm 8, Kaitlin is 10, Mom's 39, and Dad is 44. I love them all.

Upstairs Kaitlin and I like to play Barbies™. We like to set up house for them. We also like to play Playmobile™. We make them mountains for their home.

We went to a science fair at school. I made a volcano and Kaitlin made a universe model. Kaitlin and I both won first place.

Once I beat Freddy in a race at gym class. My legs were strong because I jumped waves for three hours straight and I got new shoes in L.A. I went to a pottery class in the summer. It was fun. I had a nice teacher. Her name was Mrs. French. She was fun and very nice!

Sometimes when Kaitlin and I go out on the beach we catch rock fish. It's fun. Sometimes we make a home for them. Sometimes there are rock fish on Sandy Beach too. We love that beach. I like to go hunting for starfish. I love to go wading too. (Jordin)

Photo: Dave Fischer

Boarding the M/V Aurora at Hollis, Alaska.
Leaving Prince of Wales Island.

PART I OF THE SOJOURN

September 15   **Port Hardy, British Columbia**

Well, we've started the trip in earnest now. Yesterday's entry on the computer was a brief moment of calm in the eye of a storm. We were supposed to eat dinner at Lenny and Judy Church's at 4:00, but after packing steadily all day (Kaitlin and Jordin did a great job, doing most of the actual packing in the truck as I carried things out of our apartment), we were still hauling stuff out as 4:00 came and went. In the end, there was one clear spot 2 1/2 feet long and 2 feet high right in the middle back of the truck. There was one big box to load, but it wouldn't fit, so I emptied it and just tossed stuff into the hole and shut the tail gate! Whew!! Packed (questionable!) and set to go! I had hoped to take my bike along, but it's wrapped in plastic and sitting silently under the porch of the apartment we have lived in for the past year.

A quick good bye to Nola and Jerry and off to Church's. Well, not exactly yet. Our neighbors, the Grahams and Peavys came running up, literally, as we were driving away to give us gifts, smiles, and waves. Mrs. Peavy's eyes got a little big as she saw the two bags of garbage, one at Jan's feet and one on her lap, that we were dropping off at COHO's dumpster so that our landlords wouldn't have to deal with it!

By now we were an hour late, had 15 minutes before we needed to leave for the ferry, and we're holding the still-frozen shrimp that was supposed to be the main course. When we arrived, Judy had dinner all ready to go. She had bought shrimp, so we gave her our frozen pack to put in her freezer. She and Daniel had picked huckleberries that day and there was delicious huckleberry cobbler and vanilla ice cream for dessert. Thank you, Judy. We piled the dishes in her sink and left with smiles, tears, and warm hugs.

Waiting at the ferry terminal in Hollis, with more goodbyes, were our dear friends Dave and Gay, family to be sure. There were some last minute gifts of magic and peaceful words of leave-taking tempered with promised reunion.

Now on to the Aurora, down the ramp leaving Prince of Wales Island, the first step on a LONG journey. Oh no, you mean we actually have to get the sleeping bags out of the back of the truck?! I'm afraid to open the back!

The lights came on at 6:45 a.m. as we were approaching Prince Rupert, British Columbia. Now we're gone from Alaska for probably eight months.

We wanted to check out the Canadian ferry system as an alternative to the beautiful but long drive through B.C. The terminal was right there so we drove over and found that a ferry departs in 20 minutes! We were number 17 on standby, but the next ferry didn't leave for 2 days, so we gave it a try. The lady behind the counter was very nice, as was the man who was at the head of the loading line for the B.C. ferry. We were the last ones on, and off we go, southward!!

As we opened the tail gate, the deck hand laughed and said, "Couldn't you fit any more in?" We spent 35 minutes tunneling like moles into the back of the truck from both the rear and the front (there's access from a window at the back of the cab section too), and now we have food available, clothes and towels for a shower, even a hairbrush (which was impossible to find yesterday after I took a last quick shower at our apartment), and most importantly the tent, as we are due to arrive at Port Hardy, Vancouver Island tonight at 10:30 p.m., hardly a time to be digging in the back of the truck.

Granola and bagels with cream cheese for breakfast, and we begin to feel somewhat human again. Being on the road and living out of the truck will take some getting used to, but we've done it before. I'm looking forward to it.

The Canadian ferry is very nice. Lots of windows and very light. It seems to be going much faster than the AK ferries and there's a bit more of a roll to it once in a while.

We've seen lots of Winnebagos and campers moving south like the migratory Canadian geese moving through Craig.

Times of transition in both the micro and macrocosm for us... Hopefully we'll use this chance to examine the cycles and rhythms and purpose of not only the education of our children, but the way we live our lives as well.

We went for a short walk around the ferry and, of course, visited the gift shop. Kaitlin wanted to buy a magazine. We talked about alternatives like visiting libraries as we travel. You can read the same articles for free. Living on a tight budget will be an art form before we're done.

September 16   **Miracle Beach Provincial Park**
                                      Port Hardy, British Columbia

The concept of time again—last night we got off the Canadian ferry around 11:30 p.m. The girls did a lot of the work setting up the tent and sleeping bags. Such a lot of growth in the two years since we moved to Alaska; the girls are much more self-sufficient and capable now. Jan and I joked that before the trip is over we'll get to a campsite and the girls will get the tent set up and a fire going while we play.

But this morning I was a 44 year old body waking up after sleeping on the ground. The passage of time...

We have done a lot of camping and I know my body will get used to sleeping in a bag. It felt good to wake up in the open and get a crackling fire going. I like this.

September 17   **Vancouver, British Columbia**

Leaving friends behind was a rather painful process. I kept asking myself why am I doing this again? I had just said good-bye two years ago to friends in Wisconsin. I know this trip is a rare opportunity, but then so are good friends.

As we rode the ferry, rocking and rolling, rhythmically back and forth across the water, each ripple and reflection passed like memories, passed like time and thoughts gone by of our time in Craig.

Leaving friends behind was a rather painful process. I kept asking myself why am I doing this again? I had just said good-bye two years ago to friends in Wisconsin. I know this trip is a rare opportunity, but then so are good friends.

Adjusting to life in the back of a pickup truck. Kaitlin is inside the truck, head first, looking for something. Hint: you can see her feet.

Craig was a great place for me, and a difficult place for Jim. The girls made good friends, but, even as we left, they were still appalled by the violence they saw.

I have many doubts about this trip and don't feel as if I'm 100% behind it yet. I'm here physically, but close to the surface are feelings of rage for being uprooted again, doubts about our finances and physical comfort, pain and sadness for the distance (emotional and geographical) I've put between me and my friends, the continual plague that I carry with me, always questioning my purpose, goals, and dreams of this life. Will the grass always be greener yonder? Will the PLANS always appear better than the REALITY? Is the REALITY worse than the MEMORIES?

Enough emotional reflection. How about the topic of Australia's mandatory voting law? They are on the opposite end of the spectrum of voter involvement. Do we want ignorant citizens mandated to vote, and fined if they don't? (The consequence imposed in Australia.) Would a law really create less ignorance or only better attendance at the polls?

How could/would we fine/find the many peoples that make up our U.S. population? The homeless, the transient, the poor, etc. Could we really impose that financial burden on them? Could the law be selective: those who have a home or a certain level of income per household are required to vote?

All these thoughts are grateful by-products of a conversation with Jerry, an 85-year old Australian woman from Brisbane whom I met on the British Columbia ferry from Prince Rupert to Port Hardy. She was widowed 12 years ago, and has few friends who like to travel. So, she goes on her own. She has no children, by fate, not by choice. She sees now in her golden years how valuable children would be, especially when her husband died. "They would have been a great comfort." (Not always true, Jerry, not always true.)

We talked about what it will be like for those who have chosen not to have children. She feels they will have lonesome times in the years ahead, by choice.

Showering on the B.C. ferries was a noble task. The small shower room was conveniently divided by, you guessed, the shower curtain. Appropriate. It appeared, then, that the girls and I could dress/undress on the "dry" side of the curtain while someone else showered on the "wet" side. Deceptive appearances beside, the designer put the drain on the "dry" side of the curtain. Imagine two girls, 1 adult, 6 pairs of socks (3 clean, 3 dirty), 6 pairs of underwear (yes, 3 and 3), one towel bar approximately 15" long, 4 square feet of space, no bench, an inadequate fan, no hooks, and a large drain on the dry side of the curtain. Dry is relative. I call it the dry side because it was the side without the shower head. The result? Wet clean clothes, wet dirty clothes, wet shoes, and to prevent further duress, we finished dressing out in the hall where ferry occupants traveled to and from their state rooms. One has got to do what one has got to do.

In Port Hardy we awoke to a wholesome family from Victoria. The father, a banker, the mother a disillusioned teacher, the two-year old a toddler, and the four-year old a social creature.

We talked at length about Canada's universal health care system and how it's being abused and the country's attempts to remedy the situation. One solution, possibly, is a flat fee ($10) for each visit to a medical facility, each time, to prevent people from excessive and unnecessary medical bills. Also of note was the fact that there was a monthly cost for health care!! (I was under the assumption that the citizens did not incur any expense.) The cost is approximately $70/month, half of which the employer pays. We are paying $168/month, but have to pay as much as $5,000 before our policy kicks in due to the high deductible and the 80% co-pay. Canadians receive immediate and full benefits for any medical treatment.

> **The basics of life
> are a warm sleeping bag
> and a quick fire in the morning.**

The basics of life are a warm sleeping bag and a quick fire in the morning. It has been cold the last two nights. We are definitely trying to stay ahead of frost as we head south.

The girls have not complained. They are doing well and adapting as we go. They help set up camp, wash dishes, and get the fire going. They are a little leery of paper matches, but we found some wooden matches in our "kitchen box" this morning, so they will build and start tonight's fire. A major part of this year's experience for them is to feel confident and self-reliant, good gifts to give a growing human bean.

This morning as we were walking down the campground road Kaitlin said, "I like being a kid. I'm carefree!" And she raised her arms to the trees.

As I looked around I thought of Kermit the Frog singing "It's not easy being green." The sunlight was filtering down through the pines and maples and there were at least ten different shades of green and gold. Made me think of a cathedral, and it's there every morning. It's just the kind of thing you could miss as you drive to work.

Addendum to the basics of life: a hot shower.

We are now ready to break camp and move on, at 12:00 noon. Yesterday's schooling didn't happen until 8:00 last night and there was frustration all around. We did two hours of school this morning, which was very productive. Jan helped with map skills and reading aloud while I worked with Kait on math and watched both girls do cursive writing. It was nice to have Jan involved. And then time for a hot shower, my first since leaving Craig. Clean hair makes for a clean brain.

Today we saw a slug. He was the same as slugs back in Craig because he made a slimy trail and he had a slick top. When we put a rock in front of him he went around it. He was different because he had a bumpy top and he was black! (Jordin)

September 18
Larabee State Park
Bellingham, Washington

As we were waiting for the Nanaimo-Tsawassan ferry, we saw a man speaking on his cellular phone in his car, waiting in line. Directly behind him was another man, also speaking on his cellular phone. Jordin, in her infinite, innocent childhood wisdom asked, "Are they talking to each other?" Looks are deceiving. Meanwhile the loudspeaker booms a voice saying the next ferry to load will be the 6:00 ferry to Tsawassan, scheduled to arrive at 6:10. Yes, prompt.

September 19
Deception Pass State Park
Anacortes, Washington

I'm losing track of the date, a good sign. Yesterday was a test and I believe we passed. Our truck needed some muffler work, so we pulled into a repair shop in Bellingham, WA. We originally wanted a muffler and wheel alignment. Then it began, the traveler's nightmare. "Well, we can't really align your wheels because the widgets on your steering column are shot, so the alignment would be a waste unless we replace those. They do a poor job with those at the factory, you know. That'll be another $45 and another hour of labor. And we see that you need a new tailpipe at about $35 and a new pinion seal at about $75 and another hour and a half." Yikes!! We had budgeted $400 for truck maintenance and it was all going to go at once! Well, five hours later we left the shop with a new seal, muffler and tailpipe and our same alignment. The people seemed friendly and honest and ended up charging us less than the quoted price on labor because we were there so long. Truckie drove away smoothly, ready to go and most importantly, our spirits were still upbeat.

Last night seemed warmer, but it's definitely chilly this morning. I'm glad we didn't leave two weeks later as we had originally planned.

The state park where we are staying is $10 per night with some walk-in sites for half that price. Two nights ago we stayed at a campground for $23

(Canadian) because it was late when we got off the ferry. We had budgeted $10/ night.

We were peacefully and snugly sleeping last night when a huge roaring, whooshing sound scared the bejeesus out of me. My first thoughts were either a foreign invasion or a UFO. It turned out to be a train going basically right through this state park campground. There were four trains in all between midnight and 6:00 a.m. Who in the heck plans these things? I'm glad they're not running our country (or are they?)

As we were driving down Vancouver Island, we came to the community of Courtenay, a nice looking town. We stopped, trying to catch a tour of a local paper mill, and talked to the young lady coordinating the tours. She was a local who was planning to move away shortly. Retirees were driving up the land prices and the schools were becoming more violent (guns and knives in the high school, she said) as the traditional community's roots and relationships were weakened by the surge of newcomers. This will be a main part of my investigation during this trip. Is the anger and violence that I encountered in my last teaching job indeed happening "everywhere" as some people there contended or are there some communities that are still able to hold together some values and the "small town" lifestyle? Is that a stereotype of the past? We'll see.

Is the anger and violence that I encountered in my last teaching job indeed happening "everywhere" as some people there contended or are there some communities that are still able to hold together some values and the "small town" lifestyle? Is that a stereotype of the past?

We'll see.

One of our worst camping fears has materialized—it's started raining. The truck had $200 worth of repairs yesterday; the money seems to be quickly diminishing, so do we get a motel for the night so we can stay dry? Our Reiki Training is not until Friday (five nights away). This weather could stay for weeks, seeing as this IS typical for NW Washington. Rain is the biggest disabler of many a camping trip.

We've recently made our first change to our unplanned trip: not going out to the San Juan Islands. Jim and the girls didn't want to go. I think I would have liked to. Do I need to be more assertive, even when I'm out voted? Sleep is a luxury that has not yet been afforded me. Each night brings new sounds that stimulate me and keep me alert to the early morning hours. The first night's sleep was on the floor of the ferry, the second night in a quiet, dark campground in Port Hardy where the only sounds were nocturnal animals and early birds rising and chirping their tunes for all to hear. The next night we froze in Campbell River, followed by a campground right near (on?!) one of Vancouver's freeways. Last night, the black quiet night exploded with the sounds of five trains that roared through just 40 yards from our tent. (Jim didn't hear the first one; when the second one came through, I was prepared, Jim wasn't—I thought he was going to climb right through the tent.)

The first part of this trip seems to be spent "getting there." We are packed like sardines with, it appears, too much stuff, and not enough of it will be dropped off in Seattle at the storage unit. So, the question arises, will we be trimmed down enough to have reasonable, easy access to everything in the back of the truck? Getting to the shoe bag took 10 minutes. The bag with the hats and mittens (yes, we need them) has not had the feel of human hands since it was packed six days ago. Where is it?

Nine months of travelling, five days gone, and we haven't started yet; we're still getting trimmed down, and yet have spent a sizeable portion of our budget. I'm ready for the desert and remoteness. I'm ready to take off a few layers of clothing. Right now I'm wearing a turtle neck, wool sweater, warm-up jacket, and my winter coat. I'd like to thaw out and feel the warmth of the sun against my skin, all my skin.

September 20

No train, just rain. Yesterday was our first real rainy day. It was OK as we broke camp in the morning, so the tent and sleeping bags were dry, but then it rained on and off from 10:00 a.m. through 4:00 p.m. We debated back and forth about a motel and finally decided to buy a tarp and see what happened. We bought a 20' by 16' tarp for $31. Then we went to Deception Pass State Park, traversing a huge bridge. The rain let up briefly and the tarp proved to be bigger than I had envisioned. We got our tent, the picnic table and the kids' tent (for playing, not sleeping) all set up under the tarp during the late afternoon and then went down the road to got some firewood. Three dollars for ten chunks of dry wood, so we had a fire last night and this morning as well. The weather is pushing us, but so far we are holding our own as far as our spirits. We're looking forward to hot, dry weather. Will we find it?

Plans for today call for a visit to the beach, hot showers, a visit into town to mail a box to Marge, do laundry, and then some quiet time at camp.

Discomfort is relative. Two days ago while we were getting the muffler fixed, we saw a woman with two boys, about ten and twelve years old, holding up a sign that said, "Will work for food."

September 21   **Fort Worden State Park**
                                      Port Townsend, Washington

The girls are doing a lot of exploring: going farther down the beach, climbing rock faces that stretch their abilities, going to the campground bathroom by themselves (I know that doesn't sound like a biggie, but trust me, it is), and talking of sleeping by themselves in the kids' tent. These are all exercises in inner growth that will probably come faster on this trip than during a year at home. They are untold riches for these girls as young adults...

We really liked Whidby Island, especially Oak Harbor. Horse and farm country in close proximity to the ocean. I overheard a woman talking in the dentist's office (Jord's W-arch needed repairing). She was teaching half days, so I went over and talked with her. She said the pay was decent and so were the students, depending on which of six elementary schools you worked in, and that Oak Harbor was a good place to live. People here seem friendly and there's a feeling of living in a place with some energy, but not quite so "on or over the edge."

Then we took the ferry to Port Townsend, a very laid back town that reminded us of Madison, Wisconsin. It seemed like the best possibility so far for a future home. We toured the P.T. Shipwright's Co-op with Bruce Solem, Jan's sailing buddy, and got the lowdown from him. He liked the area and especially recommended the school system in Chimacum. A lady with the Wooden Boat Foundation had spoken highly of Chimacum schools also. Interesting. Perhaps worth a return trip in the spring.

The girls are doing well with home schooling. We're slowly getting into new ground in math while really emphasizing reading and writing, both grammar and creative writing. We started building our Spanish vocabulary today while walking around the docks in Port Townsend. Such a rich learning environment, and campfires at night.

> **Such a rich learning environment,
> and campfires at night.**

Camping in cold weather is not bad when you have a place to go home to for warmth. We are not afforded that luxury, seeing as we have no home. So far it appears as if we are surviving, not living. The days are getting shorter and are busy with school, chores, and travelling. Nights around the campfire are dark, damp, and cold unless we place ourselves within "burn distance" from the fire. What's that I smell? Oh, tennis shoe sole, well-done and re-shaped.

This morning was a mad scramble to stay warm with bare hands and winter coats while we were taking down damp tents. I don't know the exact temperatures these mornings, but we're guessing in the 30's. Tolerable.

We have emotionally survived some tough days, though. I define "emotional survival" as having minimum cross words, no screaming, and a pleasant good night to each other at day's end.

Sunday we survived, in good shape, a day filled with constant rain and grey. Yesterday and today we survived a dental emergency with Jordin and the W-arch in her mouth. The band around her back left molar came off and left her W-arch loosely hanging in the roof of her mouth.

Knowing her discomfort and the possible damage to her $400 appliance, I searched last night at 6:30 p.m. for a dentist. No luck. I called our orthodontist in Juneau, AK (using my mom's calling card, thank you, Marge) to see if he had any ideas on how to keep it on overnight. (I was tempted to try a wax and gum mixture.) He had no suggestions.

The first dentist we found this morning in Oak Harbor couldn't see us for 24 hours and said he would, then, take the whole thing off. (Thanks anyway.) Our continued search landed us in the hands of a warm-hearted female dentist who re-cemented the band back on for just $10. Thank you, Dr. Cilely.

Jim and I are not as young as we used to be and are waking up with sore hips. We are sleeping on 2" pads. I think I'm into the 4" age group now.

I'm surprised at how many times I use the words "survive and tolerate" and am becoming aware that I view this trip as a burden and not as a joy. What needs to change? First and foremost, my attitude. Happiness takes courage. As a perfectionist, I guess I feel that if it's not perfect it's not worth enjoying. But the reality is that this trip will go too fast, is a rare opportunity, and I need a swift kick in the rear.

Road Schooling is more fun than public school because it is shorter and I don't have to wait for the rest of the class to be done. Mom and Dad are good teachers. I like it. But Road School and regular school are the same because we do some of the same stuff. Radical Road Schooling! (Kaitlin)

Road schooling is more fun than than public school because it is shorter and I don't have to wait for the rest of the class to be done. Radical Road Schooling!

September 22   **Wenberg State Park**
                                          Everett, Washington

There is a current that exists beneath the everyday layer of "Do I have enough money, who did the dishes last, does she love me?" Today as I did yoga on the beach I closed my eyes and entered that current. I heard the sound of the gulls and the waves and felt the sun on my face. I could have been a pre-colonial Native American.

September 23   **Kanaskat-Palmer State Park**
                                     Green River, Washington

Boy, talk about self-motivated learning! We started our Spanish studies very casually yesterday with "thank you" and "you're welcome." The girls REALLY got into it and spent probably 2 1/2 hours pumping me for all the words I knew. Well, I had one college semester of Spanish in 1970, but

> There is a current that exists beneath the everyday layer of "Do I have enough money, who did the dishes last, does she love me?"

they had me remembering words that I didn't even know that I knew (from the "musty basement" as Kaitlin would put it). Then they pulled the English-Spanish dictionary out around the campfire last night and spent another hour looking up new words. We probably have a vocabulary of 20 words now. It's fun.

The weather has been relatively dry and a little warmer the last two days. That helps immensely. We looked in the newspaper two days ago and there are warmer temps in the Southwest. We have a date with a storage shed somewhere in Seattle today to hopefully pare down truckie's load, a three-day Reiki training session in Tacoma, a quick hop to Roslyn (filming site of *Northern Exposure*), and then off down the coast. Hasta la vista, baby.

September 24

We had a great science lesson this morning. Got up and went walking (the two girls and I) as soon as we woke up. Compared different kinds of seed production in the fall season. We saw maple helicopters, moss and fern spores, dandelion fuzz balls, and two kinds of wildflowers. We also had some leaf identification of an unidentified wildflower-weed with a bright purple flower and hairy, velvety soft leaves.

September 25

Yesterday afternoon we continued the day of science. We came across two different kinds of caterpillars, one very green with yellow side stripes and big black shiny eyes. The other was a hairy one with cinnamon brown bristles and a black racing stripe down his back. We took the latter one captive and the girls made him a nice home of leaves and twigs in a converted milk jug. His name is Izzy and he is loved.

This morning Jordin checked on him first thing (he spent the night on our picnic table under the Big Blue Tarp). Was he dead or just lethargic? We talked again about how cold-blooded animals' daily cycles and activity levels coincide with the air temperature. She asked if her breath would warm him, and within 30 seconds of her gentle breath he uncurled and began moving! Giving the miracle of life—wow!!! We correspondingly are near the fire as I write this and the others are eating a breakfast of granola.

Speaking of fire, that has been one of the surprises of this camping trip so far. The state parks stop putting out firewood at Labor Day! We therefore spent a few days with no fire. It made me understand the "cold camp" that I've heard cowboys grumble about in the movies. It's hard to get the stiff and cold out of these morning bones.

However, we've become better at scrounging wood now. Two nights ago Kait and I went into a field of slash where there would soon be a beautimous subdivision and in about ten minutes we had collected enough wood for two fires, or about 45 minutes of warmth.

Yesterday we made a trip to Roslyn, the small town where they film the television series *Northern Exposure*. It was interesting to see Hollings' bar (The Brick), Joel's office, and the radio station where Chris ruminates. Double layers of reality. On the way back we stopped by the side of the road in a pine woods and spent 15 minutes collecting some dead branches. So in today's camp we have enough wood for probably three fires. Scrounging wood is just another level of taking care of ourselves that we'll need to be aware of. Can do.

I think I'm getting more used to sleeping in a bag on a pad. My hips are not as sore when I get up.

Mornings are still cold. We are doing our second day of Reiki training today. We'll stay at this camp tomorrow night as well, after finishing the training, then head south for hopefully warmer temps.

September 26

Where did this last week go? The week was busier than we all thought. We are now "trimmed down" and truckie seems to be riding prouder and easier. (Who wouldn't be with pounds shed?) Finding things is a lot easier. I asked Jim if that was the case, seeing as he does most of the digging. I predict, though, that more will go as time passes.

The Port Townsend and Whidbey Island area remains a pleasant surprise. A nice mixture of Midwest farmland and a mountainous ocean area. But, am I ready to start over AGAIN someplace else? When I left Reedsburg two years ago, I was sure I'd find no one to replace Barb, Eleanor, and Mimi. I was proven wrong. I didn't replace them, actually, but found additional friendships with Gay, Nan, Joni, Dave, and Judy. I feel like my luck has to run out at some point and that the next move will leave me without a support network. (Law of scarcity at work fueled by fear of the unknown.) For as much as Gay tells me, the law of scarcity does NOT exist, but I believe that the law of rarity does. I am concerned that AA meetings were not listed in the Port Townsend paper. Are there recovering people in the area? Are they underground?

Moving back to Reedsburg, would be just that—moving back. And I don't believe that you can ever go back.

We've had little time so far on this trip for leisure time, and I look forward to having that, especially in a warmer climate. I feel that we have one more thing to do in this area, and then the trip will begin. Truckie needs some more work and a cleaning, and then we start the migration south.

We are limited in our activities by cold weather which keeps us huddled by campfires in the evenings and early mornings.

September 27   Lewis and Clark State Park
Napavine, Washington

Fall camping brings a dimension we've yet experienced with summertime camping, and that is the shortened days. None of us wear watches, intentionally, so I really don't know when we turn in at night, but it appears that we are spending 10-12 hours a night in the tent. It is dark now by 7:30 and it's not getting light again until close to that time. We have been camping in heavily wooded areas which prevent the morning sun from warming us and

Truckie with a tarp covering the tent.

lighting our early hours.

It won't be long now that Jim and I will have had enough sleep and won't be turning in each night with the girls.

Evening:

This is great—a WARM evening. No campfire needed to warm us up!! We are sitting at the picnic table with the lantern going, reading and writing. We took late evening showers for the first time.

I believe relationships have seasons. While in Craig, Jim and I were in a blossoming, warm, summer season. Things were blooming, our relationship was tended to and nurtured.

It's hard to tell when the days got cooler and when the first frost hit, but autumn came around again for us. The cool weather turned to bitter cold days of winter. And so began our travels together.

Being in the winter season and spending 24 hours a day together does not work. Partners of a winter relationship need to spend more time apart. We aren't and won't be. Thus, we are being forced to change the season (or accept the chilling coolness) during a physically intimate adventure. Forced? Choice? Necessity? Can a season be changed? We're trying. Or, can we just let things be? There is not enough space to give each other the distance we need.

We're talking once again, the first intimate discussion being at "Deception Pass." (Appropriate?) I believe we cleared up past deceptions and did not create any new ones.

I'm pleasantly surprised at how well the girls are adapting to the trip. Tonight, as we pulled into site #9, Kaitlin jumped out of the truck, surveyed the area and said "Isn't camping fun!?" Bless her heart and spirit.

We have been extremely lucky with the weather this past week, and tonight's warmth is the frosting on the cake. Another much needed and welcome reprieve.

September 28   Seaquest State Park
Silver Lake, Washington

We stayed last night at Lewis and Clark State Park campground, just south of Olympia, WA and on the way to Mt. St. Helens. A nice unpretentious park, but a quiet jewel just the same. We pulled in about 5:00 and set up camp, then went for a walk. We discovered four or five juvenile "bunnies" leisurely munching and hopping in a space appropriately called the "Play Field." They were cautious but curious.

Then we continued on down the way to a patch of stately old growth forest. For my money, this is the kind of cathedral God intended us to worship in. It certainly makes you humble. We talked about the redwoods and tried to join hands to circle a large cedar. The two ends of our line couldn't even see each others' hands. There was a small log hut with an "old growth" exhibit. Ironically, two LARGE trees had blown over, completely smashing the hut! One tree lay over the other, making a large X with each arm probably 60-70 feet long. We walked along the logs and at one point were about 5 feet off the ground. I jumped off, but the three ladies stayed on, bouncing on the tree like a giant springboard. At first Kaitlin was a little afraid but she discovered that it was like riding a horse, you just needed to go with the flow.

**We continued on down the way to a patch of stately
old growth forest. For my money, this is the kind
of cathedral God intended us to worship in.**

She relaxed into it and did fine.

This morning as we were doing school on the picnic table by the campfire, we were visited by a group of three unidentified birds. They were very social, flying and chatting all around us, giving us a chance to note the shape and color of their beak and tail, colors top and bottom, and the black band over the eyes. After searching in our bird books, we found that they were

Gray Jays, a family addition to the Blue Jays of Wisconsin and Stellar's Jays of Alaska.

Fall is upon us now, with leaves changing and falling, but the weather seems to be a bit warmer. We are pretty comfortable with camping and seem to be finding the rhythm of this trip now. It was nice driving out of the Seattle urban area yesterday after having truckie's wheels aligned. He sings on the road now and awaits only a wash job to rid him of the vestiges of those gravel Prince of Wales logging roads.

This morning while reading from the Children's Bible, Jordin was reading about Noah and his three sons, Ham... Ham... (she looked at me with a twinkle in her eye) Ham, Bacon, and Sausage!!!

This morning while reading from the Children's Bible, Jordin was reading about Noah and his three sons, Ham... Ham... (she looked at me with a twinkle in her eye) Ham, Bacon, and Sausage!!!

The weather continues to be a blessing. This morning I walked early, able to get out of my warm cozy sleeping bag because the temperature was tolerable. We were also able to have school at the picnic table by 8:30 a.m. A productive morning. The girls are excellent students and learn very quickly.

When Kaitlin went to first grade years ago, she was disconcerted at the "all-day" schedule compared with the short, half days of kindergarten. She was sure that the work in first grade could be completed in half the time and that she could be home by noon and told us so. I believe she was correct and I can see now, clearly, how little time EDUCATION takes. The rest of the days are spent with social activities (yes, these are important), social problems (we could do without), recess, lunch time and snacks, bureaucracy and toilet needs.

Imagine a class of 28 students; 14 go to school in the morning, 14 in the afternoon. (I believe this is feasible for grades K-5) Imagine the work that could be completed with this low student/teacher ratio. Imagine the irate parents who would no longer have government subsidized, free child care all day long.

September 29

We had a hard time with school today. I think the girls have forgotten what a full day of school is like. There was a lot of complaining and a real lack of focus, so we're going to have school for a couple of hours after lunch today so they remember the long days of public school. They are learning a lot in just a couple of hours each day but it needs to be something they do more willingly. Am I being unreasonable? I don't think so. This line needs to be crossed at sometime in every class I've taught and it looks like it needs to be done here as well. Before we left on Plan Z we joked about sending the girls to the principal's office. Well, I am he and we are there...

September 30

The good weather continues so our migration has temporarily ceased so we can enjoy the warm temperatures. Yesterday our truck was never started. Jim played music, I did some beading and we all played catch and explored the park.

Most people who travel have a home to go back to. We don't. What happens if we tire of this life or run out of money? Being homeless creates a myriad of problems that "homeful" people do not encounter. Being homeless gives me a sense of being a beggar. Just the thought of being homeless is unsettling to me. The comforts a home provide seem distant now, and would be welcome.

Everything we do needs something to be unpacked from the back of the truck. For instance, to brush teeth we unload the toiletry bag, get the toothbrushes out of their holders, walk to the bathroom (sometimes blocks away, depending on the size of the campground), brush, walk back to the campsite, put them back in their holders, back into the bag, and repack what was initially unpacked. A ten-fifteen minute process. Of course, the option is brushing in the campsite with God and every neighbor watching. (This is becoming a more convenient option.)

Cooking requires the cooler, kitchen box, food box, stove, propane, and the water jug that's always needing to be filled elsewhere in the campground.

By the end of the day I'm tired, both physically and emotionally. The girls are helping with more and more of the daily chores, but not enough to split the workload into fourths.

Tonight we are camped, literally, on the edge of Interstate 5 north of Portland, Oregon at Paradise Point (a severe misnomer). I've camped in areas where I could HEAR the freeway, but never where I could SEE the freeway.

We are having problems with the zipper on the tent door, and are going to stop in Portland tomorrow morning to see if it can be fixed. Then we will make an assault on a local laundromat and watch quarters disappear into agitating and rotating slot machines. If time and energy prevails, truckie deserves and needs a wash.

Yesterday's afternoon school went well. The girls were productive and attentive. Today's work went better too. It was a gas watching them learn how to use the video camera. I showed Kait how to use it first. In 45 seconds we covered the power switch, zoom feature, the record button and the view finder. Then I turned to Jordin and started explaining. She said, "I've got it," took the camera and started up. She had trouble getting the record button the first time because her thumb was too short, but she adjusted. They took the camera and were off to film the inside of the truck cab, adding narratives about how messy the adults kept their section! What bright, fun kids!!

I feel like I'm watching Kaitlin grow up before my eyes. Jordin is growing by leaps and bounds, too, both physically and mentally, but Kaitlin seems to be crossing the line into womanhood. She's in the cocoon and undergoing metamorphosis. At times she still hugs her stuffed lion tight (we've decided that he's one of those stuffties that has received enough love to become alive, although he's quietly dignified about it) and at other times the teenage attitude is very strong. They are both well on their way to becoming independent, self-sufficient, curious adults. I'm proud of them.

October 1
Battle Ground State Park
Battle Ground, Washington

Today we went to the Tillamook Cheese Factory. There were lots of conveyer belts that were moving cheese. Big blocks of cheese went down a slide and ladies cut them into half circles and then packaged it. Then some men put it into boxes. We got some cheese. It is good! (Kaitlin)

October 2   **Elk Creek State Forest**
                                            Lee's Camp, Oregon

It's 8:00 at night and pretty dark already. We're camped at Elk Creek State Forest, a free campsite between Portland and the coast. I'm sitting in one of our lawn chairs with a crackling fire in front of me and a babbling brook behind. The tent and sleeping bags are set (Sidewalk the Stuffed Bear, Snuggles and Lion await the girls) and we just had a filling dinner of bean burritos, chips, salad, and raspberry juice. Ah, the life of a gypsy!

The last few days have been good. The fantastic weather has continued, normal for this area into October we're told. Yesterday we ventured into Vancouver, WA to do laundry, give truckie a much-deserved wash job to get off the last of the road to Thorne Bay (Alaska), and to get our tent zipper fixed—a story in itself.

The zipper had been giving us trouble, unpredictably separating as we closed it, for the last week or so. A morning tip from colorful (to say the least) co-camping neighbor Ty ("semis are taking over the highways") Keltner at Paradise Point State Park sent us to a store in Portland. They referred us to Laurie (back across the bridge) in Vancouver, Washington. We called and she willingly agreed to help us out by fixing our portable home. Two hours, $19 and a jar of salmonberry jam later we left her new suburban home with a revitalized tent. During that time we had visited a sports card shop and sold two 1958 Don Drysdale baseball cards from my childhood for $30, paying for the tent and that night's camping.

Today we visited new friends Marilyn and David in Portland. Loads of fun as they took us to the Saturday street market and a new-and-used book shop, a little shot of urban delight and people watching. It had been quite a while since we'd been to something like the market. Good food, handmade arts and crafts of high quality, live music of several varieties and lots of people to watch. It was a very nice afternoon. Still, it was nice to drive out into the country, which brings me back to Elk Creek.

Kaitlin and Jordin are sitting about ten feet away, reading by the light of our lantern. They are really enjoying the new books we bought today. Six books, that should keep them going for a few days anyway. So much growth in lots of ways. When we moved to Alaska two years ago they both had mini-lawn chairs to sit on and now they have full-sized chairs and their feet touch the ground. They are good kids and I enjoy spending time with them

Well, enough writing for tonight. I think I'll pack up the notebook, lean back and stare into the fire as the creek chuckles behind me in the dark. I think that's the poor man's version of surround sound. I'll take it and thank ye kindly!

More great weather, a repaired tent, and the coast of Oregon by noon tomorrow! We've found our first free campsite at a cozy spot beside a babbling brook. Sure beats Paradise Point!! After unpacking, settling in, and getting used to the idea that this free site has no water, I visited with a prison warden. He was checking out the parking lot of the campground; just doing his "rounds." It seems that in the past, visitors to his prison have left things here at this campground which is just across the road from a minimum security prison. (We were not aware of this prior to setting up camp!) The prisoners, during break time, have enough time to run over here and pickup little treasures. (Drugs, paraphhernalia, and weapons.) So this campground has become part of his rounds. I'll wait until morning before telling the girls we are camped next to a minimum security prison wherein sit lifers who have been accused of murder. (Facts from the warden!)

I'm feeling more adjusted to our homeless condition. Homeless? Home is where the heart is. But the flashlight is never where it can be quickly found. Okay, so we're homeless. We're all getting used to calling the tent and campsites "home." Where is home tonight? When will we be home? Kaitlin and Jordin continue on the course of adaptability.

My fragility, anxiety and rage appear to be diminishing and are not so close to the surface of my existence. I've had days of tears and total emptiness, feeling like a dry leaf in hurricane winds. No control over my destiny, no longer attached, uprooted prematurely. But, I'm adjusting. The winds of emotions have died down, the wind currents not so severe. What IS my destiny? Will I know it when it comes my way? Probably not unless it slaps me in the face.

> **What IS my destiny?**
> **Will I know it when it comes my way?**
> **Probably not unless it slaps me in the face.**

October 3   Beverly Beach State Park
Otter Rock, Oregon

Last night as we got to camp, Jan started fixing dinner and I started setting up camp. The girls scampered down the hill to the creek so they could explore. I looked over my shoulder and thought about the responsibilities of a grownup. This morning first thing, I went down to the creek and explored. We need to take care of the child within.

October 4   8 p.m.   Loon Lake State Park
Reedsport, Oregon

Tomorrow will mark three weeks we've been on the road. Time for grades I guess. There are several levels to look at here.

We've been pretty lucky with the weather (only one day of rain so far), but camping in the fall is a bit of a challenge. The mornings (and some evenings) are cool and firewood has been scarce, although at this point I'd say we've become successful wood scavengers. We have missed one or two morning fires, but never when we really needed one to warm our bones. Tonight we're having a fire with wood we've been carrying since yesterday. There seems to be enough dead wood here and there by the road so we should have no trouble keeping warm in Oregon. I have a feeling California may prove different, but we'll see.

Setting up and taking down the tent every day is somewhat time-consuming, maybe 30 minutes or so at each end. Only twice have we stayed in the same camp more than one night. That should change as the trip starts to take on a slower rhythm. We've made two changes to help cut down on the time for this chore; first, we've gone to leaving our cushions inflated during the day instead of rolling the air out and putting them in their stuff sacks. It means the back of the truck is a little less organized (the four mats slide in on top of everything else when we're loaded) and we can't see out the back window while we're driving, but you need to be clear about your priorities and leisure time is definitely near the top of the list. Besides, we can both drive well with mirrors. Second, everybody stuffs their own sleeping bag in the morning as they get up, unless they really have to pee bad! At the start of our trip I pretty much did all the set up and tear down of camp with some help from the others, while Jan did almost all the cooking.

> We need to take care
> of the child within.

In the name of Sexual Equality and Greater Harmony we've begun sharing the jobs. Jan still does most evening meals because of their greater complexity (bravo, dear!), and after burning pancakes (breakfast) and burritos (dinner) I've come to realize my abilities and limitations and handle only some of the cooking chores. We've been eating well. I've lost the 5-7 pounds of "ice cream hump" left over from the Sub Marina, have gone to eating more salad, and am feeling fit.

School is going well. As I talked about earlier, I'm learning to be less rigid about both schedule and teaching methods. Working with two bright motivated learners makes it easier. They both read a ton each day if kept in new books and given time. I've come to think that that is really a valuable way for them to spend the two to three hours daily. Their vocabulary is growing and we're always talking about what they've read, so we deal with characters, their interactions and motivations, setting and plot. They've both taken to Spanish as well. It will make Baja a much more rewarding experience.

Science is all around us every day. So far we've had mini-units on different forestry practices, plants and seeds, animal identification, and today's aquarium trip, with material on volcanoes from our Mt. St. Helens trip still waiting to be digested. Math is one area we work at daily and I feel very confident of my abilities in that area. They'll have a strong math background by the end of our school year.

The scenery has been spectacular—from the ferry rides to Washington State Parks and the Puget Sound area to the amazing size and power of the Oregon coast.

Jan and I have had a few rough spots in our relationship and that has made some days hard. The time in Craig, while a great growth and strengthening experience for the family overall, was a stressful time. A difficult teaching assignment for me, cramped living space, tons of rain, and some of the angry people we encountered there, all produced a strain that is letting out little by little now. Jan's job at COHO was a really good experience for her and it was hard for her to leave job and friends for the second time in two years. She has done a good job of dealing with the demands of the trip while waiting for her mood to lighten. She's a good woman.

After one of Jan's and my early "talks," five or six days into the trip, Kaitlin had a dream. She said that she and Jordin were trying to drive the truck. Kait was steering and Jordin was down below, trying to guess which pedal was the gas and which was the brake. We all had a good laugh the next morning as she told us about it around the morning fire, but the symbolism seems pretty clear to me. We're here, little one. The hands on the wheel may not always know where they're going, but that's all a part of being a grownup.

Yesterday we arrived at the Oregon Coast in all its glory and foggy, cold dampness. We camped near the coast and spent the evening and the next morning with the feel of chilling dampness.

Needless to say, after an exciting day of play on the coast we are now camping inland on Loon Lake, a Bureau of Land Management Campground. While on the coast today, we laughed and screamed while we watched gallons and gallons of water rush and crash into the Devil's Churn. Later we ran up and down the dunes in the Oregon Dunes National Monument.

It is so much warmer here inland. I've taken off my winter jacket again and feel comfortable.

I continue to adjust to this way of life, but look forward to an existence in a house where stoves, beds, and the roof are immediate, constant, perpetual and warm exudes and permeates all and everything. What I used to take for granted, I now crave and appreciate.

October 5   Lookingglass, Oregon

Last night we stayed at Loon Lake Park, a real beauty near Scottsburg, Oregon. There was one other couple in the park and after they left at about 9:30 this morning, we spent three hours in the first real solitude we've had since leaving Prince of Wales Island. It felt very nice, touching a place deep inside of me.

October 6   Jedediah Smith State Park
Gasquet, California

A while back I talked about a deeper current, a timeless reality underlying our everyday concerns. Today I physically touched it. It was a fallen redwood in the Stout Memorial Grove in Jedediah Smith Redwood State Park in northern California. It was a beautiful reddish brown with swirled grain, smoothed from the many hands, young and old, that had touched it before me. By its diameter, I guessed it was probably 5-800 years old. As I touched it I felt a tingle, but not in the physical sense. Almost like the shimmering as Spock or Kirk beam up... Sounds loco, right? That's OK, it felt real to me.

I'm enjoying the trip immensely. Details are starting to come a bit easier now, and I really do enjoy seeing new country and meeting new people every day. We have no schedule, sometimes going to bed by 9:00 and staying in our sleeping bags till 8 or 9:00 the next morning. During our last year in Craig my sleep schedule was more like 10 or 11:00 to 6:00. I could have pushed myself again I'm sure, but it feels good to be catching up on rest.

It feels good to be out of the public school system for a season. Sometimes I think about doing something else, but I'll probably end up back in the classroom. I enjoy kids and I think I'm good at teaching. When I started out, I always said I'd do it for 20 years, and this year is number 20. That constitutes a career I think.

October 7   **Gold Bluffs Beach**
Orick, California

Right now I am at a campground in the Redwoods. We are camped by a river. In and out of the river live some tiny frogs (and toads). Jordin and I caught them and made jails for them out of sticks, but they kept on escaping. The frogs are about the size of the eraser on the end of a pencil. (Kaitlin)

October 9   **MacKerricher State Park**
Fort Bragg, California

I feel like we've been seeing Mother Nature's Greatest Hits: Mt. St. Helens; the Oregon coast (featuring a dynamic duet with Pounding Surf and Endless Sands!); and now the California Redwoods. Talk about touching the

> I feel like we've been seeing Mother Nature's Greatest
> Hits: Mt. St. Helens; the Oregon coast (featuring a
> dynamic duet with Pounding Surf and Endless Sands!);
> and now the California Redwoods.

eternal! I can feel the wheels in my head slowing down, achieving a more efficient balance, a well-oiled equilibrium. I'm not sure what the next stage will be, but I think I'll be ready for it, more able to center myself within whatever circumstances I may find myself.

As we planned for the trip, anticipating a leap into the unknown, we were wondering what would become of two urges, consumerism and the nesting instinct. In Craig for the past two years we've not had the opportunity to be blatant consumers. The availability of basic goods was fine, but there were no real toy stores or general merchandise stores Well, that urge seems to be under control. There have been no spending frenzies yet and the opportunity has been there. Even the girls have been very responsible and mature shoppers. After touring the Oregon Ocean Aquarium the other day we went through the gift shop. We gave the girls the green light to buy, but after 20 minutes of energetic browsing, they decided not to buy anything because they found nothing they really wanted. Good job, ladies!!

It's also been two years since we had a real home (or house to be more exact, since we've said that if the four of us are together that's home). We always had the feeling of being in a temporary space and especially small quarters for the last 12 months. The urge to have a real house again is strong in all of us. Jan came up with a nice floor plan the other night. I enjoyed sitting in Marilyn and David's living room on a real couch as we passed through Portland. Kaitlin has been asking if she'll get her own room, is planning some basketball posters and is excited about having her white chest of drawers. Jordin's home urge has mainly centered around what kind of kitty we'll get when we "settle in somewhere."

Somewhere indeed...at this point the front runners appear to be Chimacum, Washington, just south of Port Townsend; and the Midwest, probably Minnesota or Wisconsin. Chimacum's plusses are a good school system, small town life, and the proximity to the ocean. The drawback appears to be high real estate prices. The Midwest offers more reasonable home prices, probably more family-centered values (a guess), and closeness to relatives. It obviously is, however, a long way from the Big Waters.

Jordin will graduate from high school nine years after we "settle in," so it seems like Jan and I will be doing some major goal-setting and long-range financial planning during the next few months. Sailing? Paying off a home? To teach or not to teach? A women's center or some kind of job counseling? Buy or build? Where to live?

I like challenging times like this. I feel alive. The trick is to keep it loose but somewhat under control and to alternate this with more settled times where we can regroup and let the wanderlust itch build up.

We've eaten breakfast and packed up camp. Truckie is locked, while Jan and the girls are out exploring the beach. I'm sitting on a log outside the men's room, writing in my notebook while the battery for the VCR recharges inside. The sun is coming out after early morning fog. I have really enjoyed our three days in the redwoods. I'm reminded strongly of Tolkien's Ents, the living tree-people. We all laid our hands on the world's tallest tree yesterday (367 feet!) and I know I felt a gentle wisdom vibrating deep within. Their life span of 600 or more years yawns at our frantic pace.

Today we'll continue south along the coast to friends in San Francisco and Los Angeles, then on to Baja.

October 10
Clear Lake State Park
Kelseyville, California

Jordin often talks in her sleep, and Jan said that last night it included a few words of Spanish!

After a long afternoon of driving, we camped near the coast. It had rained and we couldn't get a fire going so we went to bed at 8:00! We all read in bed for a while and then got lots of Z's. I think the girls needed some catching up.

Today we visited Mendocino, an old favorite of mine from previous trips to the coast. I remembered a small, eclectic artists' colony of weathered wooden buildings. For once, a favorite had not completely sold out to mindless growth. It had changed to be sure, but still retained its basic flavor and lots of class. The real eccentric art shops had been largely replaced by tourist art, but as Jan said, "Real art doesn't always sell."

As we walked through one shop, Kaitlin asked why anybody would buy a certain item, a basic glass jar with a see-through stopper top filled with sand and shells. She noted that you could probably buy four or five regular jars that would be just as functional for the price of that one fancy jar. I tried to explain the concept of extravagant consumption, but I could see that it made no sense to her and in the end I had to boil it down to the old standard, "People are different."

October 11   **Mill Valley, California**

We broke down and rented a motel room tonight, and I'm sitting on a bed in Mill Valley, CA just north of San Francisco. The girls are eating a picnic dinner and watching T.V.

Since I last wrote, we went to inland Oregon and clear sunny weather, then back to the foggy coast of the northern California redwoods, back inland to rain in northern CA, and are now back on the coast with the hopes that the weather will be clearing.

The price of gas fluctuates drastically from week to week. While in Seattle we paid $1.05/gallon; the day we arrived in Oregon a 4.3 cents per gallon gas tax went into effect, and in Portland we paid $1.22. We thought the high prices were geographical and felt sure that the prices would decrease in California because Oregon does not have self-serve stations. The general public is not allowed to pump their own gas, thus a much higher gas price. We were looking forward to crossing over into California, and were disappointed when the price of gas went UP. But now that we're in Central CA, we are seeing more reasonable prices—$1.17 is the lowest so far.

Since arriving in CA, we've encountered lots of signs at the state parks, warning us to "keep our valuables locked in our vehicle," and also warning us about thefts of cash and valuables from the vehicles of tent campers. The state parks here are more costly than the parks in WA ($4.00-6.00 more), not as well kept, and obviously not as safe. There are just too many people here trying to get by, and for many crime is a viable solution.

Our daily routine continues to be one with very little leisure time. The shortened days, especially when rainy, will send us into the tent sometimes as early as 8:00 p.m. Our lantern and a warm fire will placate us most nights, and we're in the habit now of doing paperwork, school work, writing in our journals, and correspondence by either firelight or lantern light (both in and outside the tent).

 I've tried selling dream catcher earrings I've made, but have not had luck. The coastal towns are slowing down this time of year. I'll need to find places which have a Christmas trade. It's hard for me to put a price on my own creations. I waiver between $5-$9 a pair. If I truly want to sell them, a lower price would probably be more appropriate.

 Jim has played his guitar a few times since we started, but I have yet gotten mine out of the back of the truck. I hope Jim plays this week in preparation of seeing Larry.

 Today was very non-directed. Our initial goal was to contact two friends of mine in the San Francisco area, but several phone calls failed to locate them. The secondary goal was to visit the San Francisco library to explore microfiche sources on the earthquake of 1906, then tour Stanford University to show the girls a college campus, and finally, head out of the Bay area. But we realized it was Columbus Day and that the library would most likely be closed. We tried to reach my friend Larry in L.A., but the best we could do there was hearing his voice on a recording machine at his job. We've lost his home phone number and I couldn't get it from directory assistance.

 We began to drift down through wine country, miles and miles of vineyards on both sides of the road, very impressive! There were some pear orchards mixed in, and we stopped and bought a bag of 15 delicious pears for $1.00. We started discussing the possibility of a motel, and the girls bit big-time on that one. So, I'm writing this in relative comfort in a motel in Mill Valley, just north of San Francisco. Jan and I both took hot baths and the girls are soaking and playing in the tub now. We've been averaging about $35 a day (aside from truck expenses) and tonight's lodging alone cost $52 plus tax, but I think it was the right decision. Good for the troop's morale, don't you know.

 And so this string ends at 26 nights of tent camping, a new Marousis-DeMars record. I hope it's been enjoyable for the girls. Being outdoors is something that I've really enjoyed in my adult life.

Real art doesn't always sell.

October 12   **Sunset Beach State Park**
                                            Watsonville, California

Today turned out to be another misguided day. The $52 hotel room was on the first floor and we were underneath a 3:00 a.m. insomniac TV-watcher. I called the front desk and got no answer so I went outside, looked up and read the room number off his door, went back in, called him up and in a fake foreign accent (there are a LOT of new Americans in this part of California) said, "This is the front desk. Please turn off the TV." It worked.

Anyhow, too little sleep for a night that consumed enough money for three or four nights of camping. But ah, that hot bath last night!!

Our intention today was to see several different areas of San Francisco and then scoot by Stanford on our way south. After crossing the Golden Gate Bridge in a classic bay-area fog (with Kaitlin videotaping and providing commentary), we were able to visit part of Golden Gate Park. However, after that we were momentarily disoriented by the force field of heavy urbanity and found ourselves exiting San Francisco on Highway 1 heading south. Instead of trying to re-enter like a salmon going upstream to spawn, we just went with the flow and left without really experiencing the city.

The last two or three days have seen a flagging of my spirits and resolve. At times I have wondered whether the family is really enjoying this trip. We seem to be moving constantly (fall weather is one reason why you see fewer people tent camping at this time of year), and are always short on money (I know some small portion of the desperation that must gnaw at homeless or low-income adults, except that my state is temporary and by choice).

We are all striving to make the best of this and enjoy our freedom, but it seems that one or another of us has been feeling the pinch and verbalizing it lately. Luckily, it seems that so far we haven't all had the blues at the same time. I know that this will be a good experience for us all in the long run, but can we persevere in the short run?

Tomorrow we'll continue on toward Larry and Mary in L.A., even though we haven't been able to make contact and verify that they are indeed home. I've had visions of camping in their back yard and prying off a screen to get in to use el cuarto de bano (bathroom for all you gringos!)

We took a nice long walk on the beach tonight after setting up camp at Sunset Beach State Park south of Santa Cruz. There must have been 200-300 sea gulls resting on the beach at one point, and Jordin went running and

Tonight, on the way to the bathroom, I said to Jordin, "I wish I had half the memory you have." She said without a moment's hesitation, "You do!" and then gave a tiny little chuckle. Was she playing with my head?

skipping toward them, hair and arms flying. They screeched and wheeled into the air, a huge, boiling mass of grey and white. I wished I had the video camera, but will have to settle for the remembrance of my mind's eye.

Tonight, on the way to the bathroom, I said to Jordin, "I wish I had half the memory you have." She said without a moment's hesitation, "You do!" and then gave a tiny little chuckle. Was she playing with my head?

October 13 Lake Lopez State Park
Arroyo Grande, California

These are the good times. We've been driving through agricultural lands for the past two days now (artichokes, grapes, brussel sprouts, tomatoes, pears, etc.). We just stopped in San Ardo and had a lunch of apples, green beans and chips in the parking lot of Our Lady the Redeemer Church. We set up the tent to dry in the noonday sun. I hear a concertina very faintly on the breeze. About a two-hour drive to the next camp and the crew is happy.

Last night we went for a long walk on Sunset Beach and found a note in a bottle. The bottle was green and said Chardon Wine on it. The cork was duck taped and the note was in a plastic bag with duck tape on it. It was from some people on a sailboat. (Kaitlin)

October 14

What a rare morning here at Lopez Lake. It's 9:00, sunny and warm, and we are the only ones in the campground, except for the wild turkey, deer, grackles, grey squirrels, quail, woodpeckers and an occasional ranger who might drive through, (and reportedly, a mountain lion or two).

So much of California's population is coastal, and I've been surprised (pleasantly) at how much of the inland state is, inversely, isolated. Not more than 10-15 miles inland and we can drive for hours through mountains seeing only a few cars or houses.

The homeless population is increasing as we approach southern California and the warmer climate. I've seen people on street corners with signs stating that they'll work for food; Jim saw a man wrapped up in rags today. Our country's population continues to explode and I fear we will strangle ourselves steadily and terminally. Being in rural Alaska these last few years has isolated me from urban problems, and as I tread through the cities of the lower 48, especially on the Pacific coast, I'm reminded once again of the many social problems our larger cities contend with on a daily basis.

Prior to leaving for Alaska, small town living in northern climates had kept us isolated from many urban problems. I know they exist, but I am always slightly surprised at reality. I agree with Jim when he says that the biggest problem we have, globally, is overpopulation. Controlling our population could? would? ultimately affect our environment, our social problems, our diminishing crop lands, education, and hopefully the demise of the institution called family.

But can our government mandate birth control? Probably not. But incentives might possibly help. Rather than giving exemptions for each child on a tax return, maybe they could give tax breaks to families with fewer children. There are bonuses in our economic structure for having children rather than for controlling population growth. (i.e. AFDC gives additional amounts for each child.)

The issue of birth control also needs some revamping. Until the recent trend of condom use, which is becoming more popular because of AIDS and NOT as much because of pregnancy prevention—men will wear them now to prevent their own death—almost all birth control devices and procedures were for women. Have you ever, except once in biblical times, heard of a woman conceiving without male sperm? Why, then, aren't more devices for

MEN? Where does our social system fail to teach men that conception is equally THEIR responsibility? Where does our social system fail to teach women that male's sexual "needs" are a not a woman's responsibility and duty?

Today we will arrive at Mary and Larry's in Thousand Oaks, California. A house. Friends.

In many ways this trip has made me anti-social. I prefer, at present, the campfire more than meaningless social chatter, I prefer my sleeping bag and the tent more than a strange bed, and I prefer rural wildlife more than urban wildlife. But, close friends' company I look forward to, and the girls are excited to have new playmates.

Brother Bill's birthday! Stayed about ten miles inland last night at Lake Lopez Park near Arroyo Grande, California. An incredible amount of wildlife! A flock of 30 wild turkeys greeted us as we entered the park. Lots of quail, some sort of woodpecker with a bright red cap and some deer, too. A nice quiet spot. Fall camping is cooler, but the campgrounds are a lot emptier, especially during the week.

I'm writing this at 9:00 a.m. The other two campers that were in this section have already left. We're enjoying the unaccustomed morning sun, and the girls are off stalking deer with the video camera.

October 17 6:00 a.m..   Thousand Oaks, California

It's been awhile since I wrote in the journal. We've been at Larry and Mary's in Thousand Oaks now for two and a half days and have been taking a much-needed break from the daily "Z routine," sleeping in a bed, actually taking a shower two days in a row, not taking the tent out of the truck, watching two innings of game one of the World Series on TV, and generally living an indoor (although we spent about four hours outside at various junior soccer matches yesterday) civilized life. As Jan remarked, Thursday night was probably the first time that we had slept in a room of our own for 14 months.

It seems to me that we are at a rather critical point: in Plan Z; in our relationships; in our plans for the future. I think about it a lot, and I really do believe that this experience is going to be a good period of growth and maturing for our girls, a really invaluable influence on the development and

> I really do believe that this experience is going to be a good period of growth and maturing for our girls, a really invaluable influence on the development and strengthening of their adult personalities.

strengthening of their adult personalities. This is an opportunity for me to work with Kaitlin on her math skills and hopefully restore her confidence. It's also a rare opportunity for a parent to share that incredible metamorphosis of child into adult on a daily basis. Jordin's reading ability is just exploding and I'm really enjoying her math aptitudes as well. Mary and I were talking about how kids are constantly soaking up and collating impressions from their immediate environment, not having adult distractions like death and taxes to contend with. I know that our girls are gaining a greater understanding of the world around them.

Well, all this is long term gain, and I sometimes wonder if we can deal with the short term reality that leads to the gain. No pain, no gain.

I think the weather has been one major factor here. In Washington state we camped inland and although mornings were cool, I remember days as being fairly mild, clear and for the most part, dry. However, the Pacific coast was a major part of the experience and as we moved through Oregon and California, the coolness remained and was fortified by increasing cloud cover and dampness. Tough on tent campers longing for the sun after two years in Craig, AK.

Money is another definite factor and one that we need to deal with. As mentioned before, we left with 1/3 less than our original budget. As we adjusted our spending, it effectively resulted in almost no choice on our daily food and lodging. So far, in 30 days prior to our arrival here, we've eaten out maybe five times, slept on a ferry once, in a motel once, and 28 nights in our 8' by 8' tent. With better weather we might have felt a little more like adventuresome gypsies, but reality has become tinged with feelings of being homeless and slightly destitute.

There are three major options that I can see at this point. One would be to cut our Z travels off at Christmas as we return to the Midwest, look for some kind of "permanent" job and get a home. Another is to take money out of my Wisconsin teacher retirement fund. Another is to look for temporary work at Christmas time to replenish our coffers, take a break from the tent for about one to two months and then do a two to three month travel in early spring before looking for another job. While options one and two are certainly seductively attractive, I think number three would be better overall. Maybe I could get on somewhere seasonal like UPS for the Christmas rush and Jan could work as a tempo office worker for a while. Again, who knows?

While at Mary and Larry's, Kaitlin had another abandonment dream. She dreamed that we were leaving her in the middle of the night. She came downstairs, shaking, and joined Jan and I in bed and ended up spending the night sleeping between us.

Last night we got a sitter and the four adults went out to eat Chinese food to help mark Jan's passage into her 40th year. The sitter said that both of our girls were really missing us. I think they are both feeling the anxiety of our unsettled life and unclear future. It would be nice to be able to take that away, but this is probably another opportunity for growth. I think the "security" that most people use as the cornerstone of their daily lives is very much an unstable illusion. Disease, an accident, or even random social violence can take your health or your life at any time and material possessions are certainly not a "given." In the end what we have left are our own mental and physical resources and the love and support of those around us.

I think the "security" that most people use as the cornerstone of their daily lives is very much an unstable illusion. Disease, an accident, or even random social violence can take your health or your life at any time and material possessions are certainly not a "given." In the end what we have left are our own mental and physical resources and the love and support of those around us.

The Desert Classroom

October 19

From Friday to Monday we had fun at Bethany and Brianna's house. On Sunday I got new shoes. They are black and purple, my favorite colors. They are size four and a half. My feet grew from size two and a half to four and a half. I like my new shoes a lot!

After I got my new shoes we went back to the house

and swam in their pool. We slid down the slide and made big waves. After we got bored with sliding we played mermaids in the pool. We also played pool tag.

While I was there I also played basketball on their hoop. Dad videotaped me playing. I also played soccer with Brianna. I went to her game and practice too.

In their backyard they had two swings, a slide, monkey bars, and a hanging metal bar with rings attached. We did flips on the bar and hung by our knees. We swung on the swings and had swinging contests. We slid down the slide and played in the little wooden house. It was fun!

I also got new jeans, went to the fair, watched TV, went to the park, had Mom's birthday, looked at Watson the snake, took a bath, and last of all... did not camp! (Kaitlin)

October 20   **Anza-Borrego Desert State Park**
                          Ocotillo Wells, California

Today we learned what a siesta is and why they're necessary. During the first month or so of the trip we were looking for warmer, drier weather. Well, we've found it in Anza-Borrego Desert State Park, two hours east of San Diego. High of 85 degrees, low around 55. Very pleasant last night around the campfire in a T-shirt and shorts, with a warm gentle breeze blowing and millions of stars twinkling above.

This morning we spent two hours in the Visitors' Center, talking with Aaron, a very friendly and enthusiastic senior volunteer. He spent some time describing three or four of the best spots for short to medium hikes and then took us to the "back room." Wow! The first thing that caught my eye was a stuffed mountain lion. There were bobcat and Mexican raccoon pelts, a bighorn sheep skull (those horns are incredibly heavy!), the upper jaw of a sabertooth tiger, the lower jaw of a mastodon (this area used to be a grassy plain), arrowheads and pottery from local ancient Indian cultures. Very interesting. We are in an ecosystem as opposite as possible from rainy Craig.

Exploring our surroundings here beats any science textbook.

The time at Larry and Mary's was critical. I for one was at a pretty low point. Parts of this trip are definitely hard work, but in re-reading my journal entries as I typed them from the notebook into the computer set up in Larry's den, I realized that our travels have indeed been a rich experience for us. It will be interesting as the girls grow older to see what memories they bring away from this time. Come to think of it, it will be interesting to see what memories stick out for Jan and me.

October 21

A beautiful morning. Jordin woke up at about 6:45 to go to the bathroom, looked outside and said, "Oh you guys, get up!!" We came out to a beautiful desert sunrise. I had just gotten out the video camera for the sunrise when two coyotes nonchalantly trotted across the campground road 25 yards away. I was so excited I could hardly get the camera going, but I got lucky and the second coyote walked through my sights. Gotcha!

October 22   San Diego, California

I spent the weekend in Anza-Borrego Desert State Park.

In the desert there are lots of animals. My favorite animal was the mountain lion (I didn't see one, thank goodness!). I saw a stuffed cat sitting on a rock in the Visitors' Center. A mountain lion skin was in the Center too. It was very soft. Some other desert animals are the lizard, beetle, jack rabbit, kangaroo rat, bighorn sheep, coyote, bobcat, and fox.

Plants are all over the place. My favorite plant is the Desert Lavender. It is a plant that has light green leaves with a little fuzz. When crushed it gives off a very nice smell. It is pretty big. Other plants are beaver tail, teddy bear, and ocotillo.

The things we did in the desert were very interesting. We went hiking to Palm Springs and went to Font's Point. I enjoyed my stay at Anza-Borrego Desert State Park!!! (Kaitlin)

10:22 a.m.

We're heading into the mountains toward San Diego and Sea World, leaving Anza-Borrego Desert behind. I really enjoyed our time there. It was my first real stay in the desert and I found it to be as spiritual as the Black Hills. Seemingly arid and barren at first glance, we found the area to be teeming with a variety of plants and animals.

The girls each completed a five-page Jr. Naturalist booklet as a family project. It taught us all about different desert animal and plant species and how they adapt to an environment of very limited rainfall, an average of 6.8 inches annually in this case. Desert plants often have small or waxy leaves to reduce water loss, or leaves that are light-colored to reflect light. One plant, the palo verde ("green stick" in Spanish) has bark that is actually a pale green color to reflect light (which turns to heat when absorbed). We saw a wide range of animals including beetles, hummingbirds, a snake, black-tailed jackrabbits, mice, a kangaroo rat, and two coyotes. The kangaroo rat is even more adapted to desert life than the camel, the famous "Ship of the Desert." It never drinks water! According to Rosemary, a volunteer naturalist at the Visitors' Center, it gets moisture from the nuts and seeds that it eats and it has special kidneys that somehow recycle the water in its body so that it doesn't need to urinate. I heard an owl during the night.

Camping here was nice; we had comfortable evenings around the campfire and warm mornings with dry tent and bags. It was also nice camping in the same spot for three nights. We took excursions yesterday to Font's Point, Split Mountain and Palm Grove; we've had extra time because of no driving or dealing with setting up and taking down camp. All together a nice restful and renewing time in the desert.

The girls are doing well with schooling. We've done tons of science in the last few days, as well as the usual one to three hours of reading every day. Math skills continue to build as they're getting better with addition and multiplication flashcards. During the last week we've done a lot with writing, using the framework of individual story maps which list main points that they want to include in their work, then brainstorming ideas together, and finally writing with introductory sentences and paragraphs.

Jan and I have been finding more peaceful waters together. During our stay in Thousand Oaks we revised our original budgetary aims. In the first month of our travels we averaged about $35 a day (excluding truck repairs). Since pulling into Larry and Mary's we've averaged about $10-12 more per day. We're still holding to a pretty austere budget, but not totally bare bones. It feels better. After all, this is literally a once in a lifetime trip and we need to enjoy it. The problem is that we are going to have to either cut short the trip or add more dollars to our treasury.

Dear Maegan,

Right now I am in San Diego. We are staying in a hotel with a pool. For us that is pretty rare. Usually we tent camp. So we are enjoying it!

About two weeks into the trip we visited the Redwoods National Park. We saw the biggest tree in the world! It was 367 feet tall and 44 feet around. Most of them you couldn't see the top! It was awesome!

And just yesterday we left the desert. We camped in Anza-Borrego Desert State Park for three days. The hottest it ever got was 85 or 90. When you think of deserts you think of sand, right? Well, this desert had about a million plants (not really a million plants). It also held about a million animals (not really). I really enjoyed it! I hope I can visit it again.

And while we were in San Diego we went to Sea World. We saw a whale show, a dolphin show, and a sea lion show. There were also some exhibits on fish. It was really hot! We also got sports cups that say Sea World on them. It was fun. My favorite show was the killer whale show. One whale was named Shamu. Dad and I sat on one of the bottom seats in the bleachers and got soaked! Very wet!! It was fun!

   After Sea World we went to the Santa Anita race track. We watched some of the best horses in the world run. I filmed a race on our video camera.

            I MISS YOU!!!

                                    Love,
                                    Kaitlin

Dear Brittany,

   I miss you too, very much. I hope (think) we will be back in winter.

   We went to the giant Redwoods. They are very big. When you peeled off the outside bark you would find dark reddish brownish wood. When a fire hit, some of the outside bark would break off and burn the inside. The tallest tree would be 367 feet tall. Taller then a football field.

   We were where the bottom of the sea was. It was neat. But there was no water. And there was a big crack in the earth. We drove right through the crack. The crack was formed by the ocean and an earthquake. It looked like it would all fall down. It was neat.

   The crack was part of the desert. When we went to the desert we saw lizards, bugs, coyotes, birds, a rattlesnake, and a stuffed (real) mountain lion. We did a workbook too. And got a badge. It was fun.

   Guess what? WE WENT TO SEA WORLD! We got to see lots of animals. There were even horses. Not sea horses either. They were Clydesdales. They were very pretty. We also got to see dolphins, penguins, water turtles, parrots, and Shamu. We got to get some cups with killer whales on them. We got to see Shamu and baby Shamu put on a show. Dad and Kaitlin got wet from him, splashed with his tail. He could splash 14 rows of seats. It was neat!

Love,
Jordin

October 23   **Campland RV Park**
San Diego, California

We went to Sea World in San Diego today. It was worth the high price of admission. The theme for the dolphin show was "One World" and there was a segment that featured the dolphins and their trainers playing together and shadowing each other. It was an interesting presentation. I like science fiction a lot and it struck that chord with me, communication with another intelligent race. They're beautiful animals.

We also saw sea otters, sea lions, a HUGE walrus, sharks and untold variety of both fresh water and salt water fish. And of course the Big Guy, Shamu the Orca. For the orca, the "splash zone" was the first 14 rows of the stadium, as opposed to four rows for the dolphins. The dolphins had politely sprayed some water on a few people here and there without getting everyone in their "zone," so Kaitlin, Brianna and I stayed in row #4 for Shamu (early recruits Jordin and Bethany had the good sense to emigrate to higher ground before the show began). Well, Mr. Shamu definitely did the job. At the very beginning of the 25-minute presentation, he made two passes around the outside edge of the tank, with three huge flipper splashes on each pass! We were soaking wet with 55 degree salt water!!! Kaitlin loved it. We moved to the top of the stadium, where sun and cool wind soon eased our chattering teeth. To see an orca gracefully slip the bonds of gravity and fly through the air is an amazing sight.

If only the tent could talk... packed up yesterday morning in the solitude of Anza-Borrego Desert and unpacked tonight in "Campland" in the very middle of San Diego—with a hot tub and pool! The ladies are there now and I'm sitting in the truck writing.

Jordin has had a sore throat the last two nights. Hope she sleeps well tonight.

As we were breaking camp in Anza-Borrego we met a guy who was just coming in. He had traveled extensively, including Baja, so we talked with him for a while, playing the old travelers' game of trading stories and trying to sift the kernel of truth from the embellishment. He was knowledgeable and practical about Baja, providing us with some very useful information. It was obvious that he too relished traveling, finding himself in new territory and interacting with unfamiliar people in new situations. It was reassuring to meet a kindred soul.

October 25   Thousand Oaks, California

Yesterday we took the girls to the Santa Anita Race Track, a real classy place where you could lose a lot of money in a big hurry. The outside facade was very stylish architecture that recalled past days of grandeur.

We placed one $4 bet and our horses were actually running 1st and 2nd heading into the home stretch, but were overtaken in the last 20 yards. Seeing the thoroughbreds was a thrill.

There was also a free concert by Sha Na Na in the infield between races which I really enjoyed. Live music is in my blood—loud guitars and rock and roll.

Today we went to Brianna's dentist to have the girls' W-arches checked before we headed into Baja. The dentist was a nice guy my age who enjoyed hearing about our travels and told us how he had backpacked through Europe for three months. Then he sighed and said, "That was before I was married. And I just had a baby boy too." He went on to talk about how he had spent years in schooling and 15 years building up his practice and how hard it was to get away now. There was a definite longing in his eyes. He ended up charging us only about 1/3 of what he could have gotten. I took one of his business cards. We'll send him a post card.

I'm reminded of a short story by Gordon MacQuarrie, from the book *More Stories of the Old Duck Hunters* (Willow Creek Press, Oshkosh, WI, 1983). A man who works in an office begins to feel the need of extended time out of doors and away from his work environment. He makes arrangements for a solitary canoe and tenting trip and sets out.

During the first few days his hands and back are sore, the bugs eat him alive and he burns some meals. He wonders if he has lost some of his prior enthusiasm for the outdoor life. But slowly he notices a transformation. His hands become calloused, his body becomes lean and hard, he relishes the solitude, his mind becomes clear and focused again. In the end he stays away longer than planned and comes back renewed.

I see signs that our travels are leaving behind some of the early stages of difficulties. It still has its ups and downs of course for this is no easy undertaking. But we are becoming leaner and harder on some levels. May it continue!

October 27   Campland RV Park
                                  San Diego, California

Mary and Larry's was a welcome respite. We had our own room, the den, while the girls slept upstairs in Brianna and Bethany's room.

During our visit, I saw my 40th birthday come and go, celebrating with Chinese food and a soak in their hot tub (both two favorite items in my book). I purchased a AAA membership on my 40th (not a planned coincidence) and wonder if there is some kind of significance.

We left Mary and Larry's for a stretch and spent three wonderful days in the Anza-Borrego Desert. The large, stone-made bathrooms were clean, had flush toilets, but no roof!! Imagine a clear evening sky full of stars posing as the bathroom ceiling. (People attempt to create this image on their walls and ceiling with plastic stars and moon that glow in the dark. I know. Kaitlin bought some in the hopes of some day having her own room again.) Yes, these bathrooms were some of the cleanest, but also the most incomplete, creating a celestial view.

For me, the desert was the best part of the trip so far. The days were clear and hot, the nights were equally as clear and pleasantly cool.

At present, we are camping in an urban San Diego campground that belies the concept of over-crowded, but has three of the best pools I've seen anywhere: a hot jacuzzi; a warm (100 degree) large pool; and a rarely used "cool" pool that chases most folks out in 2-3 minutes. Within 20 feet of our tent are three vehicles and two other tents. I guess I should feel lucky that the sound of traffic never ceases, otherwise I'd be listening to my neighbors sleep, dormitory style.

I spoke with my Mom last night on the phone, and she informed me that there are major forest fires in this area. Although we have not seen them, we are constantly living with their residue. Everywhere ashes are coating any surface that will accept them, the tent, the truck, the table cloth, our granola, the milk in the glasses, bread, silverware, etc. etc. etc.

Southern California has done the job of thawing us out and darkening our skin, but it has also vacuumed the pocketbook. The coastal campgrounds are expensive, over-crowded and usually near a freeway.

I believe we've spent as much here the last 10 days as we spent in the first 30 days of the trip. I'm wondering if Jim or I will need to work at some point. I don't like scrimping—if we are well-off enough to do this trip, then why have we been acting so poor? Because we are if we want the trip to last through May. The bottom line is we'll run out of money if we don't act poor, but I'm tired of saying "no" to everything except basics. We've yet to buy a bag of cookies or some other treat. We cringed at the bill for the first motel. For me to enjoy this trip more, I need to feel like we are financially capable of buying a bag of Oreos™, a box of tissues (rather than campground toilet paper), a game of miniature golf, or a meal at a restaurant once in awhile.

Jim and I talked about this when we first arrived at Mary and Larry's and decided we had to be more free with the money, even if it means dipping into retirement funds. We need to be able to treat ourselves occasionally and act like we're on vacation rather than a painstaking, limited budget, money-saving marathon.

Tomorrow we head into Baja. I have mixed emotions. I'm uncomfortable about not being able to speak their language, and we have a noise in the truck that mechanics have neither identified nor fixed. Services in Baja, I've heard, are limited. Hang in there, truckie!! I am looking forward, though, to a more deserted countryside, as I'm tired of the LA-San Diego sea of humanity and pollution. I'll keep an open mind.

As I told my Mom, don't expect to hear from us until at least mid-November (two-three weeks from now), but don't be surprised if we call within a few days. I told her I wouldn't call until we were back in the states.

We were at the San Diego Zoo today and Jan mentioned seeing some Twinkies™. Jordin piped up and asked, "What's a Twinkie?" Imagine an eight-year-old American not knowing what a Twinkie is! We've raised our girls differently than many, and today shows that as plain as day. (By the way, we later showed her a Twinkie in a grocery store.)

We are staying in Campland again. The pools and hot jacuzzi are a great attraction to us. Jan has worked with the girls, and their swimming has greatly improved in the last two days.

I met a 24-year-old pastry cook from Switzerland at poolside yesterday and talked with him for awhile. He was a very happy, curious guy and I really enjoyed the contact. He definitely had a twinkle (not a Twinkie) in his eye. He and his friend had just been in southern Utah and he said the nights were below freezing, very cold.

Tomorrow we'll stock up on canned goods, water, gasoline, and head across the border into Baja. Looking at the map last night we targeted several camping spots as far south as San Antonio Del Mar, 180 miles south of the border. We'll play it by ear, planning initially to come back in seven to ten days.

October 28   Boulder Oaks, California

Wow! We tried crossing into Baja through Tijuana today, hitting the border, going south, about 2:30. The border guard spoke fairly good English, but you could tell the comprendo wasn't 100% and he wasn't real sure where we could get the tourist cards that seemed to be a necessity according to the advice we had gotten. We pulled through the border, went a half block and pulled into a place that said "Mexican Insurance." Well, actually I pulled into what I thought was the driveway. It turned out to be a place for taxis only. I backed up, trying not to get hit by four lanes of cars accelerating past the border. There was also a huge hole about three feet deep in the concrete. Look out for that too!

There was a guy wildly gesticulating for me to pull into the next drive while pointing to the insurance sign, so I did. We all looked at each other as we got out and locked the doors. It turns out the guy not only couldn't speak English, but couldn't speak at all. He kept grunting and gesturing as he ushered us into a building where there were two women behind the counter. The one that spoke better, broken English was pretty aloof and told us that we could get insurance there, but the tourist cards were "back toward the border." Right. Our choice was to try to go against four lanes of screaming traffic or park truckie and walk back. Neither one seemed like the right choice so we got in and set off into the traffic, hoping to see an opportunity for a U-turn.

We soon realized that we were into the thick of Tijuana, with no U-turns coming up, speeding into Mexico with no tourist card and no Mexican insurance. People were driving crazy, with little regard for lanes and I was really watching my fenders for benders! Quickly we were submerged in the flow of Tijuana!! I was concentrating on the road, other drivers, and any traffic signs that might give me a clue to where we were heading. My peripheral vision was showing me a colorful kaleidoscope of tons of people on the sidewalks, two-story shops selling anything imaginable, and everything written in Spanish of course. After three or four blocks, I saw a street two blocks over to the right and parallel to the one we were on and it seemed to be going the opposite way just as madly as ours was heading south, so I winnowed my way to the right lane and turned. I spotted a sign that said San Diego and within minutes we were waiting in line to go through the border again.

Jan was picking her thumbnail and not saying much, looking through our AAA guide to Baja for something that would help make sense out of what we had seen in the last 30 minutes. To their credit, the girls only asked once, "Do we have to go to Mexico?" This boat is a democracy and runs on a majority vote. A voice vote was not necessary here. After we hit the border and went through our two inspections, we kept rolling north. Certainly in the running for the shortest tour of Baja ever, but relieved.

Now the bottom line for me is that, yes, I was nervous as we approached the border and, yes, I was concerned for our safety as we rolled through Tijuana. I don't think I would have felt the same during my extensive travels when I was in my 20's, and that bothers me. Why the change? There are several possibilities. I was more naive then, believing that the world was basically a safe place as long as you kept your eyes open and your wits about you. I don't really believe that anymore. If it ever was, it certainly isn't now. Also, I'm older, no doubt slower and less physically able to defend myself. That probably contributes to a feeling of insecurity in situations which seem unfamiliar or "threatening." I'm married now and have two daughters. I'm looking out for a family instead of an individual. When I traveled before I was most usually in the company of one or more males.

I've never been afraid of aging, believing that the wisdom and experience that comes with age gives a greater understanding and appreciation of the ironies of life. I still believe that, but my reaction yesterday is somewhat unsettling.

When we bought groceries for Mexico yesterday, our receipt had a coupon on the back for $1 off on a kids' haircut. Kaitlin had been talking about getting hers cut, so we did it. She had 8-10 inches cut off. It looks good, kind of a Peter Pan look. She's really enjoying the change!

As I filled out the campground pay slip I marked down October 27 and it was really October 28. I've lost track of the date, a good sign.

October 30   Anza-Borrego State Park
Ocotillo Wells, California

Yesterday was strike two for Baja. Mexicali proved to be less chaotic than Tijuana, but Mexican border officials gave conflicting versions of whether or not we needed the famous Tourist Card, and nobody seemed very friendly or helpful. This time we parked on the U.S. side and walked across. We spent 20 minutes or so in Mexicali, bought some ice cream bars in a drugstore, then headed back across the border. Returning to our country felt good.

We saw a full moon rise last night, danced with our moonshadows, slept soundly with the tent windows open all the way, and awoke this morning to see a pink desert sunrise as the full moon was just setting. A day of $0 expenditure, reading, playing with toy horses and taking hikes.

We talked with the park ranger this morning. He's been visiting Baja for 20 years and really felt that it was worth the trip. He suggested getting our tourist card and Mexican insurance on this side of the border and just driving through. Neither Jan nor I like the thought of giving up so "easily" on this part of the trip, really one of the few goals we had planned ahead. I think we are going to stay in Anza-Borrego Desert for a while, but perhaps Baja is not as far in our future as I was thinking.

We're back! We weren't gone long, just a short miserable one and a half hours in Tijuana. Chaos on parade. Masses of steel, humanity, and garbage. Unsafe, in my opinion. We were sucked and vacuumed into a rhythm that belongs to Tijuana alone. Help was not available to us, it was clear that we weren't welcome there. We wanted to get Mexican car insurance (mandatory, we were told, because without it you'd see the inside of a jail cell if you were in an accident) and a tourist card. Directions for obtaining these were inadequate, as was a place to park so that we could search on foot. We turned around and got in one of 13 lanes to re-enter the U.S. Each line was 1/2 mile long with street merchants and beggars making last feeble attempts to pull U.S. dollars from the pockets of U.S. citizens, or anybody else who had pockets that jingled.

The merchants have their sales pitch polished: instead of "You buy one?" They said, "Which one you want?" When I shook my head, he said in surprise, "Neither?"

After the first of two gates to re-enter, we were told to wait at the inspection station. We did. After what seemed like half an hour, a woman came by, initialled the card on our windshield and without any questions or observations of us and our loaded vehicle, said we could go.

How do you spell relief? U-S-A.

My feelings after returning were briefly of relief. They changed, quickly, to feelings of failure for not tackling something that shouldn't have been so difficult. Baja was one of the few "planned destinations" of our itinerary, and we chickened out. Wisely so? I don't know. We let Tijuana be the jury and judge of Baja. No, we didn't. Tijuana was the burning hoop we needed to jump through, and we weren't strong enough or willing enough, or maybe we were wise enough. (Note 6/3/94: Spoke with a friend just returned from CA, and was informed that his friends who are frequent visitors to Baja said local attitude toward Americans has definitely changed.)

A few days later, wanting to rid myself personally of that feeling of failure, and because we just knew in our hearts that we still wanted to go, we <u>walked</u> *through the border at Mexicali. We attempted to get a tourist card from an "Officio" and was told we didn't need one. A set-up for later and further into the country? He was not friendly, not willing to discuss it, and was adamant in his decision. We tried again at the "Turismo" center that was partially open to the outdoors, and mostly vacated. In the back behind a sliding glass door were a few people, including a man in uniform who we asked about a tourist card. He would neither acknowledge our question nor our presence; simply, we weren't there.*

Those two encounters, in addition to Tijuana, frosted the cake, or more like, shot the lame horse. We returned, once again, to the U.S.

Since then we continue to get mixed reviews on Baja from other travelers, and Jim and I still ask each other, often, if we are willing to try again. Third time is the charm? Or, three strikes you're out?

November 1

Last night was an unusual Halloween. Earlier in the day we had met two couples camped just down the road from us. One couple was from San

Diego, the other was retired with a home in Tucson, a boat in Oregon and on the road with a van. Our girls got dressed up as a black cat and a princess and we went trick or treating to their camp. We sang a little song wishing them Happy Halloween and the girls collected compliments and some Reese's™ Peanut Butter Cups. We sat around their campfire and traded travel stories and watched the full moon rise over the desert mountains. Today we inherited 2 1/2 boxes of firewood from them and a tip on a nice spot to visit in Mexico.

We visited Agua Caliente County Park later in the day. It's about six miles down the road from our free camp site here in Mountain Palm Springs. What a find! Two dollars per carload to get in and use their cool pool, huge hot pool jacuzzi and showers. An authentic oasis!

It is so quiet in the desert.

Yesterday was Halloween. We went to some people's camp and trick or treated them. They gave us two candies each. Kaitlin was a black cat and I was a princess. Later when we went to a store we bought some more candy. It was good. (Jordin)

November 2

I've seen that a traveling existence promotes autonomy from service-oriented sectors. I've taken the initiative to look at, purchase, and replace the air filter on the truck. (A simple task, no doubt, that any idiot could do, but also just one of the many things that most of us hire a mechanic to do for us instead.) We've repaired the broken glove box, saving ourselves $44 just in parts (and probably twice that in labor). There's more we could do, and I hope we learn.

Medical services are not as quickly utilized as when we were living a non-nomadic life. Reiki is applied instead, and that along with patience and time cures most ailments.

Orthodontics I could have done on my own had I been confident enough to trust my intuition. My diagnosis on both of the girls' "W" arches were correct, and they needed to be removed. I wasn't sure I could, I know now I could have, but they are out, professionally removed.

Self-reliance sports more freedom and choices.

I'd like more opportunity to barter. Jim and I have talents to offer in exchange. Is bartering a thing of the past? Probably not, but just harder to find.

November 3

I'm territorial, like an animal that marks her territory and expects others to honor it.

We arrived here at Bow Willow campground because it had picnic tables, fire rings, water, and was free (due to lack of toilets, which the girls have turned into an art: digging, depositing, refilling, and marking). We were pleasantly surprised to see we were the only campers, scouted out our new home, set up, laid out nude in the sun, scoped out pit toilet areas, hung toilet paper on branches, put the table cloth on the table, set up the tent, and basically felt like we had found home for the week. We saw signs of road runners, birds, rabbits, etc., and were looking forward to the wildlife, isolation, and quiet.

Until the R.V. Invaders. Every, every (I do not exaggerate) site in the campground was empty except ours, but where did the R.V. pick to call home with their two yapping dogs (goodbye to wildlife)? Yes, right next to us!! I don't know why other people camp, but my goal is always solitude and as much of mother nature as I can find. That was quickly gone with a few back-up instructions from Midge (the name is changed to protect the invaders, although I never did ask her name) as they steered the trailer within 25 feet of us and my territory.

Anger? No, Rage! I quickly stomped over there and as politely as I could, I asked, "How long you folks plan on staying?" Midge replied, "Oh, a few days." Grrrrrrrr. I stomped back and informed my family that we were moving, lock, stock and barrel. And move we did, around the bend to a, once again, isolated spot. Just a quick note, in case you were wondering if I expected miracles, by wanting isolation in a "campground." For your information, yes I was, solely because this was the "off" season, with few visitors to the area.

But as we were packing, I continually wondered "why". Why would someone do that? Were they cognizant of their rudeness? I wanted to ask, so I headed on over, again. I chickened out, spun around and came back to *the chore of packing up. But the feelings, the nagging questions and rage wouldn't go away, nor did the shock of being invaded by choice.*

I decided that there have been times in my life when I've chosen rageful silence over assertiveness, and that it was time to change. I mustered up more courage, marched on over, smiled (fake, with the hint of glaring, but also to appear ignorant rather than assertive for fear of being punched), and asked why they parked next to someone when there was an entire empty campground. I may have been the one to appear ignorant, but the answer was something like, "We've been coming to this spot for 20 years (blah, blah, blah) and this here hill (pointing to the slight elevation in the earth to the west of us) makes the sun set at 3:30 rather than 4:10 in the other part of the campground (blah, blah, blah), and we don't like the heat.........." (Kaitlin, after hearing of my conversation with Midge's Mate, asked why do they camp in the desert if they don't like the heat? No ignorance in that girl.)

So now this is the second day of our new territory, and this home suits me just fine. We have no neighbors within view or ear shot. We've marked our territory with chairs, a clothesline, a tent, the truck, and the endless round of pit toilets that the girls enjoy digging. Kaitlin usually digs the toilet, one or both of them uses it, and Jordin fills it back in and does landscaping so that no visual signs remain, except for their grave marker, a rock. (The terrain and our lack of a shovel do not allow us a big, communal pit toilet.)

Last night we sat around the campfire. We got the wood from the Halloween people. We sang songs and told jokes. When we looked up there were lots of stars. (Jordin)

November 4

Dear Grandma,

I got new sandals. Because I had a Morton toe. A Morton toe is that the second toe is longer than the big toe. To get my sandals we went into El Centro. Kaitlin got sandals too. It was fun!

Sometimes when we go to a campground there is a pool. The campsite we are staying at now has a campsite next to it. And that campsite has a pool. We might be able to go swimming today. Sometimes when we go swimming we bring our My Little Ponies™ in or our kooshes in. It is fun.

When we were in bed we heard coyotes bark, yip, and howl. And we saw them too. I saw one and dad, mom, and Kaitlin saw two. The one I saw was all yellowish greyish and the tips of his ears were black and on his tail there was a tip of black too. Coyotes mostly come out at night and early morning to hunt. It was neat.

In math we are doing fractions and flash cards. And we do adding with dice. We are reading from Teenage Mutant Ninja Turtles™ and the Children's Bible. Dad reads The Black Stallion as we get ready for bed. It is fun.

P.S. See you soon! Miss you!

Love,
Jordin

Dear Grandma,

I am having fun on the trip. Every day we have school (except on Saturday and Sunday). We have about two hours a day. I have one or two pages of work in my notebook a day plus flash cards. I am learning fractions.

About a week ago was Halloween. We were in the desert. Down the road from us were two couples. We dressed in costumes and sang Happy Halloween to them. Jordin and I got two Reese's™ Peanut Butter Cups each.

It was fun!

A week and a half ago I got my hair cut. I had been wanting it for weeks. We went to a haircutter. We had a coupon to save one dollar. I got eight to ten inches gone! I like it a lot!

Right now we are in the desert. Yesterday morning we heard coyotes. It was awesome. They don't howl like wolves do. They just yip and yap. It was interesting!

Almost right smack in the middle of the desert is a hot springs. The people made it into two pools. One is indoors and so hot that the kids can't go in it and another outdoor pool that is lukewarm and two feet deep that the kids go in. It is fun! Miss you lots!

> Love and sunshine,
> Kaitlin

November 6

It is so quiet in the desert that sometimes it feels like my ears are plugged. The quiet massages my ears and soaks into my brain. It soaks into my brain and calms my soul. My soul is calmed and I remember who I am.

We've been back in Anza-Borrego for over a week now. Some free camping to ease our budget, some solitude to balance out all the Southern California urban bustle and road noise we've been in lately. Clean, clear air and sparkling starry nights. Shooting stars. Hills that change colors as the day progresses and the sun follows its daily appointed rounds. Darting lizards, burbling quail, waking to the yips of coyotes as the sun comes up, and nocturnal visits from the inquisitive, comical kangaroo rats.

I've had some real ups and downs so far on this trip, but if indeed I start building up my psychic strength and flexibility and regain my cosmic perspective and sense of humor, this is where it will start. Gracias, amigo. Muchas gracias.

> It is so quiet in the desert that sometimes it feels like my ears are plugged. The quiet massages my ears and soaks into my brain. It soaks into my brain and calms my soul. My soul is calmed and I remember who I am.

November 8

Last night I woke up in the middle of the night. I went outside the tent to go to the bathroom. When I was done I heard coyotes. They yipped and yelped and one was really close. Then we heard a crash and a scream. A coyote had his meal! The moon was really bright and not quite half. It was really awesome. (Kaitlin)

November 9

I woke up in the clear desert air, and recalled reading a book written by Sue Bender, telling about her stay with Amish families, searching for direct simple values in her life. It reminds me of what is most dear to me.

Jordin, I love you for bringing so much joy and love into our daily lives. Your direct gaze is so full of twinkly. I admire the way that, even being the youngest of our family, you persist in asking when you don't understand something, even if it brings you to tears of frustration. You are a brave and joyous soul. I'm glad you are a part of my life.

Kaitlin, I love you for your unquenchable curiosity and burning clear intellect. You have taught me much. Your new pixie haircut seems to have loosened the ballast on your spirit. You are aware of your metamorphosis from child to woman and are enjoying the dance. You are a bright and shining star. I'm glad you are a part of my life.

Janet, I love you for all the questions you ask. Your irresistible energy has probably saved me from becoming stuck in the mud of middle age. You also persist in asking when you don't understand, even if it brings tears. You

Anza-Borrego State Park
Student-led parent/ teacher conference for Jordin

have grown so much during our adventures since leaving Reedsburg. You are
a loving woman, my other half, and I'm glad you are a part of my life.

Jim, I love you for your ability to stay on the right path in the face of
adversity. You are learning the strength of honesty and flexibility. Follow
your heart and keep your music alive, my friend. You are an ancient traveler.
I am glad for the life that flows through you.

November 12   **Scottsdale, Arizona**

I read a newspaper article about three weeks ago and a quote keeps
running through my head. The interviewer asked a woman who had just
visited Buckingham Palace what she thought of it. With Princess Di and
Prince Charles obviously in mind, the woman replied, "I'd rather live in a two-
room flat and be in love."

I read a newspaper article about three weeks ago and a quote keeps running through my head. The interviewer asked a woman who had just visited Buckingham Palace what she thought of it. With Princess Di and Prince Charles obviously in mind, the woman replied, "I'd rather live in a two-room flat and be in love."

November 13

We are staying at the home of my cousin Andy and his wife Laurie, whom I just met for the first time. They are both warm and gracious hosts, and seem to genuinely enjoy our girls. It feels like home, and that's a very welcome feeling after a long stretch on the road.

November 17   Picacho Peak State Park
Picacho, Arizona

After four nights at cousin Andy's in Scottsdale and one night at Bill Bremser's in north Phoenix, we headed out late this afternoon. It was nice spending some time in homes, but Kaitlin yesterday and Jan today both made comments about being ready to camp again. Me too.

It rained the first three days in Phoenix. The ground there is hard and doesn't handle extra water very well. Lots of gushing washes and semi-flooded streets.

An important event took place for me. Andy is a teacher in one of Mesa's junior highs, and he asked me to talk about Alaska to his 7th grade geography class Monday morning. Junior High is not my favorite age, and I was leery about stepping into a classroom again, but it went well. Very well. And I enjoyed it. Normal kids doing normal things in a normal setting. Not perfect, just normal. I think I can handle going back to teaching, and probably even enjoy it. The healing continues...

We visited the Phoenix Art Museum for almost two hours today before leaving town. I enjoyed it immensely, especially a special exhibit of "cowboy art" and some pop art. The girls are old enough to enjoy it too. Another step in growing up.

Parts of Arizona and New Mexico had snow while Phoenix was getting watered. We'll be watching weather reports in the newspapers and picking our way carefully now. We may end up back in the Midwest within a week or so, ending this phase of Z, but we'll be back in the Southwest for spring training.

I remained territorial at Anza-Borrego (AB), hating when people would choose a spot next to us. Don't they care about privacy? What big-city dweller ever spends silent, truly silent, moments? (How could they with all the noise pollution?) A camping neighbor was minimal company to them.

I was extremely hesitant to leave AB and was grateful that both our first and last night there found us alone, alone in the dark, starry, silent night. My hesitancy was due not only to the warmth and beauty, but also due to knowing that in the near future we would be making social visits to friends and family in Phoenix whom we've never visited. Yes, and Andy's wife we've never met. Was I ready to be social? Was I ready to leave my territory and intrude in someone else's? How do these people live? Do they want us to visit them? Will we be welcome? I had doubts and questions as we left AB and her warmth and beauty.

AB also provided our family a very creative environment as we all began making dream catchers for Christmas gifts. (They all looked gorgeous hanging from the campsite ramada.) At the Agua Caliente pool a woman overheard comments about my dream catchers and earrings, and I sold my first pair. I then sold her a willow dream catcher and was commissioned to do two more. Creative energy is financially supporting for the first time. What a buzz. When I left Agua Caliente General Store that final day, I left behind a display of earrings, and four dream catchers. People actually liked and wanted my creations. I am honored and feel like the dream catchers are a symbol of my life at this time.

What is my dream, my goal, my own personal direction and choice? Making these dream catchers represent daily life to me, not the subconscious, nocturnal dreams. Follow your dream. Find the dream, first.

And tonight we left Phoenix. The visits are over and we are back to our own tent, a room of our own, fresh air, and the, what else, hum of the freeway. Tonight, it's okay.

> I am honored and feel like the dream catchers
> are a symbol of my life at this time.

Dear Papou,

The trip is going well. In Casa Grande (Big House in Spanish) I got an awesome hat. It says Phoenix Suns on it. The bottom of the bill is green. The rest is purple. I like it a lot.

Yesterday we walked along the canal on a paved path. I brought my basketball on the walk and practiced dribbling and passing. The canal is Phoenix's drinking water. It comes from the Colorado River.

At Andy's and Bill's we saw a Suns basketball game on TV. The first game they lost to the Houston Rockets. The game at Bill's they won over the Golden State Warriors. They played well!

At Andy and Laurie's house we went to the Phoenix Museum of Science and Technology. We played with magnets and saw some animals. There was a booth where you could trade faces with someone else. There was an Infinity Chamber where it looked like you kept on going forever. There were lots of experiments you could try. I liked it a lot!

Love,
Kaitlin

Dear Papa,

I will see you a week from today! We are at Bill's house. Bill is a friend of dad. Bill has a cat named Boots. Once Boots went head first into the wall. Then she went side first into the other wall because she was chasing a string. Once she was going to the bathroom and she was burying her poop and a piece of poop got stuck on her claw and she flew it away from the litter box.

We also stayed at Andy's. They have a pool in the back yard. And they have two dogs. Kaitlin and I slept in a bed that was a King size bed. We slept with pillows down the middle. It was fun.

When we go to campsites sometimes there is a pool. Once one pool was two feet deep. Another one was four to six and a half feet deep. I could touch the bottom of the pool of six and a half feet. Andy had a pool too. But it wasn't heated. It was 56 degrees.

I saw a movie. It was called Turtles II, Secret of the Ooze. The turtles would go into a show place and some people would sing and the turtles would fight and then go up on stage and dance.

Hope you are having a good time cause I am!
See you soon!

Love,
Jordin

November 19   Cochise Stronghold
                                      Dragoon, Arizona

We sure had to work to get here, driving over seven miles of the bumpiest gravel road we've seen since Prince of Wales Island, but we're in another inspirational spot: this is Cochise's Stronghold. Cochise was a warrior and Apache leader who headed resistance to the whites in SE Arizona from 1860-1872. He died in June of 1874 and is buried somewhere in these hills. The area has the usual desert plants—yucca, various cactus, etc., but also 20-30 foot oak trees of some kind and water as well. The rocks are large slabs and boulders, several shades of tan, deeper browns, and red.

It was cold last night, but still nice to be camping in the clear air and out of the noise of city and freeway. We'll stay here for another day before moving on.

A blazing fire is a dire necessity at 5,000 feet in the Dragoon Mountains, southeast of Tucson in mid-November. Last night was cool, and we assumed the day would warm us up, but the tree cover prevented a continuous warm ray of sunshine, and by 3:00 we were just as cool as we were this morning at 10:00. Yes, the warm part of the days here are brief. We stayed in the tent late this morning; absent was that moment when the sun heats up the tent to an intolerable temperature and everybody dives for the door and fresh air. Instead, tonight, we'll dive for the door from chairs rooted to the edge of the hot, dancing flames of the fire.

We are alone at Cochise's Stronghold, bathed in silence. As we climbed each large boulder today, I imagined the natives finding refuge in the crevices, caverns, and shadows. The terrain here is beautiful, while the thought of Cochise's predicament is, inversely, very sad and depressing.

Jim and the girls seem anxious to be heading north to family, while this climate and terrain draws me in and tries to keep me here. Would I tire of this area and climate zone if I lived here? The test will be our reaction when we descend upon the frigid cold of Iowa, Minnesota, and Wisconsin. Will we like it there? The people? The terrain? I fear boredom with a tame life.

November 20   Rock Hound State Park
                                 Deming, New Mexico

The silence was shattered last night, and exploded with voices of six adolescent, hormone satiated, drug ingested, adventuresome boys looking for a Rainbow Gathering; they were excited and anxious to find the "hippies" that were to be congregating somewhere near here and were ready to party. (Actually, they were already partying.) Every other word that was formed by

*their lips was "f___" or derivatives there of. Equal time was given to "cool"
and "dude." Fortunately, we found their predicament (the search for the
Rainbow Gathering) through a brief encounter (conversation) wherein they
wanted something flammable to start a fire. Something explosive would have
suited them fine, while I thought a match would have been enough. When
hearing of their search for the gathering, we instead got out the map (prior
to that moment I think they thought WE were the only two hippies at this
gathering) and showed them where we had heard their destination was, based
on two gentlemen's (questionable) visit to this same spot the previous night
(in error) while also looking for the said event. They forgot about their fire,
and immediately loaded into the van to continue their quest.*

*This morning before we stepped out of the tent, the six boys once again
appeared, obviously not having found the gathering, and feeling more the
affects of a hang-over than their inquisitiveness. With somewhat clearer
heads (relatively speaking), minimal sleep, and the still strong
adventuresome spirit, they again looked at our map under the light of the sun
rather than the single ray of a flashlight. They, once again, were on their way.
Good luck boys. Be here now, guys, for that's where you're having fun, and
besides, it's an old hippie term.*

*With all the people looking for this gathering, I wonder if there will
be more spectators than hippies. Gather on.*

*Today the goal is a shower, for based on the smell in the truck, we all
need one. It's Saturday, and the last day water touched this body was
Wednesday. Bring on the water, preferably hot!*

As we left today we stopped at a small Chamber of Commerce-Tourist
Information Bureau in Sunsites, Arizona, just south of Cochise's Stronghold.
For $2 we bought a back copy of Arizona Highways magazine (rather than a
$25 hardback biography) that had several articles about Cochise and his
stronghold. There were no photographs, but an eyewitness account of
Cochise at age 56, a "most remarkable man...His height, five feet and ten
inches; in person lithe and wiry, every muscle being well-rounded and firm.
His countenance displayed great force."

A man who had roamed this area all of his life without seeing anyone
other than Indians, was now trying to fight off the encroachment of the
incoming settlers, trying to protect the land and a way of life that was
endangered.

Tonight in Rock Hound State Park by Deming, Arizona I was on my way for a leisurely walk around the campground when I was hailed by Ed, an eastern Oklahoma octogenarian with a twinkle in his eye. He held a bleach bottle in one hand, which he explained was his "quickie" toilet at night or in other times of need. He explained how he had installed a second 12-volt battery in the pop top camper in which he and his wife travelled. It ran the fluorescent lights and heater of course. If it ran out, he switched a key and pulled power from the front battery. What happened if the front battery went dead occasionally? He had a 16-foot jumper cable that he attached to the back battery and gave himself a jump start! He had sold Keebler™ cookies for 30 years... "But here I am, holding you up, telling you just about everything I know." No problem, Ed.

I really enjoy talking with elders that have made it that far in life with their sense of humor intact. It's a good sign. It gives me hope. He reminded me so much of my own grandfather. Thanks for sharing your twinkle, Ed. I think some of it rubbed off.

November 21   Caballo Lake State Park
Caballo, New Mexico

What a day! Woke up in Rock Hound State Park and waved goodbye to my buddy Ed as he and his wife pulled out this morning. Happy trails, friend.

Ate breakfast and packed up camp. Then Jan went for a walk and the girls scampered over to a campground playground with a slide and swings. I did some yoga and stretching in the warm sun. When Jan came back I went for a two-mile walk-run. I haven't done any running for at least three years, but since my bike didn't make the final load out of Craig, I thought I'd try it again. Sore knees was the problem before, but I'm stretching beforehand and walking to cool down afterward. I'm also taking it slow. No ill effects so far

---

I really enjoy talking with elders that have made it that far in life with their sense of humor intact. It's a good sign. It gives me hope. He reminded me so much of my own grandfather. Thanks for sharing your twinkle, Ed. I think some of it rubbed off.

and it feels good once I get going.

Then on to Truth or Consequences, New Mexico, the town that changed its name from Hot Springs in the 1960's when it hosted a broadcast of the old *Truth or Consequences* TV program! We drove 100 miles one way, hoping to find hot mineral springs used since Apache days, but rumored to be closed down! After some initial confusion, we got our reward!

We drove through town twice with no luck, seeing some empty buildings and what seemed to be a town a little down on its luck. But our third set of directions proved to be the brass ring! Turn right at the Ford dealer, past Indian Springs Bathhouse on Austin Street, all the way to the end where a combination youth hostel-mineral bath awaits. A couple lunching casually on a veranda, some artistic signs and decorations painted here and there, a young "hippie" playing a wooden flute, and a full-sized tipi in the background. I knocked on the manager's residence and a smiling bearded giant replied, "$4." (It later turned out to be a very worthwhile investment of $10 for all 4 of us.) A converted minnow farm, three cement "baths" overlooking the river, each about five feet by five feet, four feet deep, each with progressively cooler water with the hottest being 107-109 degrees according to the manager's wife (or mother—we weren't quite sure). She had an amazing attitude—wanted to make it work, but didn't advertise because "How would I handle all the business? I like my privacy." Ah, we climbed out reluctantly after almost two hours as the sun was hanging it up for the day. We'll return if we're within 200 miles next time!!

We drove 20 miles south to Lake Caballo State Park, and ate pancakes for dinner. We bought a $5 bundle of wood at a roadside bar/store just as we turned into the park, so I'm writing this by the soft crackle of a campfire. The girls have already turned in after I read them a chapter from *Sea Star,* a follow-up to *Misty of Chincoteague*, another horse story by Marguerite Henry, a family favorite.

We'll wake up tomorrow on a bluff overlooking the lake. I know the truck will at least cast a glance back to Truth or Consequences as we head out. Aaaaaaaah!

November 22   **Oliver Lee State Park**
Alamogordo, New Mexico

Holy Jumpin' Jehosophat, Nebuchadnezer! Was it COLD last

night!!! The rangers this morning said the overnight low was 31 degrees, but I'll bet it was at least three or four degrees cooler where we camped by the lake. Jan (with her two blankets on top of her sleeping bag) and the two girls in their down bags were warm enough, but I was never quite warm until morning light. The interminable length of a cold night in a sleeping bag is one of my very first camping memories from the age of nine or ten. And now I have a fresh memory to add to the pile.

Today we visited White Sands National Monument, huge white dunes of gypsum, which is used to make wallboard and plaster of Paris. It was eerie—the white sands had drifted across the road, and where it was plowed off it looked just like snow. We took off our shoes and climbed the dunes, then ran screaming down the other side.

Dear Dave,

We went to see Jenny and Mike. We picked up Jenny at school. And Jenny had some birds and the family had a kitten. First we went to eat at a burger place, then we went to see a volleyball game. We camped in their side yard. And when we got up Jenny and Mike were gone to school.

We went to a place called Cochise's Stronghold. Cochise was an Apache. His stronghold was some mountains. And we climbed them. I got a magazine that told about him. After Cochise died Jeffords took over Cochise's tribe. Jeffords was Cochise's blood brother. It was fun going there.

We went to see the giant Redwoods. They were huge. The outside of a Redwood is reddish brownish. The inside is red. When a fire hit the outside bark would burn in some spots and make a goose pen. A goose pen is where all the inside is gone. We saw the biggest Redwood. It was 367 feet tall. Taller than a football field.

We went to a campground called Campland. Campland has a big pool. The pool was four to eight or nine feet deep. It was 100 degrees. I practiced swimming. I played with my koosh. It was fun.

Love,
Jordin

P.S. Miss you very much.

Dear Dave,

The trip is going well. We went to see Jenny and Mike. We picked up Jenny at her school and brought her home. Then we went out to eat at a burger place. We saw Jenny play volleyball. She did a good job. When we got back to their house Mike was back from his football game. We camped in their side yard. I liked seeing them and getting the cards from Mike, a Charles Barkley and a Larry Johnson.

At Casa Grande (Big House in Spanish) I got a Suns hat for five dollars. I like it a lot! At dad's cousin's house we saw a Suns game on TV. They played lousy and lost to the Rockets. While we were in Phoenix we saw the America West Arena. It was huge! At dad's friend's house we saw another Sun's game. This time they played well and beat the Golden State Warriors. I like seeing the games.

At Cochise's Stronghold State Park I looked up the price of basketball tickets for the Minnesota Timberwolves. We bought some tickets to see the Timberwolves play the Phoenix Suns on January 7, 1994. I can not wait to see Charles Barkley, Kevin Johnson, Dan Majerle, Danny Ainge, Oliver Miller, Frank Johnson, A.C. Green, Mark West, and Christian Laettner.

And about three weeks ago I got my hair cut. About ten inches gone! Mom thinks it is short and perky. I need a trim now because my hair grows fast. I like it a lot!! When we were at San Diego we went to Sea World. We saw some exhibits on fresh water fish, and some on salt water fish. The first thing we saw was the dolphin show. The dolphins jumped over a rope that was 25 feet above the water. We also saw the Clydesdale horses you see on beer commercials. The last thing we saw was a killer whale show. Dad and I sat in the front row. When the whale went by we got soaked with freezing cold salt water. And it was sort of cold outside. We almost froze to death! But it was fun!

MISS YOU!

Love, Kaitlin

November 23   **Brantley Lake State Park
                                    Carlsbad, New Mexico**

A moonlight walk in Brantley Lake State Park— my spirit soared.

November 24   **Brownfield, Texas**

We spent three hours today touring Carlsbad Caverns. What a fairyland! We met Andy, the cave gnome/park ranger, an elderly gent with a white goatee who really enjoyed the drama of his workplace. Although the cavern was lit throughout, it was a kind of dreamy light, almost like being underwater. As we walked along the asphalt pathway, Andy materialized at Jan's elbow. She asked how long these formations had taken to form. He silently shook his head back and forth slowly about four or five times and then said, "Too many variables, too too many variables." He then went on to explain that there would be no noticeable changes in any formation during a human lifetime (Holy moly, some of these things are at least 20 feet high!!!), and that growth depended on factors like rainfall during a particular season and mineral content in a certain area. He then took us over to another section and showed us an incredibly clear fossil of a snail which was four inches in diameter.

We saw a rock called the Lion's Tail in Carlsbad Caverns. It looked like a lion's tail. It had a long white stick thing with popcorn on the end and it hung from the ceiling. It formed from drip drops and coldness. It was neat.

There was a rock called flowstone. It was named Crystal Spring Rock. It was called that because drops of water came from the roof and formed a rock and the rock dripped into a hole in the floor and made a pool. It was pretty! (Jordin)

I think that having lunch with the homeless people is not going to be fun. We will look rich. I think the people will be poorly dressed compared to us. I do not think I will like it! (Kaitlin)

I think eating with the homeless will be yucky. I think it also will be NOT FUN!! We will look nice and I think they will look raggy. Some will look nice (kind of). (Jordin)

November 25   **Wichita, Kansas**

Thanksgiving Day in Amarillo, Texas. We planned to camp one more night before doing motels on our way north, but a real cold snap hit us on our way from Carlsbad into Texas, so last night we stayed in a motel. It felt good to sleep in a bed.

Today we had turkey and the trimmings at the Salvation Army. We were apprehensive beforehand; the girls were definitely uncomfortable, and Kaitlin in particular voiced her discontent.

The helpers there were very kind and not judgmental of us or the others. There were four or five kids ranging from about 10 to 16 and they had a genuinely caring attitude. One lady, a first grade teacher in Colorado, had driven three hours to help, while there was an older lady who reminded Jordin of Grandma Marge. Two Salvation Army officers, a man and a woman, were very generous. One of their helpers slipped a $10 bill into Jan's hand (because of our kids I suspect.) I'm not sure I would have accepted it if he had handed it to me, but by the time I saw it, it was a done deal. (Janet tried rejecting his offer, but to no avail.)

The appearance of the homeless was much as we had expected, and I can readily understand that after our extended camping bouts. It's hard to look your best if you've spent the night in a sleeping bag or wrapped in a blanket and there's no warm water or mirror in the morning. The kindness in several of them surprised and touched me, however. It is so easy to dehumanize people because of their appearance. Most of us are insulated from any kind of real contact with people much different than "our group."

There was a black man with a stocking cap and a straggly beard sitting across from me. I noticed that he was eating with only his left hand, his right hidden beneath the table. As he warmed to the task, however, his right hand came out and joined in. The thumb was horribly malformed, bent back and up at right angles over the rest of his hand. I made a joke with him about the size of his piece of pie. He looked up, surprised at first that someone was talking to him. (Contact with others must be very minimal.) He made a return comment, smiled and went back to eating. (And why weren't there any women here? Where do homeless women go?)

There were two pony-tailed brothers about my age who had lived in Alaska for 15 years prior to 1980, near Delta Junction. The older brother was very talkative and seemed fairly comfortable with being there, but the younger brother, who had a boy of about three or four, seemed a little more ill at ease, even though he was friendly as well. We talked for awhile before the meal, and as they were leaving they wished us good luck on our journey. Same to you, brothers. I enjoyed our contact.

There was an older man, silver-haired, sitting next to the black man with the crippled hand. His manner of speech showed him to be an educated man, but his eyes were pink and unfocused and he had a 2-day growth of stubble on his face. He talked continually as he ate even though no one was responding. He talked of going to St. Catherine's Church the day before where he had received the coat that he was wearing. The night before got down to 8 degrees, and I'd bet that he spent the night on the streets.

A young man across from Jan packed in two heaping plates of food and part of a third. The helpers seemed surprised when I declined a second helping. My hunger was that of a man who had eaten breakfast that morning and three meals the day before. I also knew that I would be eating again that night and the next day. There's a big difference.

The man at the end of the table finished and stood up to go. As he did, his coat opened and a plastic deli salad tray half fell out. It was filled with crumbling croissants. Afterward we had a talk with the girls about that. They couldn't understand why someone would need to hoard food on Thanksgiving Day. We had a very meaningful talk about homeless people and chronic, continuing hunger.

Now some of these people had been dealt a bum hand by fate and some had undoubtedly earned what they had coming. Life is a long and winding road.

It was a very full and meaningful Thanksgiving Day.

We just went to a Salvation Army store to have a Thanksgiving lunch. It was very good! The people were not ragged like I thought. Most were like us. There were lots of people eating all the food. There was turkey, mashed potatoes, dressing, green beans, and rolls. I liked the food a lot. For dessert there was pie. Jordin had two slices of pie! All the plates were piled high with food. There were lots of people helping. One guy had two and a half plates of food and two pieces of pie. He had on a hat and looked like a messier version of us. (Kaitlin)

> We just went to a Salvation Army store to have a Thanksgiving lunch. It was very good! The people were not ragged like I thought. <u>Most were like us.</u>

It was OK. The food was good. I even had two pieces of pie. I saw a lady and she had an accent. She was about 60 or 70. She reminded me of Grandma.

A guy gave Mom and Dad a $10 bill. I was very surprised. The people were better than I thought. They were not very raggy. (Jordin)

November 27   Coralville, Iowa

Camping in New Mexico was not any warmer, so we made a quick dash to Carlsbad Caverns. For one brief 24 hours, the weather warmed, then with a change of the wind that was strong enough to lift the tent and all its belongings, the temperature plummeted 40 degrees and by the time we climbed out of the tent in the morning, it was below freezing. Okay. So maybe I am ready to head north (north?) to family, beds, a roof over my head and a furnace to warm this old body. (I am forty, if you remember.)

We left Carlsbad Caverns on Wednesday, planning to camp one more night south of Amarillo, Texas, and then hopefully, one more night in Oklahoma or Kansas, having forgotten what November does to temperatures in the Midwest. Plans are always subject to change, as is the weather.

As we drove across miles of Texas plains, the windows on the truck began to get cooler and cooler to the touch. By 5:00 we knew we couldn't (wouldn't) camp. We pushed on to Amarillo, arriving, blurry-eyed at 10:00 p.m. in a motel where I proceeded to fall into a hot bath.

Thanksgiving morning dawned clear and very cold at eight degrees. (That could have been one chilly night of camping, and we were glad we weren't.) There was great discussion and dissention in room 136 regarding where we should spend Thanksgiving Dinner. Jim held strong to his desire to share a meal with the homeless at the downtown Salvation Army. The girls were completely distraught with that plan and totally against it, while I had many mixed emotions ranging from fraud (I was homeless, but by choice and with ample funds to buy dinner, although we are running low and know we'll run out sooner than the trip's end) to pride to empathy. Did any of these qualify as a justification to receive a free meal with those less fortunate than me? Could I justify doing this, could I do it without justification? Would I be embarrassed?

The other determining factor for me was to start driving earlier in the day, and putting some miles behind us. If we had lunch at the Salvation Army, we wouldn't be on the road until 1:00, at least.

Education, by experience, won out and we arrived at the Salvation Army one half hour prior to meal time, which was to be at noon. The girls were not happy campers while we waited to go inside, and became more miserable as the time drew nearer.

I was nervous, hesitant, doubtful and almost backed out when the T.V. crew from the local station pulled up in front. But, I had waited out the morning, and knew somewhere deep inside that this could be okay, if only I could stay away from the camera.

It was. No one judged me, as I had thought they would. (Those who judge others assume others will judge them.) The meal recipients were more like me than unlike me, and were very accepting of those around them. The volunteers were empathic, kind, warm, loving, and unselfishly spending their holiday giving of themselves and their time to help those in need. One volunteer had driven three hours, from southern Colorado, with her kids to help out.

It was a strong emotional experience that forced me to work at keeping my tears at bay for the whole meal. The girls spoke not one word and only worked at trying to make a dent in a huge mound of food that included turkey, light and dark, stuffing, mashed potatoes, green beans, rolls, cranberry relish, and pie for dessert. (We donned Jordin with the name "Jordin Two Pie" for obvious reasons.) We sat in the dining area with the others who did not want to be on T.V. Whew.

We left, sincerely grateful, engulfed in strong emotions and $10 richer. (A kind man gave those with children each a ten dollar bill.) Fraud? Do you wonder how I can accept that? I tried not to, but I know that what I'm giving my children this year is an invaluable experience that is costing us more than we had saved, and I know that frugality has become a part of our existence in order to continue this trip through the school year. We limit ourselves unmercifully at times in order to make the money and this trip last, and yet try to experience those things we feel are educational, important, and necessary, like new shoes, and jeans (hand me downs or used, via garage sales). We've purchased Oreos™ only three times (I refer to these wonderful delights often solely because they are one of our true eating pleasures) in three months, buy snacks very seldom, and camp free when we can. (But we have yet cheated any campground on an overnight fee. We've been advised and encouraged not to pay fees in certain campgrounds because no one will be checking for days, but we have continued to support the theory that what goes around comes around.) We are choosing to live honestly.

When we left Amarillo, we knew that sometime in the future we would be on the other end of the food line and soup kitchen, and were grateful for what we had received nutritionally, emotionally, and intellectually. The girls perked up, but were obviously shocked by the experience. I respect their courage: they were extremely hesitant, but walked in with determination and have now grown because of it. We asked them to write about the experience, but their difficulty in doing so made it evident that they kept within themselves, and were not their usual observant selves. When we inquired about certain men (interesting, that it was mostly men), it was clear they hadn't noticed too much. They must have been petrified, but they did it, learned that the homeless were "not as bad as we thought" (quote by the girls) and have one more experience that they would not have had sitting in a class of 28 behind a closed door and four walls.

> **Kaitlin and Jordin learned that the homeless were "not as bad as we thought" (quote by the girls) and have one more experience that they would not have had sitting in a class of 28 behind a closed door and four walls.**

The cold weather showed no signs of letting up, so we drove hard and arrived in Coralville at the house of my sister Mel, her husband Jeff, and son Travis at 6:00 last night. We had covered 1,300 miles and parts of 6 states in 3 days. The girls did a lot of drawing and reading, Jan worked on her dream catchers, I attended to Buck the Silver Truck's autopilot system and steering, and we all memorized the words to several country songs, the highlight being Alan Jackson's *Mercury Blues.*

We are facing a shortage of funds at this point, and again are dealing with doubts about the trip and a yearning for a home. They say that the holiday season is often the hardest for people with stress in their lives and I guess we qualify. We will be trying to find work to earn money, visit people without wearing out our welcome, make sure that all family members have some kind of Christmas present, keep school going for the girls, keep working on Jan's and my relationship, and generally keep the sanity level in the black. Ho, ho, ho!

November 28

Kaitlin and I went to see the Lady Hawks women's basketball team from the University of Iowa. They are the third ranked team in the country and were playing Louisiana Tech, ranked fourth. At first Kaitlin didn't really want to go because she was having so much fun playing Teenage Mutant Ninja Turtles™ with sister Jordin and cousin Travis. But I kind of insisted and she ended up really enjoying it. She likes basketball and talks about wanting to play college basketball, and yet all her role models and heroes are pro players, male of course. They're great players and fun to watch, but a kid needs someone like them for that all-important imagination, the place where they actually picture themselves performing at a higher level.

It was a super game. The Hawks were down by as much as nine or ten in the first half, then put on a burst in the last three minutes of the first half to take a one point lead at the half. The second half seesawed back and forth, but Iowa finally prevailed, 70-66. There were big rebounders (6' 5" and 6' 4"), midsize athletic shooters (5' 11" to 6' 2") and dribblers (5' 3" and up), lots of different models to choose from, and it was GOOD, SOLID BASKETBALL highlighted by tough D. Lots of fun.

If we're still here in another week we'll go again.

November 29

Dear Gay,

In California we went to a campsite. It was called the Anza-Borrego Desert State Park. I saw tons of lizards, and we saw coyotes. And we heard coyotes too. I saw a kangaroo rat. When I clapped my hands he jumped straight up. He jumped straight up two feet! It was fun.

We are at my cousin's house. His name is Travis. He has tons of turtles. And he has a Game Boy™ Jurassic Park thing. He has brown hair. We play turtles a lot. And we play that we are the turtles too. It is fun.

Travis has a lot of turtles. The turtles I'm talking about are Teenage Mutant Ninja Turtles™. They are toys. They are like turtles with bandanas and wrist and elbow and knee bands and they have weapons and belts. And they stand on their feet. Their names are Donatello, Leonardo, Michaelangelo, and Raphael. We play with them like they are fighting and going on adventures.

We went to the San Diego Zoo. It was neat. We saw polar bears that had algae on their fur. We went to see the lions but the mama had cubs and she was in the back room. So was the dad. I saw a Guam Rail. They look fuzzy. The girls had a little thing on top of their head. It was like a quail's little thing on their head. They were tannish brownish. It was fun seeing them.

Love,
Jordin

Dear Gay,

When we went to San Diego we went to the San Diego Zoo and Sea World. When we went to the zoo we saw lots of animals. Elephants, giraffes, and lots of other ones. One parrot named Batman could hang by his beak on a metal bar! We saw two Chinese leopards fighting. The girl beat up the boy. It was fun!

When we went to Sea World we saw three shows. We also saw the horses you see on beer commercials. They were huge! We saw a dolphin show and a sea lion show. When we saw the whale show we sat in the front row. When the killer whale went by, we got splashed. We were soaked! It was fun!

In California we stayed at the Anza-Borrego Desert. We saw two coyotes and a rattlesnake. We also saw kangaroo rats, hawks, a tarantula, lizards, rabbits, and deer. We also heard coyotes.

Yesterday I saw a Lady Hawkeyes game. It was awesome! I also went to the gym and played basketball for two hours. In Minnesota I am going to see a pro game. Suns and Timberwolves, January 7, 1994. I can not wait to see it! I got all the information on the tickets ready from my magazine. I can not wait to see Charles Barkley and Christian Laettner play. They were both on the Olympic Dream Team.

Love,
Kaitlin

P.S. How are Magic and Toots?

November 30

School was hard today. We started in on equivalent fractions, and I had to speak to Kaitlin three times about sitting up and paying attention. Finally I had to give her extra work as a punishment. The tears came, but she paid attention from then on. While the girls were finishing their letters to Gay Medina, I had Jordin correct some spelling and the tears came there too. I feel a responsibility to make sure they're solid when they head back into the public (or private, who knows?) school system, so I do what I need to do, but sometimes it's not easy.

December 6

Today I watched a video about me when I was little. I always smiled on the movie. It was funny! I kept falling on my butt. I had dark hair. I always had big hands from when I was a baby. (Kaitlin)

December 7   Roseville, Minnesota

We stayed at Mel, Jeff, and Travis's for eight days, although I spent the sixth and seventh of those days at my Dad's house. I hadn't seen him since Mom's death last January, and he has had a hard time with the parting. He still goes up to visit her at the cemetery. There have been changes. The TV was only turned on when I watched the last half of a basketball game. (It used to be on all the time.) We talked more than we had for a long time. It seems like he is enjoying himself socially at times, and I hope he can find some degree of happiness and contentment.

I have really enjoyed the time we've spent with friends—Larry and Mary and kids, Andy and Laurie, Bill Bremser, Mel, Jeff and Travis, my brother Bill, and my Dad.

And now we're on the road to Grandma's and a host of friends and relatives in the Twin Cities area of Minnesota. We'll be seeing friends in Wisconsin after Christmas, and scouting out potential places to work and live in Minnesota and Wisconsin.

December 8

Dear Pat [Griffin],

While we are in Minnesota we are going to see a pro basketball game. We are going to see the Timberwolves play the Phoenix Suns. While we are in Arizona I got a Suns hat. It is purple. In Arizona I also got all the information together for the seats. We saw two Suns games on TV.

We also went to the desert. We saw lots of animals and plants. We saw a rattlesnake and a tarantula. It was cool! We saw lots of cacti. You get spines in your finger. It was the Anza-Borrego Desert State Park in southern California.

On the trip we visited White Sands Park. All of the sand was pure white. There were dunes 20 feet high! We built sand castles and ran around in our bare feet. It is in New Mexico and they test bombs and missiles there too.

This year we had Christmas at my Grandma's house. She has a fake tree she puts up every year. It has a top thing for the top of the tree. We put lots of lights up on the tree. We set up a little village too. It was fun! We turned out all of the lamps at night. All of the lights made the room light.

Love,
Kaitlin

Dear Barb [Griffin],

When we went to Texas we went to a Salvation Army and had lunch there. The town was called Amarillo. It was Thanksgiving. They had good food. They had turkey, mashed potatoes and gravy. And after that I had two pieces of pie. I saw a lady that had an accent. She was about 60 or 70. She reminded me of Grandma. A guy gave mom and dad a $10 bill. I was surprised.

We went to the San Diego Zoo. I saw a bird called the Guam Rail. They were fuzzy. They were a light brownish tannish color. There were like eleven in the zoo. There were no more on the island of Guam.

We went to the desert in California. It was called the Anza-Borrego Desert State Park. When we were at the desert we saw some coyotes. They were very pretty. And we heard them too. They went yip, yip, yip, BARRRK. When I was sitting I saw a kangaroo rat. They are like kangaroos only smaller. And I clapped my hands and he jumped two feet up. It was funny.

We are at my Grandma's house right now. And we just set up the tree. We put on icicles, balls, snowflakes, and angels. And we put up a village with lights in them. And when we turned off all the lights except the tree lights and the village lights it was fun.

Love,
Jordin

P.S. Hope you liked the letter.

December 13

We've been at Jan's mom's house for nearly a week now, and we're feeling very comfortable. People have welcomed us into their homes. It feels nice to have a roof over our heads, a bed to sleep in, and a stove and sink.

I've been painting the basement rec room to help Marge. I enjoy painting because the rewards of your labor are so quickly apparent, while fresh paint on a wall makes a room look nice.

I've been staying in bed longer than usual because 4-8:00 a.m. seems to be Jan's best time for sleep and I don't want to roll out of the sack and wake her, but my normal cycle is to get up around 6:00. This morning, since we were going to visit the Mankato area today, I did get up earlier so I could finish part of the basement before we left. As I was painting, I heard a dog yipping in the early morning stillness. It made me think of the coyotes in Anza-Borrego. I've been checking the Southwest temps in the paper.

December 14

Yesterday we took a day trip to St. Peter and Mankato, 90 miles southwest of the Twin Cities. We were scouting out possible nesting spots for this coming spring, and the news was good! St. Peter was just what we were looking for, a small town (9,000+) with a college (Gustavus Adolphus). It seemed clean, and although many of the houses were older, they were well kept, and the schools looked fairly new.

We stopped at the community rec center, obviously the old school, and were surprised by the beautiful wooden gym floor and the number and variety of rec programs for both kids and adults. The three ladies we talked to there were very friendly.

As a bonus, real estate seemed affordable. I was beginning to wonder if there were decent houses anywhere for under $100,000.

December 16

Dear Nikki,

We went to the San Diego Zoo. At the zoo I saw a bird. It was called the Guam Rail. It was a pretty tannish brownish with a white blob on its neck. They were on the endangered list. The only place you can find them is in zoos. There are no more on the island of Guam.

For Christmas this year I asked Santa for a volleyball, knee pads, books, toys, and surprises. I wrote Mrs. Claus a letter. It was fun!

When we were at Grandma's we decorated the tree. We got to put on tons of lights. And we put on decorations. It was very fun. Only nine more days till Christmas. Then we can open up all the presents. And we get out all the Christmas books and tapes.

Right now we are at my cousin's house. We are going to make his bedroom look like the Stone Age. With dinos and palm trees and stuff. We are going to tape together paper and draw stuff on it.

Love,
Jordin

P.S. We are going to see you very soon.

Dear Nikki,

The trip is going well. Are you excited about Christmas? I am! Did you write a letter to Santa Claus? I did! And I even made an envelope for it. It was fun. I'll tell you some of the stuff I put on my list: some posters, some basketball cards, a basketball signed by Michael Jordan, *Home Alone 2* the movie, a T-shirt, and a pair of shorts.

When we were in San Diego I got my hair cut very short. Eight to ten inches gone and I have bangs again. I got it cut because it took an hour to brush after showers. I like it a lot!

In St. Paul we saw *Jurassic Park*. Did you see it? Some parts were scary and some parts were funny. I liked the part best when they ran across the field from the dinosaurs and they hid under the log.

While we were at my grandpa's house we saw movies of Jordin and I when we were little. And you were in it! You were only about 10 or 11 or 12 in the movie. It was neat. We were riding three wheelers and you kept bumping me. It was funny!

Love,
Kaitlin

P.S. We will see you after Christmas. I can't wait!!

The trip to St. Peter had an interesting effect. It was clearly a community where we could all easily imagine ourselves living: dance and volleyball for Jordin, a sixth grade girls' basketball club team at the Rec Center for Kait, friendly people, affordable real estate and potential employment for the big folks, and a college, with its sports and cultural events, for all. When we started out on this trip, it was very open-ended, at times almost threateningly so. But now there is a foreseeable end to Plan Z. It's not of primary importance whether or not we actually end up in St. Peter, only that such a place actually exists and that we have been there.

When I was in my early 20's I quit working for a while, looking forward to all the things I was going to do with my new leisure time. I was going to do a lot of reading, painting, and music, a real renaissance. After about three weeks, however, I found myself not doing much of anything. It could always wait until later or tomorrow. After another two weeks, I started a part-time job working 20 hours a week. That was just right. I still had extra leisure time, but I found that the hours spent at my job made me much more productive during my "off" hours. I have a feeling that St. Peter may do just that to the remaining three months of Plan Z. Does that make sense?

The endless complexities of us human beans never ceases to amaze me.

And for now we're on our way back to sister Mel's. We'll have "Christmas" there on the 18th and then back to St. Paul for the "real" Christmas on the 25th.

December 18

I remember sitting around various campfires, really enjoying the outdoors, looking at people who had closed themselves in their RV's for the evening, lights and TV's on. For a species that has historically spent so much time out living in the elements, we homo modernus sapiens seem very content to spend most of our time within the confines of four walls and a roof.

So we've been off the road phase of Plan Z for three weeks now, and I've spent most of that time in houses, either sister Mel's or Grandma Marge's. I went for a long walk today and it felt so good. My legs and back are more limber and there's a ruddy glow on my cheeks. For supposedly intelligent beings, it certainly seems that we periodically have to relearn some pretty basic and important lessons. Balance is so hard to maintain.

For various reasons, neither Jim nor I found work during the holiday season. Being and maintaining a free spirit won out over the need for additional funds. I know we'll pay for this, but at present it just didn't fit into our plans.

December 23

I spent 12 hours yesterday finishing the painting in Marge's basement. It looks really nice. I started out by painting the rec room, which was a piece of cake, but then I tackled the laundry room, which proved to be a cake of a different color. The cement block walls had never been painted so I had to put on a prime coat to seal it first. There were several pipes close to the wall to paint over, under, and around. I was glad to fill in the last brush stroke.

I enjoy painting. It's pretty straightforward, especially with the improvements in the covering ability of paint these days, and the end result is something you can really admire.

"Tomorrow's Christmas Eve," Kaitlin continually reminds us. This is the first year without Santa Claus in our house ("our" house? More on that later...we are staying with my Mom.) So now the lack of presents under the tree is a worrisome thought. "If Mom and Dad are Santa, and we know they

*are Santa, why don't they just put the presents under the tree?" And so go
their thoughts and the endless questions, did I get a volleyball, where are the
presents, aren't you going shopping, have you gone shopping, etc. etc. etc.?
Jim and I, for the first time without the help of Santa, accept full responsibility
for the girls' presents and all the emotions, good and bad, that will
accompany them this Christmas. We continue to remind them that "Plan Z"
is a big present this year and they are reminded of it when their cousin heads
off to school or they see school busses drive by Grandma's house.*

*We've been living with others since the Friday after Thanksgiving,
and we've adapted fairly well to the lifestyles, mannerisms, and routines:
who watches the nightly news, who pees during the night, who eats a hearty
breakfast, who likes wholewheat, who dries their dishes, who lets them drip
dry, who wakes up slow, who stays up late. We've learned to be humble house
guests and are service-conscious each day: cooking, cleaning, laundry,
babysitting, errands.*

*Because I am homeless, I don't feel like a visitor in these homes, I feel
like a leech, a beggar. My past attitude that people are glad to have us visit,
has been reduced to humility and gratitude. I try to be overly generous of my
services and time (I have plenty) and of my money (which we lack). I don't
want people thinking that we have no where else to go, and that that is why
they've been chosen. But, do we? Have they?*

*It's zero degrees and we could be in the desert, warm, tan, and
wondering what our family and friends are doing yet another holiday season
without us. (Who? Oh, Jim, Janet, and the girls.) It's time, I guess to make
our presence known at a family gathering. The wanderers that we are.*

*But with all my doubts, I'm glad to be home for Christmas. Mel, Jeff,
and my Mom have been most gracious, accommodating, and welcoming of
our intrusion. Ah yes, family.*

*Yet, the urge of freedom and the road south has begun its beckoning
already, just one month after arriving here in the Midwest. No restraints, no
excessive white sugar and white flour, more fresh air, sunshine, wildlife (lots
here, all human) open spaces and warmth. New spaces, new sites.*

*Have you ever noticed that advertisements which portray women
show them mostly naked, while men are mostly clothed? Imagine Iacocca in
a high cut swim suit, Italian style, every ripple and wrinkle showing, while
ads for exercise videos showed Hillary fully clothed in a sweat suit?*

Have you ever noticed that advertisements which portray women show them mostly naked, while men are mostly clothed? Imagine Iacocca in a high cut swim suit, Italian style, every ripple and wrinkle showing, while ads for exercise videos showed Hillary fully clothed in a sweat suit?

December 24

Christmas Eve Day in St. Paul. It's below zero this morning, but I just went for a half hour walk. It feels good to get out and move about, gets the blood circulating a little faster, y'know. Good for the body, good for the mind.

Last night we were watching a TV program on wolves. It talked about how the Indians had admired the wolf because, even though it gave strong allegiance to the pack, it remained an individual. The film maker had been studying a wolf pack in the Sawtooth Mountains for several years and was able to point out unique differences in the personalities of the individuals in the pack.

At one point in the program some kids were playing with wolf pups. I watched Kaitlin watching the kids and wolves rolling around together. Waves of wonder, amusement and gentle laughter rolled across her face like white fluffy clouds on a summer day. We have spent so much time together that we really know each other. That knowledge makes us so aware of subtle shadings in each other's moods and personalities. I think we sometimes take that for granted, but it's a rich and rare gift that will last us to the end of our days. We are family.

I'm reading a book by Mike Lew called *Victims No Longer*, published by Harper and Row. In talking about people's reluctance to enter therapy he says, "People who would never dream of waiting until their car broke down before changing the oil, who would be shocked at the idea of not cleaning their house until the Board of Health forces them to, see nothing illogical in waiting until they're in crisis before seeing to the care and maintenance of one of their most valuable possessions—their emotional well-being."

As I'm typing this on the computer in Marge's den, I look out the window. It's definitely a white Christmas in Minnesota, about three inches on the ground. The season of winter is here.

PART II OF THE SOJOURN

January 4, 1994   **Roseville, Minnesota**

School was great today! We did our studies in the truck on the way back from our seven-day visit to the Reedsburg area. The girls did math and G.R.O.W. (Geographical Regions of the World) questions and we worked together on reducing fractions to lowest terms. At the end of that time Kaitlin actually asked if there were flash cards to do!! The attitude was positive and the work was very good. It really motivated me to do some prep work tonight for some new areas tomorrow. We're going to start a unit on the classification of animals into groups of invertebrates and vertebrates. We're also going to look at latitude and longitude. They continue to eat up any new math concepts that I show them.

The visit to Wisconsin was fun but tiring. Highlights were time spent with old friends Mimi and Gene, Eleanor and Steve, Barb and Jerry, Nikki, and Nancy, and phone contact with Doc and Marlene. There are just too many people that we wanted to see and even more that wanted to see us, however. We split each day into three or four visits, leaving some people feeling that they hadn't seen us enough. We lived there for eight years and were very active in the community, so there are lots of people we want to see when we go back and it just ended up being too much. We had planned to stop in River Falls for our "scouting mission" to see if it was a possible living spot for next year, but we didn't see a motel with a pool and snow had started to fall in earnest, so we headed on "over the river and through the woods" to Grandma's house in St. Paul. The storm dumped 6 inches of crystalline powder on the area. It's beautiful!

January 6

An interesting article by Juanita Darling and Tracy Wilkinson of the *LA Times* was carried in the St. Paul paper this morning. It dealt with violence in school districts as reported in a survey of 700 districts by the National School Boards Association.

Eighty percent of the districts reported increases in school violence in the last five years, with 35 percent saying the increase was significant.

Reasons for the increased violence were seen as the breakdown of the family, portrayal of violence by the media, alcohol and drug abuse, poverty, and easy access to guns. Thirty-nine percent of urban districts reported a shooting or knifing in school last year, but while the highest increases were reported in urban districts, both suburban and rural districts reported increases as well.

"In an effort to deter violence, school districts have used an array of tactics: suspending students, increasing police presence on campuses, teaching students alternative ways of handling conflicts, and setting up separate schools for disruptive students." With the exception of conflict resolution, all these are punitive in nature and do nothing to address the underlying needs of these "students." Ask any elementary teacher (and many secondary teachers as well I suspect, although I haven't worked in a high school in over 20 years) about the kids that come to school every day hungry for both food and love, the kids who are so needy that you can give them literally everything you have to give and not even hit the bottom of the well. I could name specific students in every class I've worked with over the past seven years or so who had needs so great that I could only begin to help. I'm at a point now where I'm not sure I have anything left to take with me into my next classroom. I fear that I may have been sucked dry. At times I don't even have enough left for my own two daughters.

> **Ask any elementary teacher (and many secondary teachers as well I suspect, although I haven't worked in a high school in over 20 years) about the kids that come to school every day hungry for both food and love, the kids who are so needy that you can give them literally everything you have to give and not even hit the bottom of the well.**

The article went on to say that the St. Paul School District, with additional police officers, evening security guards, hall monitors, and electronic surveillance devices, now spends about $1 million a year on security measures. Most of this money comes from a general instructional fund, thus compounding the problems besetting our educational system.

About two weeks ago I noticed another article in the paper. It was about negotiations in Stillwater, the town where Jan lived when I was courting her 18 years ago. One of the major concerns of the teachers was not the usual wage or benefit options, but what to do about violence in the classroom. When I visited Loganville, the small elementary school in Wisconsin where I had taught for the six years prior to moving to Alaska, one of the topics of discussion was the increasing amount of behavior problems seen in that school. Both of these districts would be classified as rural districts.

We have seen places where the tide of violence seems to be held at bay for the time being, St. Peter, Minnesota and Chimacum, Washington specifically. It seems that a concerted community and family-based effort is the key.

We will, of course, try to relocate in one of these spots. We'll see.

January 7

This is the big day—the Minnesota Timberwolves vs. the Phoenix Suns!!! Pro basketball, anticipated for about 8 months and about to become reality. We spent some time this morning looking through Kaitlin's basketball card collection and a magazine on pro basketball. We looked at the Timberwolves update in the newspaper this morning, listing the Suns' Kevin Johnson as a doubtful starter because of an injury. That's okay, just as long as Sir Charles Barkley takes the floor. That's why we're here!!

January 10

Dear Claire,

    Merry Christmas! A few days ago I sent your present. This Christmas I spent at my grandma's house in Minnesota (St. Paul). For Christmas I got a basketball autographed by Michael Jordan, a poster of Michael Jordan, basketball cards, leggings, a T-shirt, a gift certificate, a teddy bear in a rocking chair, and a sweatshirt. It was fun!

After Christmas we went to Reedsburg, Wisconsin. I saw all of my old friends and my baby sitter. I had a sleepover with one of my friends and we played football.

When I was in Reedsburg I went sledding on a HUGE hill. At the bottom you kept going for a long ways! It was fun! One sled was like a skateboard without wheels and you stood on it while it went down the hill. It was called a snowboard.

On Friday, January 7 we went to a pro basketball game! Minnesota Timberwolves vs. Phoenix Suns. It was fun! The Suns won, 110 to 103. Charles Barkley got hurt and did not play much. I got two magazines.

I MISS YOU A LOT!

Love,
Kaitlin

P.S. If you want to send me a letter just mail it to Box 532, Craig. My mom's friend will pick it up and forward it to us. I will get it!

Well, Sir Charles took the floor, but after falling to the floor and hurting his knee, he ended up playing only 13 minutes. It would have been nice to watch him in action longer, but what we saw was special. He is definitely an extraordinary entertainer both for his physical skills and his very apparent sense of cosmic humor.

The game was well played and very entertaining. Christian Laettner sat out with an injury, but the Wolves still looked pretty good to me. The Suns had some veteran presence down the stretch (Danny Ainge with 34 points) and prevailed, 110-103.

Jan sat next to a woman who works as a corporate sponsor liaison with the Suns! They shot the breeze, and my not so shy wife ended up with the lady's business card and some possible tickets to a Suns game when we head back down to Phoenix! Awright!!!!

So here we are planning another trip, this time to southeastern Wisconsin to see more friends and then on to Chicago to visit my aunt, uncle, and cousin. This trip will be about two days shorter, with fewer people to see.

Dear Mrs. French,

How are you? I am fine. Home schooling is fine. We do lots of math, geography, writing, and reading. And Spanish. In math we are doing fractions, averages, and looooong division. We do school in about two hours.

We went to the desert in California. It was called Anza-Borrego Desert State Park. There were lots of animals. Rabbits, snakes, birds, and kangaroo rats. They are like little kangaroos with little tails. Once I saw one and clapped my hands and he jumped two feet in the air. It was fun.

We saw the giant Redwoods in California. They were huge. When a fire came through it would burn out the inside and not the outside. It would make a goose pen. The tallest tree was as tall as a football field.

Yea! It's Christmas! How did your Christmas go? Mine went good. We had Christmas at my grandma's house. We got to decorate the tree early. It was fun.

Love,
Jordin

P.S. Miss you a ton!

January 17   **Des Plaines, Illinois**

We're well into the next Wisco foray now. To Jan and the girls it seems no less hectic than the last time. We are again going house to house, one night one town, the next night another town and set of old and valued friends. Jordin and Kaitlin have gotten good at scouting out the "feel" of their new surroundings and interacting in appropriate ways. I'm really proud of their growth!

We stopped at Chrys and Tim's house on Saturday. They have two girls who are each one month older than our girls. There were some math papers on the refrigerator, so I casually, but professionally, perused them. I talked to Sara and Rene about what math topics they were working on in school. I'm pretty confident of our home schooling in reading, writing, social studies, geography, and spelling, but I wanted to check it out in math. Chrys and Tim, both teachers, seem to feel that the schooling their girls are getting in Delafield is good, and still both Jordin and Kaitlin were working on topics that those girls hadn't seen yet. That made me feel good. We are indeed covering the bases and more, as I had hoped.

It has been soooooooooooo COLD! We thought the zero degree weather in Minnesota was bad. We've been in the Chicago area the last two nights and it's been 20 below zero both nights, with wind chills 50 to 60 below! We've been inside all the time. Visions of spring training and short sleeve shirts are beginning to float through my mind.

January 18

It was hard for me to yield, daily, to the ebb and flow of each household, but I survived nearly two and a half months of being a house guest. The visits to friends, seeing a new one daily for 7-10 days at a time was emotionally exhausting. I found myself crying, mostly due to physical and emotional exhaustion. I felt like I had to be "on" and entertaining every moment in dwellings where the temperature didn't exceed 63 degrees for days at a time. I was frozen! We were in a new bed every night, specialty meal nightly, no exercise because the wind chill was below a minus 50 degrees, and I spent each moment trying to be gracious. (Except in between houses when I would bitch, moan, kick, and scream that I couldn't do yet another house. But I always did and spent a lot of energy raging.)

But the bottom line is that we rekindled old friendships, and for their support, kindness, and hospitality I am grateful. Barb lent me her ear late into the night as I vowed I couldn't continue with this trip, but knew that I would regret quitting, if I did.

The longer visits actually turned out to be the best as we were able to settle in the flow of their lives and visit as the days passed on. We had longer visits with Dale and Gina, Mel and Jeff, and my Mom. Thank you for sharing your lives with us.

I am in an art museum, the Art Institute in Chicago. There is a picture I like because it is a girl who learned to sew very young and she looks like me. The picture is very colorful. Some of the colors are pink, yellow, white, brown, blue and yellowish-orange. That is the color of her hair.

Lots of people stop and look at the picture. I think it is nice. (Jordin)

January 19

Over the past three weeks we have spent short amounts of time with many old friends. It's almost like a series of freeze frame photos because we go from place to place in such a short amount of time. We've seen many of our friends dealing with similar issues (individuality, marriage and changing relationships, jobs, money, and child rearing just to name a few of the biggies). What has been interesting to me is the variety of approaches and results.

I feel that my generation has unfortunately been responsible for the decline of discipline in our society, in general, and in the schools, specifically. I can remember raising issues when I was a senior in high school that eventually led to the easing of dress codes and hair length requirements. A moral victory that gave me a feeling of empowerment. Not too big by today's standards, but perhaps the beginning of a movement that has gotten out of control. We wanted to push back the barriers to individual freedom of expression. I still think that is the right philosophy, but where does it stop and

I feel that my generation has unfortunately been responsible for the decline of discipline in our society, in general, and in the schools, specifically.   A sense of personal responsibility is needed to balance out that desire for personal freedom and expression. Too many of my generation have been unwilling or unable to put out the extended effort needed to teach their children a sense of responsibility.

who has the right to judge where the new barriers should be erected? A sense of personal responsibility is needed to balance out that desire for personal freedom and expression. Too many of my generation have been unwilling or unable to put out the extended effort needed to teach their children a sense of responsibility.

But on this trip I have once again begun to believe in my generation. Oh, not all of us—the weight of general failure is all too obvious around us, but in a part of us, those that I know and have grown to love over the last 30 years or so of my life. On this trip I have seen people trying to do the right thing, to teach their children that sense of balance that just might make the future a better place. I have seen people giving of themselves so that their children will be better people. It's not always the easy road, but it is the right road. At least for myself, I have no doubt.

I like the children of my friends. They have welcomed Kaitlin and Jordin into their homes and willingly shared with them. They have looked at me with shining eyes and held up their end of the conversation, not backing down just because I'm bigger and older. The old line "Why, I knew you when you were only so high!" has begun to take on real meaning for me. I think if you like what you're seeing, then that is one of the real dividends of aging. And I do like what I'm seeing on this stage of Plan Z.

Thanks on this leg to Robert and Mary, Ginny and Don, Chrys and Tim, Thia and Uncle George and Cass, and Poor Ole Patti for their warm hospitality during one of the coldest stretches in recent history.

January 21   **Roseville, Minnesota**

Dear Claire,

The trip is going well, but I miss you a LOT! I don't know exactly what day I am coming back, but I hope it is soon! I think it will be in June or July. When I get there we can go to Sub Marina a lot together.

As an answer to your question I did make the dream catcher. I made it in a desert campground in California. It was about 85 degrees when I made it! HOT!!

Speaking of weather, how is the weather in rainy, dull Craig? I am writing this letter at my grandma's house in St. Paul, Minnesota. The coldest it ever got was 24 degrees below zero! Can you believe that? I almost froze in my bed! And you know what else? There are ten inches of snow! Dad and Jordin and I have been playing football in the backyard. It is hard running through ten inches of snow with boots on.

School is fine. I like having Mom and Dad for teachers, especially when school is only two and a half hours long!

But I miss you a lot and sometimes wish I had some friends my age (ten) to talk and play with.

My Christmas was great! Do you know what basketball team I like? Anyway, I like the Suns. I got a Suns T-shirt, a brand new basketball signed by Michael Jordan, and a sweatshirt.

What I am sending in this letter is a care package because you miss me so much. (I miss you too!) It includes an envelope with a smiley face, a picture I drew, a letter, and copies of the newspaper Jordin and I made (you and I can make one!) with lots of information. I hope you enjoy it!

How is the fort on the beach (I forgot the name. Oops!) Are you making aquariums with the tarps and plastic bags?

I wish I had my own room. I am tired of camping.

Do you know where Conrad moved to? Who is in his house now?

I hope I can see you soon!
I miss you a lot!

Love,
Kaitlin

P.S. The lizard is part of the care package. I colored one side already. You can color the other half. It can be our best friends' lizard.

Dear Shona,

Miss you very much! Guess what!! We are coming to Alaska in June or July! And we get to stay for about two months!

I am writing this letter in my grandma's house. There are ten inches of snow in the back yard! We like to play football in the back yard. It is hard to run in ten inches of snow.

It is fun here. But not as fun as when you were with me. When I come up to Craig we can go to the Sub shop and play (and eat ice cream!) Miss you very, very, very, very, very, VERY much!

Love,
Jordin

P.S. Hope you are having fun without me. (Just joking!)

January 23

When we visited Uncle Dale's cabin we went on the lake. It was frozen solid. The ice was two feet thick and had 24 inches of snow on it. The lake is called Big Thunder.

When George and Gail came over we went on a walk in the woods, and George threw Kaitlin and me in the snow. I almost froze!

When we went on the walk we played in the snow. It was up to my waist and it was hard to play in. We walked about two miles.

When we were there I drove the four wheeler. A four wheeler is like a snowmobile only it has wheels instead of skis.

At his house we had our own room. It was nice. We got some teddy bears that Gina made. She let us use her legos to make ships, gliders, trucks, and a house.

They had two dogs called Golden and Blaze. Blaze was older than Golden. They both had cubes that we played with. It was lots of fun there. (Jordin)

January 26

The girls are really on a rip with home schooling right now! Last Friday they spent three hours putting together their own newspaper on the computer, setting up shop in Grandma's den, and selling copies to us for 37 cents! The next day they asked me to get the two Social Studies textbooks (world history and U.S. history) from the back of the truck so that they could do a research report totally on their own! I've had no complaints about their work for the past two weeks, and they're really doing a super job of learning and retaining new concepts. Wow!! To a seasoned and somewhat grizzled educational veteran like myself, this is like dying and going to heaven. Thank you, sweetie pies. I'm enjoying this phase more than you could imagine.

> **Wow!!**
> To a seasoned and somewhat grizzled educational veteran like myself, this is like dying and going to heaven.

January 27

The one year anniversary of the passing of my mom. I quietly remembered her at several points in the day. She was a good friend.

And as they say, the plot thickens. We have heard rumors from two friends back in Craig. The grapevine says we've lost the lease on the lot that the Sub Marina sits on. If true that will involve a HUGE pain in the you-know-what, moving the building, equipment, and deck. This may affect the projected summer income that we were counting on to ease the transition at the end of Plan Z. Jan and I went for a walk tonight after dinner to discuss options. We'll see what happens.

Our sojourn south is beginning, saying good-bye to "Northern" family and friends, travelling down to Iowa for another visit. Our daily visits to friends in Wisconsin and family in Illinois were full of emotions, memories, and meals. Everyone was welcoming, cooked delicious meals, and then sent us on our way to another house of friends and food where we indulged again. I feel as if I'm floating in fat that my body hasn't seen in 15 years. The wind chills are still below a minus 50 degrees, so I've done very little walking. My moods are plunging while the scale is climbing, and I'm saddened by the friends and family I'm leaving behind again.

The stress of moving from one house to another created quite an emotional frenzy for me as I tried to be gracious while my pants were tightening. I was so comfortable being with old friends and family (old family?) who have been an important part of my life. I thank each and every one of you.

Teaching the girls to crochet.

A month later, Jordin proudly
displays her crocheted blanket.

February 2   **Coralville, Iowa**

Once again we're at Mel and Jeff's, poised for our descent into the southland, watching the weather maps and biding our time until temperatures reach the tent camping cutoff of at least 32 degrees consistently.

Jan would like to find hot springs in Arkansas and I've thought of doing a home school unit about the Mississippi River as we go south. How far we follow Old Man River remains to be seen. An article in yesterday's paper listed Louisiana as the most violent state in America. Right. Violence certainly seems to be a theme in this year of travel. We have violence in schools, we have violence in the streets and cities, with Tonya Harding we have violence in the ice skating rinks, and we have a committee forming to "discuss and monitor" violence on cable TV. Right. Discuss and monitor but probably not curtail. After all, the market calls for it, the producers answer the call.

Today was a good day. Jan went into Iowa City to check on some dream catchers that she had made and had put on consignment before Christmas. She was apprehensive, but found that they had sold four, and she came away with a check for $42 and some artistic encouragement! She and the girls spent some time in the bead shop across the hall and purchased some nice beads.

Jordin learned how to crochet from her mom today. I was really surprised at her perseverance. They had started working as I headed out on a long walk (about 14 degrees, with a stiff wind from the northwest). When I came back she was finishing up a small blanket for her teddy bear, Snuggles. A job well done and the pride of a craftsgirl, with a grin from ear to ear.

Travis got a full size basketball hoop for Christmas and it's set up in the rec room, with the basket at six feet. Kaitlin is having a ball slamming it! We played three games today after Trav got home from school. The three cousins against the Old Man. I didn't stand a chance. They pass the ball pretty well and then hold my legs if there's a rebound. Jordin starts playing demon defense on me as I take the ball out at the half line and then if that doesn't finish me off, Kaitlin comes in from behind to slap it away.

I'm somewhat apprehensive about the final stages of Plan Z. I've enjoyed the sights and the time with extended family through the holiday season. Home school is on solid ground now, but there are lingering doubts about extended stints of tent camping, temperatures in Texas and New Mexico, our cash reserves, the future of Sub Marina, and job hunting. I'm pretty confident that all will turn out well in the end and that this venture will be a very positive experience, but there will undoubtedly be some more stressful times before we reach shelter again.

February 5

There was an article in this morning's paper about the settlement between the local teachers and the school board. The headline concentrated on kids that brought weapons to school, stating that this was one of the main concerns of the local teachers. It went into great detail about certain weapons that were to be banned and even went into a couple of specific incidents that had led to this point.

Wow! No wonder test scores are down. How can this "learning environment" be effective?

Went for a mid-morning walk today and it really felt like the early stages of spring. I could hear a cardinal singing and the sun was bright while the ice on the sidewalk has retreated considerably over the past few days. This is one of my favorite times of year. I can remember the sound of melting ice and snow dripping from the roofs and running in the gutters and how it made the soil smell in the Iowa of my childhood.

Weather update from today's paper. Little Rock: high 58, low 44!!

February 7

The below zero weather that was predicted for Iowa this week has failed to materialize. Today's temp was 15 degrees above zero with a windchill of minus 19, but it felt okay. I went for a long walk and enjoyed myself immensely.

I watched part of a video on the Navajo culture and was reminded of the eternal side of life. We follow the daily ins and outs of life and feel the ups and downs, but behind it all is the cycle that is much longer in duration, the cycle that can lend stability to our mindset if we can keep it in sight...

Uncle Jeff works for the phone company and today we visited his building. There was lots of clicking because of the phones being picked up and put down.

There were a lot of wires in the building. Little wires went into big wires that went out into the town of Coralville. And there were HUGE batteries! They were three feet tall!! They had the batteries just in case the power went down. It was cool.

This is what happens: I call my friend Shona. I would

There was an article in this morning's paper about the settlement between the local teachers and the school board. The headline concentrated on kids that brought weapons to school, stating that this was one of the main concerns of the local teachers.

dial the phone first. The signal would go down the wires of my phone. Then a computer would signal to Shona's phone. Then we could talk.

Phones now use electricity, but the newest ones use light signals. (Jordin)

February 9

We went on a school "field trip" to the Johnson County Sheriff's Office today where my sister works. It was extremely interesting, not only to see the setup of rooms, equipment, jails and duties done by different people to keep our social fabric intact on a daily basis, but also to see the environment where Mel spends a large part of her time.

There was a room on the second floor, the actual incarceration area, that spoke to me. It was a small inauspicious room at the end of a short hallway that was filled with jackets on hangars and pairs of shoes and boots. One of the girls asked what that room was, and we were told that those boots and jackets belonged to the prisoners. They were taken away from them while they were in jail, and the inmates were required to wear bright orange coveralls and slippers, designed of course to impede any escape attempt.

As the others moved on, I lingered to look over that pile of shoes. There was a pair of very new black cowboy boots, several pairs of construction boots, quite a few brands of tennies, and one VERY worn pair of lowcut, scuffed white tennis shoes. I could almost see the occupants, so t'speak. I formed a theory in my mind that you could tell the future of any criminal based on the condition of his or her shoes (although on average, only 2% of the inmates are female according to our guide). That pair of cowboy boots was destined to take some Iowa cowboy on a ride once they got out. The lowly tennies, however, told a different story. The prognosis is not good.

Bet I'd be right more often than not.

Maybe we could save tax dollars that are now being spent on costly jails and rehab programs. Buy a guy a new pair of shoes. Feel like a million bucks and walk the straight and narrow.

Ah, these daydreams of mine!

> Maybe we could save tax dollars that are now being spent on costly jails and rehab programs. Buy a guy a new pair of shoes. Feel like a million bucks and walk the straight and narrow.

February 12

Went to see Robert Bly, American poet, speak in Cedar Rapids. Although I expected him to speak more to the "male experience" (a follow-up article in the newspaper quoted him as saying he was "past that," whatever that might mean), I enjoyed his presentation. He read from some of his poems and talked about how they had come about. He also read from Bill Stafford's work (I'm not sure of the name). I enjoyed that as well. Bly had a very active sense of humor and obviously a lot of directed energy. He spoke of his growth through the stages of life.

I went with my brother-in-law, Jeff, and enjoyed the time with him as well. He spoke of going out with his grandfather into the woods and rivers of eastern Iowa as a boy, and how that had shaped his appreciation of the outdoors. A memorable evening all together.

We're leaving tomorrow morning. Weather reports for "down South" still look pretty mixed, with yesterday's paper reporting an ice storm in Arkansas. Well, it's getting to be spring and that is a pretty unpredictable season, but the general trend is toward warmth and light. I'm ready, but I still have mixed feelings about hitting the road. I hope we are able to enjoy the last stage of Z, not merely "get through it."

I've enjoyed the stay in the home of my sister and her family. It has been a home for us and I feel that we've shared a closeness that will easily warm future reunions.

February 14   Blytheville, Arkansas

Valentine's Day and back on the road. We left Coralville, Iowa yesterday with six or seven inches of snow on the ground. Two hours south, as we crossed the Des Moines River into Missouri, the snow disappeared like magic. We entered into the Kingdom of Spring. Early Spring to be sure, but Spring nonetheless. No snow, the fields are grey and brown, the sun is warm, so green will come. The goddess of fertility awakens, stretches, and yawns. Time to punch in for another season.

We had a good taste of winter. Eleven weeks in the Midwest with stretches of record cold temps sated our appetite. And it was sure nice to spend time with family. Real nice. Although it's good to be on the road again, I wasn't sure about this, but it feels right. No specific time table or destination. There's lots of map work as we make our way south and west.

Visited Mark Twain's boyhood home in Hannibal, Missouri. There was a small museum next to the house. It had artifacts, newspaper clippings, and old photographs. Kaitlin looked at one photo of 60ish Sam Clemens and observed the he looked like he had a "sharp temper." Sam had a razor sharp wit, and although he seemed somewhat pessimistic about mankind in general, he definitely got in and mixed with the masses. An interesting man.

Driving in and around Hannibal it was easy to picture the way of life that he wrote about. Life was slow and the river was the town's lifeblood. A youngster with time on their hands and an active imagination could find lots of adventure here.

February 15   Lake Catherine State Park
                                   Social Hill, Arkansas

Last night was our second night in a motel for this leg of the trip. We're ready to camp, but just a little nervous about nighttime low temps, which have been in the low to mid 30's. Predictions are for a significant warmup, however, so we may be tenting soon.

It's been fun watching the Winter Olympic Games on TV at night, we've seen luge, skating, and skiing. I love the background interviews and the uncertainty of the competition. Will the favorites hold up to the pressure or will some young upstart come out of nowhere to dethrone them?

Large sections of Arkansas are still without power because of last week's ice storm. It will be interesting.

As we were at a roadside rest today, I had the tailgate down and was making sandwiches for lunch. An older man who had a heavy Polish accent came over and started talking to me. He and his wife were from the Chicago area and they were headed to Hot Springs to check it out as a possible retirement site. He had an inquisitive mind and was pumping me good-naturedly about living in Alaska and our decision to travel for a year. His wife was sitting in the car and had evidently figured that it was time to go. She opened the car door and then closed it decisively (I saw this over his shoulder). As his head jerked around, he smiled at me and shrugged his shoulders, and said, "Have a nice trip!" You too, my friend.

Dear Jenny [Fischer],

We spent Christmas at my grandma's house and my cousin's house. I got a poster, a volleyball shirt with the number 11 on it, some good sweatpants, and a lot more stuff I can't remember. Christmas was very fun! How was your Christmas?

Yesterday I got my first basketball. It was the Big 8 Conference for '94. The basketball is a woman's size. These are some of the states on the basketball: Kansas, Nebraska, Missouri, Iowa, Colorado, Oklahoma, Oklahoma State University, and Kansas State University. I like my basketball a TON!!

Right now we're at Hot Springs, Arkansas. We stayed in a motel for two nights in a row. But last night we camped for the first time in weeks. It was 26 degrees out. We helped dad set up the tent, campstove, and get pine cones, sticks, and wood for the fire.

Love,
Jordin

P.S. Hope your school year's going good. Are you playing softball?

Dear Mike [Fischer],

Right now we are in Arkansas.

When we were in Minnesota we saw a Timberwolves vs. Suns game. In the second quarter Charles Barkley got hurt. He bruised his knee when he got knocked down. He is still out. Kevin Johnson and

Christian Laettner didn't play either. At the end the score was 111 to 103. Suns won.

While we were in Minnesota at my grandma's house, there was a lot of snow. One foot of snow! When we went to Uncle Dale's cabin farther north, there was two feet of snow! Uncle Dale's cabin is by a lake. It was frozen and we walked out on it. Aunt Gina buried us in the snow. It almost froze me stiff.

In about a week we are headed down to Arizona for baseball spring training. I don't know what teams we will see.

When we went to the basketball game, mom sat next to a lady that worked for the Suns. The lady might try to get us free tickets for a Suns game!

How was football season?

> Your friend,
> Kaitlin

February 16

Radio weather forecasts yesterday led us to believe that the overnight low would be 38 degrees. Well, our coldest night in New Mexico was 29, so we figured we'd break out the tent again at Lake Catherine State Park, just west of Hot Springs, Arkansas, "boyhood home of President Bill Clinton." The radio this morning informed me that it had gotten down to a "chilly 26, folks!" Wish I had that weather forecaster in the tent with us last night. Anyway, it's 9:20 a.m. as I'm writing this, and we're sitting in the truck with the heater on, overlooking misty manmade Lake Catherine, finishing up home school, and figuring what we're up to today.

Noon. Still here. We've decided to stay. It's a nice break in the action to stay in one spot longer than a night. (Leave the tent set up and have more leisure time.) It's probably in the upper 50's, still cool but sunny. Jan is working on redoing two of our camp chairs and the girls are playing. They have the old sleeping bag spread out on the ground and are stringing rope from tree to tree, busily setting out the perimeter of play for the day. Barbie™, Aladdin™, or horses, along with two active imaginations, will probably flesh out the details.

Hot Springs is known for its hot mineral baths, which were here before Bill Clinton. (I think my paternal grandparents took a trip here in the early to mid-50's.) We toured the Fordyce Bath House, which has been fully restored and preserved as a National Historic Area. Incredibly beautiful marble and woodwork, with huge skylight panels of stained glass. Workmanship of another era, to be sure.

February 17   **Arkadelphia, Arkansas**

When Kaitlin, Dad and I went down to the lake last night we got some wood for the fire. Kaitlin got a poker stick for the fire. I sawed a piece off and carved my initials J.D.M. The knife slipped and cut my thumb and it hurt a TON!! (Jordin)

February 18   **Lake Bob Sandlin State Park**
                                                    Mt. Vernon, Texas

We spent two cool nights and parts of three very nice days at Lake Catherine State Park. At first the girls were really antsy to keep moving, but pretty quickly settled in and "took possession" of the area. They soon had ropes between trees, with treehouses and beds made out of Minnesota Twins Homer Hankies from the 1991 World Series (thanks, Grandma!)

The days were warm and sunny. Hard to believe that only four or five days ago I was shovelling snow in chilly Coralville. Today as we drove out of Arkansas and into east Texas there were banks of wild daffodils. Spring in mid-February!!

We took a bit of a jump today in home school math. Even though it was Friday and the end of the week, I decided to show Jordin how to divide with two-number divisors. She had 30 seconds of petulant frustration with it, but was soon flying! I decided to push my luck, and showed Kait how to use a three-figure divisor! She has progressed to the point where she has solid enough skills to be confident in new math endeavors. She tried and conquered! I'm really proud of their work and effort.

It's just getting dark now and we're about to light tonight's campfire in Bob Sandlin State Park, an hour northeast of Dallas. It seems 10-15 degrees warmer tonight, which hopefully will hold for more comfortable snoozing.

> These are the golden moments.
> This is the reason why we came.

Two nights in a sleeping bag with the hood of my sweatshirt on is enough. There was a Texas cardinal and his slate grey mate that gave us quite a show tonight at dinner. Because of Jordin doing a research report on cardinals last week, we've been on the lookout. They flew from one side of our camp to the other for 30 minutes and then the female capped it off with a bright, piercing song at dusk.

A quarter moon lit the road sufficiently for an after-dinner walk. It was warm enough that I took my sweatshirt off toward the end.

It must be 8:00 now, and I'm writing this by campfire light. The girls are composing their own rap song about our travels, while the wind is sighing in the tops of the pines. These are the golden moments. This is the reason why we came.

February 20   Dinosaur Valley State Park
Glenrose, Texas

Well, the sleeping has indeed been warmer, but a little on the wetter side. It was drizzling as we woke up yesterday, so after a filling breakfast of pancakes from scratch, we scrambled to set up the tarp ("blue skies") over the tent. The girls got the idea of setting up their tent under the tarp too. I had helped them set it up three days ago, and this time they basically did it themselves. I've noticed a real growth in their confidence level and willingness to help now compared to the first part of Plan Z!

Anyway, in the course of playing in their tent during the day, they decided to sleep in their own tent that night, a first. They went to bed with bravery and confidence.

About 3:30 a.m. it started lightning and thundering, with some sprinkles as well. I first heard Jord calmly calling me, "Dad, can I get up and go to the bathroom?" Well, then Kaitlin woke up and they decided to move back to the "Big House" at 4:15 a.m., and shortly thereafter the heavens opened. It rained hard! The lightning continued and two or three huge thunder boomers made us jump.

Arlington, Texas
The tents are drying outside, while the pillows and sleeping
bags are drying inside the laundromat.

Dinosaur Valley State Park
Kaitlin is standing in a dinosaur
footprint, approximately 8" deep.

The wind blew hard from the side, and Kait and I were basically afloat by 8:15 when we started to break camp, but our gear did the job and kept human flesh dry and warm. We stopped at a laundromat in Arlington during a sunny afternoon break in the clouds to dry two sleeping bags, two pillows (belonging to guess who), four air mattresses, both tents and assorted clothes and stuff sacks. While Jan was in the laundromat, I set up one tent in the parking space next to the truck and had another tent draped over the open camper door and various stuff sacks hanging off the tail gate and side doors. I just had to get out the camera and take a picture of this one. One car had to drive through the parking lot twice to look at us! In two hours we were dry and heading off to Dinosaur State Park.

We visited the John F. Kennedy Memorial in Dallas today. The whole exhibit was in the sixth floor of the Texas School Book Depository building, where Lee Harvey Oswald allegedly fired the shots that killed JFK. There were photos and film clips of Kennedy and the events of his administration. Historians debate what did happen and what might have been, but to me his importance in style was real and significant. Can style be as important as substance? I think in rare instances, yes. At 14, I was, admittedly, at an idealistic stage in my life when he was killed, but even now, looking back at the film clips, he shows an easy grace and sense of humor in his public interactions. There is a sense of energy, purpose, and joy of involvement that underlied the substance of his time in office.

I think his assassination, followed by the deepening of the Vietnam conflict and Watergate, led to a dismal time of doubt and loss of purpose for our country. Disillusionment and cynicism are still a significant part of our political makeup.

The visit was very emotional for me. The girls did a good job of absorbing as much as they could. They know a lot for their age, but it's hard to understand this darker side of humanity. As adults, I think we acknowledge its existence, but wish it weren't so. Such is the ongoing struggle of light and dark.

February 21   Odessa, Texas

Two images from a wakeful period in the night... When I first awoke, it was just light enough to see the outline of Jordin's teddy bear, Sidewalk. His arm and leg were thrust up into the air. A youngster in the neighborhood. I missed the girls when they were sleeping in their tent the other night. I hope when they're adults they realize what joy they gave me as they grew up.

After a while I listened to Jordin breathing in her sleep on one side of me while Jan did the same on the other. Jordin's cycle was shorter, so they weren't totally in sync, but every once in awhile they'd breathe together, grow apart, and then together again. It reminded me of porpoises swimming alongside the Alaska ferry, periodically coming up for a gentle blow and then gracefully sliding beneath the waters.

We spent 45 minutes this morning looking at fossilized dinosaur tracks in the bed of the Paluxy River. Real tracks, millions of years old! It was a grey, misty morning and easy to imagine those lumbering giants moving in herds, pursued by the smaller, quicker carnivores.

February 22   **Davis Mountains State Park**
                                            Fort Davis, Texas

Another night in a motel. Bonnie Blair and ice dancing on the Olympics, lots of thundershowers in West Texas. Senor Weatherman assures us the sun will return today so we'll once again try to camp.

Later in the day—bingo!! They were right. Blue skies again, although cooler and windy. We bought two additional blankets in Odessa and will try to stay warmer tonight. Dry at least.

Last night we stayed in a Best Western motel. It had a pool. We even got to swim in the dark. At the shallow end it was three feet deep and at the deep end it was eight feet.

We pretended that we were whales and that Dad was our trainer. Then we played mermaids and Dad was a bad guy. Dad and Kaitlin and I played totem pole. Dad gave us boosters into the air. I even did a flip! (Jordin)

February 23

Dear Travis,

On Monday night we checked into a motel. It had a big pool right outside our door. It was indoor. We went swimming at night and in the morning. On the roof there

Kaitlin and I wrote a rap song and we practiced it a lot. Then dad filmed us. Here is some of the song. "We travel around in a truck called Buck. He's a 4 X 4 and he don't get stuck. We don't have a boat but we don't care. We can go anywhere!" It was very fun doing the rap song.

was a skylight that covered the whole roof. When you floated on your back you could look out the skylight. Dad and mom chased us around the pool and swam with us. One time I stood on dad's arms and he pushed me into the air. I did spins and bellyflops. It was fun!

Yesterday we went to the McDonald Astronomy Observatory. We saw stars really close up through a powerful 24-inch telescope. The moon was so bright it hurt my eyes! We watched a videotape about the universe. In the giftshop there were glow in the dark shirts. There were also posters, tops, bouncy balls, postcards, toys, and more!

Love,
Kaitlin

Dear Travis,

Kaitlin and I wrote a rap song and we practiced it a lot. Then dad filmed us. Here is some of the song. "We travel around in a truck called Buck. He's a 4 X 4 and he don't get stuck. We don't have a boat but we don't care. We can go anywhere!" It was very fun doing the rap song.

One night we slept in a little tent. It was a rainy night too. And it was all thunder stormy. The little tent was soaked,

Gila Cliff Dwellings

**McDonald Observatory, where
the girls manipulated both the
dome and the telescope.**

but we went into the big tent. At least the big tent was dry.
It was a bad night.

Love,
Jordin

P.S. How's school going?

February 24

It's cold!!
According to best available intelligence, it got down to 22 degrees last
night. Another family record, but as Jordin said, "I don't want to set any more
records." Right. We put the girls' smaller blue sleeping bags over their down
bags like a cocoon. They stay warm once their body heat warms up the bag.
Jan likes heavy layers. She sleeps in a hooded sweatshirt, a sleeping bag,
under three or four blankets, and an overlayer of coats. Ditto for me, minus
one blanket and the coats, add sweat pants. It's been chilly but bearable.
We made a timeline for social studies during home school today. It
showed the beginnings of recorded human history from the hunters and
gatherers at about 10,000 B.C. through Egypt at 3,000 B.C. and Greece at
1,000 B.C. The girls asked where we were, and I showed them a sliver of time
that represented our "modern technological era." Then we visited Dinosaur
Valley State Park and saw footprints from millions of years ago. It spaced me
out. We are indeed a grain of sand.
We've spent six or seven hours during the last two days at McDonald
Observatory near Ft. Davis, Texas, where we saw a video on the solar system
that talked in terms of billions and hundreds of millions of years. Yikes!!
The observatory was a great experience. We started out at a Star Party
on Tuesday night, watching a video and pondering various exhibits in the
Visitors' Center. After dark we looked through a 24-inch telescope at a star
cluster in Orion's belt. Jord said, "Wow! They're dancing!"
The next afternoon we went on a guided tour of the main observatory
and the huge 107-inch telescope. Mark Bridges was our very knowledgeable,
personable guide. The real highlight for all of us came when Mark asked
Kaitlin and Jordin to be his assistants in demonstrating how to move the big
telescope, open the dome, move the floor, turn the dome lights on and off, and
generally work the controls. What a celestial gas! This is where feelings of
confidence and motivation start. In writing about her experience, Kait said

she felt "strong." They loved it, and proud Dad got it on videotape. Thanks, Mark!

Kaitlin is now motivated to become an astronomer. We had a neat talk about college today. It took a little bit to get across the concepts of a semester and a four-year program with a major in astronomy and all the "go-with" courses in science, math, and a foreign language. It was exciting for all of us.

February 25   Las Cruces, New Mexico

They say all's well that ends well. Finding a spot to sleep last night got a little complicated. We left Ft. Davis around lunch time, heading for Guadalupe Mountains National Park on the Texas-New Mexico border. It was pretty there, but high altitude and strong winds led us to believe that it might be cold at night. As we drove through the campground for a look-see at the campsites, there was a couple from Minnesota sitting in their car. With all the open spaces, it was the only way to get out of the wind! There were some majestic rock outcroppings at the entrance to the park, but we left them behind and drove on to warmer pastures.

We headed for Hueco Tanks, a park 70 miles west, toward El Paso. As we were driving there, Jan noticed an article in the newspaper about an international rock-climbing event to be held there on Saturday, two days hence. "Campground Full," said the sign, so we drove on to El Paso.

Across the Rio Grande River was incredible poverty. Ciudad Juarez, Mexico. There was trash everywhere on the outskirts of town, so we passed it by. The next possible camping spot was north of Las Cruces, New Mexico, 60 miles to the north. By now it's probably 5:00 or so. We stopped at a K-Mart so Kaitlin could shop for basketball Kevin™, boyfriend of Skipper™, who is Barbie's™ little sister. Not beach Kevin either, just basketball Kevin. OK? Got it? Then we finally got to eat pizza.

Then on to Las Cruces and north to a State Park, down a dirt road. Get there... and the gate is locked at sundown, which of course was about 40 minutes ago!! Aaaaaaaaaaaaaaarrgh!

Back to Las Cruces (about 15 miles) for a motel room. Getting late, getting frazzled. Motel #1: no non-smoking rooms left. #2: a shower, no tub. #3: only one $61 non-smoker left, too expensive. #4: too seedy, but delicious aroma of Indian cooking coming from the rooms behind the office. #5: we didn't even get out of the truck as we drove by, a bit seedy as well. #6: Bingo! OK, bed down after a little late night Olympic TV.

Today the sun is shining and fruit trees are in flower in Las Cruces. Onward, Buckie.

February 26   **City of Rocks State Park**
                                   Faywood, New Mexico

We've been back on the road for two weeks and have managed to dodge rainy, cold weather, but have yet to dodge the wind. We've been here in City of Rocks for three days, and will stay three more, enjoying the warm days and comfortable nights. At present, the wind is making itself known, but I believe it will calm down again this evening.

The pear started as a pair, or was it a threesome? The first one Jim ate and pronounced "not ripe." The last two were then moved from their confines of the dark cooler to the heat and sun of the dashboard where they rolled right on left hand curves and rolled left on right hand curves. They rolled off when we started and hit the windshield when we stopped. They viewed Dallas, I-10 beyond Odessa, Texas, and then highways south to the Davis Mountains.

The second one was then eaten, once again by Jim, and he pronounced it "not good, throw the last one out." But how can you throw out a pear that has travelled miles in a cooler, miles on the dashboard, rolled and hit the floor at least a few dozen times, and ridden next to me on the seat when I began to worry about too much bruising? And as I write, I wonder where IS that pear? I'd throw it out if I could find it, maybe. (I might try a bite just to pronounce my own sentence of its condition.) I'm inclined to believe that when I ask Jim of its whereabouts, he'll pronounce it "gone." (I doubt by means of ingestion.)

I'm so anxious at times to "nest" that each place I like I'm ready to look for land, a job, and call it home. I enjoyed the Davis Mountains, and the McDonald Observatory where we visited three different times and where Kaitlin's interest in astronomy sparked.

This part of the trip is going so much better for me. Why? Because I see an end and know that this is rare and it's time to buck up and enjoy it. Financially, things are looking better as we will be getting an influx of cash called a refund from the IRS. The days are longer and warmer, while the nights are shorter (but not always warmer), and we're staying in places long enough to relax, write, read, walk (lots, as I try to lose the 5-10 pounds I gained as a house pest, I mean guest.), do yoga, and leave the tent and its contents stationary for days at a time!

February 27

Our third day in City of Rocks State Park, just north of Deming, New Mexico. The weather is dry and warmer. A nice change. We've heard coyotes the past few mornings.

Last night was super. After dark the sky cleared off, so we pulled our chairs away from the campfire and did some family stargazing. We named our own constellation, a rather indistinct cluster of stars to the lower right of Orion's belt, which we dubbed the "Shopping Cart." The full moon rose over the ridge and through some clouds. A night to remember.

Yesterday we tried to go 80 miles north through the hills to Gila Cliff Dwellings National Monument, but truckie's brakes heated up and became squishy. I discovered this as we were heading slightly downhill and around a bend. What a feeling! That had never happened before, and we thought it best to turn around even though we were two thirds of the way there. It was a bit scary on a high country twisty turny road, but on the way back the brakes cooled off and were fine.

February 28

We went to see the Gila Cliff Dwellings, where some natives used to live. The dwellings were 700 years old. To get there we had to cross a creek five times. It was called Little Creek.

In each cave lived 40 to 50 people. The roof was black from the soot of all their fires. I would like to live in a cave like that because I think it would be fun. But the winters would be so cold, I would not like to live there then. (Jordin)

March 1

Another sunny day at City of Rocks State Park, our last. Tomorrow we head to a county park just southwest of Tucson. We plan to spend the following day at Kitt Observatory and then head to cousin Andy's in Scottsdale.

I'm starting to do follow-up work now on locating a job for next year. I have cover letters and resumes done and am completing my application to River Falls, Wisconsin today. I plan to plug our computer into the outlet in the men's bathroom here, the only available plug in the park. What a hoot! I have four other districts' application forms and hopefully a few more waiting at Andy's house, forwarded from Jan's mom in St. Paul. After the wave of paper work, the next step will be to make myself known to secretaries and administrators through phone calls.

We are in a great space with home schooling now. The girls are energetic, cooperative, willing, and interested. Today Jan continued her work with the nutrition unit. In math we started working with negative numbers (the girls ate that up!), and in Social Studies we continued talking about the rise of Rome. We read about Hannibal and his elephants and then Julius Caesar; Jordin likes him because of the connection to Little Caesar's Pizza. (Pizza is her definite food of choice.)

Yesterday we made a successful trip to the Gila Cliff Dwellings north of Silver City. We drove through high pine forests to a pass at 7,800 feet. It snowed heavily for about 45 minutes, big floating flakes. It was gorgeous, but visibility was 300 yards or less in some spots. It let up about the time we got to the site of the cliff dwellings.

We walked three quarters of a mile along the bed of Little Creek in a canyon carved through volcanic rock. We made a turn in the trail and spotted the cliff homes high above us. What a sight!

We were able to walk through the site, which was home to 40 or 50 prehistoric Indians for at least 40 years in the 1300s A.D. I was telling Jan that coincidentally I was just reading about that same time period in our world history book, preparing for home school. Michaelangelo and Leonardo were creating divine artwork in Europe at the same time that these people were abandoning their primitive home, leaving no written record behind. Why did life (civilization?) develop so differently in these areas?

The 700 year old walls, made of flat stone slabs held together with mortar carried up from the creek bed far below, were 75% intact in the original form according to the trail guide brochure. There were small storage areas and larger living rooms with central fire pits. The smoke from their fires had coated the cave ceiling with dark black soot. It was easy to imagine these people living here.

Archaeologists had discovered corn cobs, a smaller variety six inches long, which the natives supplemented with wild game and gathered food. Skeletons found at the site measured 5' 1" for the women and about three inches taller for men.

The weather had cleared for our return to camp, and we were treated to gorgeous vistas, with layers of rock ranging from gold and red to brown and black. At one point Kaitlin noticed a large herd of elk; we backed up and shot them on video.

No back talk from the brakes today. Thank you, Buckie.

March 3   Scottsdale, Arizona

In the education trade, a new byword is the "teachable moment." I other words, catch the kid when they're ready to learn something, and will go in easier and stay longer. Makes sense. Well, we are living in a extreme example of that now. Our visit to Kitt Observatory wa interesting, although not quite as striking as McDonald Observatory. Ki had more buildings, but was not as strong on the public relation However, we did buy some materials about the universe at Kitt, which wer at a level the kids could absorb, and absorb they did! On the two hour driv to Phoenix, they were buried in their books and astronomy magazine surfacing only to fling another amazing cosmic fact into the front seat fc our inspection.

March 4

We went to the Scottsdale Art Fair today with cousin Andy and ne friend Dennis Tovar. The weather was gorgeous, sunny and about 8 degrees. I look around and see green grass and feel like I've landed on foreign planet. We strolled around for two hours and then actually bougr some art: we bought three large and two smaller color photographs c Bryce Canyon in Utah and a place called Corkscrew Canyon in norther Arizona. The girls purchased two smaller pictures of horses. I also bougr a lithograph of a painting that I really felt a connection with. In metaphorical way it showed the ascension of a soul into heaven after deatl

March 7

The four of us went to America West Arena last night to see th Phoenix Suns play the Utah Jazz. The tickets, at No Charge, were a outgrowth of Jan's conversation with Marliss Stahle, the marketin assistant for the Suns who Jan sat next to at the Timberwolves game bacl in Minnesota. It was a great experience. It's a beautiful arena, with vocal supportive fans and lots of entertainment. Unfortunately the Suns failed t show up for the fourth quarter and ended up losing to the Jazz 103-92 They looked tired down the stretch.

We intended to see the Cubs and Giants play baseball today but i was rained out. We seem to be a curse on the city of Phoenix; it's raine four out of the eight days that we've stayed here. I still like this place a lo

On a continuing theme, violence in schools, however, this
seems to be no exception. There was an article in
tonight's paper about kids dropping out of high school
here because they have had violent run-ins with other
kids. One student estimated that about 40% of the kids
he knew brought weapons to school. Teachers
mentioned fear of violence as well.

though; the weather is nice (most of the time), the people seem friendly and relatively unhurried, and there is a lot going on here.

On a continuing theme, violence in schools, however, this seems to be no exception. There was an article in tonight's paper about kids dropping out of high school here because they have had violent run-ins with other kids. One student estimated that about 40% of the kids he knew brought weapons to school. Teachers mentioned fear of violence as well.

March 8

The sun was out today and we made it to a ballgame, a spring training first for the whole family. The Milwaukee Brewers, our old hometown favorites, beat the California Angels 11 to 4, featuring home runs by Tom Brunansky and B.J. Surhoff. We really enjoyed the whole day.

We got to the ball park about 12:30. Coming from the parking area we passed a concession stand where they were selling hats and balls. I looked at one of the nice white baseballs, dreaming about the long shot of getting an autograph. A nice older gentleman behind the counter pointed to a practice field where three of the Brewers were practicing bunting and said that we'd be likely to get an autograph if we went over there and were patient. Sure enough, Kevin Seitzer and Jody Reed signed balls for Kait and Jord. What a thrill!

We ate the traditional ballpark hot dogs, sat in the sun and rooted for the Brewers. They played a fairly solid game and came from behind to take the lead. Near the seventh inning we saw eight or nine Brewers leaving by a side gate, so we quickly left our seats and tailed them. They were running bases on a practice diamond. While we quietly sat on the bench in the "dugout" area, watching and waiting, they began leaving by the outfield exit and we were in hot pursuit! Kaitlin and Jordin ran ahead and scored with Tom Brunansky and Daryl Hamilton. Bruno called Kaitli "Buddy" and Jordin "Sweetheart." They were absolutely gushing! A tal dark-haired handsome guy flirting with them!

After the game we waited by the exit gate and got seven mor autographs, including manager Phil Garner, coach Tim Foli, and B.J Surhoff. As we headed to the parking lot, Buck the Truck was the only on left, but it was worth the wait. What a day!!

Dear Grandma,

The night before last we went to a Phoenix Sun: basketball game. They have a huge arena downtown in Phoenix. We saw the Suns play the Utah Jazz. The Jazz won, 103 to 92. I wore my Phoenix Suns cap. All o the good players played. Nobody was hurt. At the entrance people were handing out free Phoenix Sun: sports bottles. The gift shop had lots of Suns stuff, like shirts, caps, jackets, cards, and more! It was cool! The tickets were free. Each one was worth $22!

This morning when I was eating breakfast a Andy and Laurie's house I lost my first molar! I wa: eating and my tooth started to hurt. I put my finger up there to check it and it was gone! I spit out all of m: cereal quick! I saw it sink under the milk and cereal All of my cereal was bloody and my mouth was bleeding Jordin got me some tissue and I stuffed it in my mouth Mom took the bowl over to the sink and found my tooth It was big!

Yesterday we went to a Milwaukee Brewers vs California Angels spring training game. I liked it a lot We had hot dogs and pop. The Brewers won, 11 to 4 During, before, and after the game we got autographs. got 11! Before the game I bought a $5 baseball. We went to a place where four or five guys were practicing As they came out I got two players to autograph m: ball! As we were walking to the field we saw anothe

)layer and he gave us his autograph Then we went)ack and bought a case for the ball. Then we went back o the game. In the fourth inning Tom Brunansky hit a hree run homer! It was awesome! During the game we :aw some players leave. We went after them. They vere running because they wouldn't play any more. Vhen they left we chased them. We caught them and ;ot Tom Brunansky's autograph! After he signed it, I :aid, "Thank you." And he said, "Sure, buddy!" After iis I got Daryl Hamilton's. By then it was the eighth or iinth inning. After the game was over we went looking 'or a place where we could get lots of autographs. We vent behind a fence by where the players leave. It took i long time because they were doing running exercises. At one point we were waiting for a half hour. Then lots)f players started coming up. I got about six at that ;pot. All together I got these autographs: Tim Foli, Jody Reed, Phil Garner, Kevin Seitzer, Greg Smith, B.J. 3urhoff, Brian Barks, Tom Brunansky, Alex Diaz, Daryl Hamilton, and Turner Ward. Dad took 20 photos of lifferent things. I miss you!

Love,
Kaitlin

Dear Grandma,

Just the day before yesterday I went swimming. The day was very hot, but the pool was about 70 degrees. The day was about 90 degrees! Laurie and Andy have two dogs. The young one's called Maggie and the old one's called Chelsie. Maggie went into the pool with us, and we threw her tennis ball for her. The tennis ball went into the pool. Sometimes Maggie can catch tennis balls in her mouth and it goes SWAK!

On this trip we went to an observatory. It was called McDonald Observatory. They had a 107-inch telescope (28 feet long). If you wanted to move it you had to do it by

buttons (that you pushed). And Kaitlin and I got to pus
the buttons. It was cool.

Yesterday we went to a Brewers game. Th
Brewers played the California Angels. The Brewers wo
11 to 4. Before the game Kaitlin and I got a baseball eac
The baseballs cost $5. And the guy selling them said, "
you get an autograph I'll give you this case for the baseba
for two dollars." And we got two autographs! So the ma
gave us each one (for two dollars). Then we got like fiv
more autographs. We saw players walking by, and w
saw Tom Brunansky. I had to run very fast to catch him
When I caught him I asked him for his autograph. I wa
only up to his waist. He took such big strides I had to jog t
keep up. And he called me sweetheart. He was very, ver
nice.

Love you lots,
Jordin

March 10   **Dead Horse Ranch State Par**

Cottonwood, Arizon

There are degrees of cold nights. Last night, camped in Dead Hors
State Park (how did that name come to be??) near Jerome, Arizona, I slep
without hooded sweatshirt and sweat pants. I did, however, rely on one c
our new auxiliary blankets laid over my sleeping bag. Perfecto. I eve
took my socks off in the middle of the night, a rare treat. We're trying out
new bedtime technique, hanging our lantern from the inside peak of th
tent. It seems to warm up our inside space, but possibly increase
condensation on the inner walls as the night cools down. Tinkering wit
the basics. (We always keep the windows open for ventilation.)

I met Jesus in my dreams last night. Now I'm not one who believe
in church-going. I feel that most religions are too dogmatic and inflexibl
for my tastes and too many people use church attendance as a once a wee
salve on their conscience, justifying questionable weekday actions an
morals. But I am spiritual. I try to live by the Golden Rule and I definitel
believe in some sort of life after death.

Well anyway, in my dream I was in a crowded room. Peopl
milling, and the buzz of background conversation. Someone said, "There'
someone you should meet," kind of like getting introduced to someone at

> I met Jesus in my dreams last night. I never actually formed a picture of a face or body, but I knew he was there. I had a white aura around my upper body, with flames shooting out the ends of my fingers. Shazam!!

arty. I turned the corner and found myself in his presence. I never ctually formed a picture of a face or body, but I knew he was there. I had a white aura around my upper body, with flames shooting out the ends of my ingers. Shazam!! I was calm, but alert. I remember kind of soaking up the energy and then someone asked me to sit down. There were a number of us itting on folding chairs. Soon after that it began to feel like a sermon. The magic was gone, so I slipped out the side door.

Jan did some re-figuring on our preliminary tax return today, and found that we are getting back about $1,000 less than she had previously estimated. That calls for measures of austerity. No more art purchases, no motel room if we can help it, and planning our day trips carefully to keep mileage down somewhat. I think we can do it. Benign weather helps a lot. Warmer temps and longer hours of daylight enhance our outdoor experiences, which in turn eases pressure on the budget.

We had a family spring training session today, playing catch and having some batting practice at Riverside Park in Cottonwood.

March 11

Where oh where is that pear? No one seems to know of its whereabouts. Yikes. If it's still with us, we'll know soon from the stench.

We've been back to cool evenings and cool mornings again, and more wind. I find wind irritating, annoying. As I look back through pages of my mind, I remember always disliking the wind. Tonight we raced against a windy eye-of-the-storm, trying to put the 10 x 20 foot tarp over the tent. But the wind won, ripping out a corner grommet, ripping stakes out of the ground, and acting more like a sail than a rain protector. Bag the tarp, I said, and we folded it back up after 45 minutes of wrestling with big blue. The storm has so far tracked around us (except for the initial wind), leaving a beautiful dusting of snow in the higher altitudes. As the clouds cleared and revealed the mountains once again, they emerged slowly, with a new coat of white.

Today we spent time in Sedona, Oak Creek Canyon, and Slide Rock State Park. As with most hot-spots in the U.S., population explosions had

> Humans sure can ruin a good thing.

changed the aura and attitude of what was once the small town of Sedona.
As of '88, it was incorporated and it's grown to a full-blown mini
metropolis. Humans sure can ruin a good thing. Rape, pillage, and
commercialize. Population growth needs to be curbed. Who do you limit?
Can you and still be called a "free" country? Can you and still say we
give our citizens "rights?"

I've had success with my dream catchers, and have sold some in
California, Iowa, and Minnesota. Agua Caliente in Anza-Borrego sold
everything I left there and want more! I'm waiting on payment from the
first batch, and then will send more dream catchers and earrings their way.
What a good feeling to make a product and have someone else like it
enough to pay me money. This is a real thrill.

We drove to Sedona today. It's a beautiful area with enormous
reddish-brown rock outcroppings. On the way we stopped at a very
impressive horse ranch. A travelling troupe of Budweiser Clydesdales
were staying there in preparation for tomorrow's St. Pat's Day Parade in
Sedona. They are majestic creatures, dwarfing us but benignly letting us
pet their massive sides.

As we drove away, Kaitlin wondered if there was such a thing as
professional horse rider. She said, "You know the neat thing about Plan Z?
It's gotten me interested in lots of things, like astronomy, baseball, and
horse riding." Neat indeed. Perceptive thought there, m'dear. Precisely
one of the hoped-for outcomes of this trip!

March 12

We dodged a bullet last night for sure. After we returned from our
day trip to Sedona we noticed ominous black clouds sailing over the
neighboring mountains. Sheets of slanting precipitation obscured their

> Kaitlin said, "You know the neat thing about Plan Z? It's gotten me interested in lots of things, like astronomy, baseball, and horse riding." Neat indeed. Perceptive thought there, m'dear. Precisely one of the hoped-for outcomes of this trip!

peaks. Yikes, it looks like it's coming our way! The wind began to pick up and the decision was made to batten down the hatches and cover up with the Big Blue tarp, memories of the Dallas flood of '94 still fresh in our minds.

As we were getting the tarp out, the wind really started kicking in. The girls were playing in the tent and as Jan and I were wrestling with the tarp we started to hear whoops and giggles. Kaitlin poked her head out a screen window and said, "Wow! The corner of the tent lifted off the ground and tossed us!" Oh, great. We managed to get two corners of Big Blue staked out and two tied with rope to the scrubby Arizona trees. Just then one of the stakes flew out of the ground and one of the grommets holding a rope popped. I began to wonder if we were in over our heads. The storm kept advancing like a stalking cat in the background. We finally figured we'd haul in the tarp and ask Ma Nature for mercy. It worked! The wind shifted and having left a dusting of new snow on the surrounding peaks, the storm moved off over Jerome.

We hung the lantern in the tent and snuggled in for a family night in the "den," Kait reading, Jord doing animal art, Jan making dream catcher earrings, and me doing work on job applications.

We woke up dry and that's the bottom line.

March 13

Yesterday we visited Tuzigoot National Monument, ruins of a native hilltop settlement. It is a beautiful site, with a commanding view of the river valley below. They cultivated beans, squash, and corn, caught fish in the river and hunted deer and various small game. Life must have been good, but in the late 1300s or early 1400s they apparently abandoned the area. This seems to have been a significant time for the natives in the southwest. Gila Cliff Dwellings and Chaco in New Mexico (as well as others) were inexplicably abandoned around the same time. There are three popular theories advanced by the people who get paid to know (but

Deadhorse Ranch State Park
Savoring Indian Fry Bread, coated with cinnamon and sugar.

Deadhorse Ranch State Park
Home cooked pancakes on the camp stove.

apparently don't in this case). The first is a drought that lasted for several seasons and made farming a losing proposition. The second is that the population outstripped available resources and the folks had to range farther and farther afield for food, building materials, and fuel. The third is some type of social disintegration. The first two are more probable, but the third is intriguing to me.

In a relatively closed society such as these pueblos must have been, most of the community members were blood relatives. In some instances this leads to a remarkable degree of tolerance for various idiosyncrasies, but it can just as often lead to the opposite. Jealousy, envy, greed, and anger can be magnified, and grudges can be held for years even when there is a physical separation of hundreds of miles. What would it be like to see the person every day? But individual differences would not account for the seemingly widespread abandonment of a way of life that had endured for over 700 years. What happened here? They left no written history, no obvious clues, only the stone and mortar foundations of a town that once echoed with the voices of a living, breathing community of men, women, and children.

According to archaeologists, 42% of the bodies found buried at the site were children eight years or younger. Only 4% lived to be 45, my age. I would have been respected as a village elder. I would also have been dead in the near future.

We had a great family baseball game today in a field near the lagoon. Jord and Kait were on one team, at bat, with ghost runners when needed. I pitched and Jan fielded. Two days ago we taught them about getting in position to take a relay throw from a deep hit to the outfield. Today we taught them to round first and take the extra base on a throw to third or home. They caught right on. Kaitlin started using the adult aluminum bat and handled it better than I expected. We played for close to an hour on a warm, sunny morning and all had fun!

March 15

Our third morning of baseball. Jordin is now batting with the big aluminum bat for a few rounds and then switching back to the smaller wooden bat. They have certainly gotten the hang of aggressive base-running, forcing Jan and I into throwing errors a couple of times by unexpectedly rounding a base. It's really fun to see them developing confidence in another area.

> Both girls have started writing their books this morning. Kaitlin is going to write a mystery with horses in it, and Jordin is writing a story about a horse and a kitten who are good friends and bedevil a mean dog on the farm. They're excited and so am I.

Made three phone calls this morning and found more places to send in job applications. Contracts are being distributed now, and teachers have a month or so to turn them in. That's when a district generally begins the hiring process. I'll be finishing up and sending out ten applications in the next few days to join the one that already went out to River Falls, Wisconsin. Then I'll be making phone contacts and looking for interviews.

I feel good about looking for a teaching position. The "time off" and the opportunity to work with Kaitlin and Jordin have pretty much cleaned my mental filters of the frustrations I've had the past few years teaching. I feel capable of doing a good job now on both the interview circuit and in the classroom, wherever that may be.

We could do this trip cheaper in regards to groceries, if we chose processed foods. For instance, generic macaroni and cheese can be purchased for 69 cents (probably less in some stores). I make it from scratch, probably costing $2-3.

If we ate a diet of mostly canned, processed soups, rather than homemade (campstove made) dinners, we could eat for less than one dollar per meal. White bread can be purchased at a cut-rate price, while whole wheat demands a higher price. I thought of making dessert bars, but held off because Jim and I are trying to lose some excess baggage (fat!). The bars would have cost close to $5-6 for a 9 x 13 pan; so instead we bought a one pound bag of store bought, generic cookies for 99 cents.

So, our food budget is higher than a processed diet would call for, but part of the education for our girls is learning good nutrition.

For the first time on our trip, we are making a campground our home—staying for 11 days. We are killing time, waiting for Sub Marina's tax return to be finished in Phoenix. The cost will be one-tenth of an Alaskan CPA's price.

Spring training sure has been a family highlight for us. Baseball at its finest: smaller stadium, friendlier fans and players, cheaper and better seats, and lots of sunshine. Every seat was good, the players approachable, and the sky blue. Batter up!!!

Dear Pat [Griffin],

How are you? I'm fine. We're in Arizona right now. It's warm and sunny and about 75 degrees at noon. Sometimes we wade in the creek near our campsite.

In Phoenix we went to a spring training game. Brewers 11, Angels 4. We took lots of pictures and used up a whole roll of film! Dad got a picture of almost all of the players. In the fifth inning Tom Brunansky hit a three-run homer! After the game I got his autograph. I also got these autographs: Daryl Hamilton, Tim Foli, Jody Reed, Phil Garner, Kevin Seitzer, Greg Smith, B.J. Surhoff, Brian Barks, Alex Diaz, and Turner Ward. Eleven in all! At the entrance we bought a baseball (and a plastic holder) for the players to sign. The stadium was really small so all of the seats were good. On the side there was a grassy hill that people could sit on with blankets. It was really cool! We got seats on the bleachers about in the middle. At the end of the game (when we got most of our autographs) we waited behind a fence by where the players come out. At one point we were waiting 45 minutes! When we left we were the third to the last car to leave! We didn't have the pictures developed yet but when we do I'll send you some.

Love,
Kaitlin

March 16

It's 8:30 in the morning, with the sun shining and a warm breeze stirring. Birds are contentedly twittering all around us, taking care of details on their plane of existence. The green checkered table cloth is on the picnic table and we've finished breakfast and have started on school. Both girls have started writing their books this morning. Kaitlin is going to write a mystery with horses in it, and Jordin is writing a story about a horse and a kitten who are good friends and bedevil a mean dog on the farm. They're excited and so am I.

This is our seventh night at Dead Horse Ranch State Park, and we've signed up for four more before heading back to Phoenix and, hopefully, another spring training game. We've found a rhythm to our days here: wake up to the yipping of coyotes, the Irish tenors of the local animal community, read in our sleeping bags for a while, occasionally reading the good parts out loud to each other, then out the tent door when nature calls. By then the sun has started to warm the earth and dry off the overnight dew or frost from the picnic table. After a breakfast of granola or pancakes, we have an hour and a half to two hours of home school.

After school we have our family baseball game, playing catch, batting, and running the bases. Yesterday we topped off our hot and sweaty game with a visit to the flume leading into the park's lagoon. Its cold water was running fast down a three-foot wide cement trough. We took off our shoes and socks and went wading, water flying up around our ankles (Kaitlin said she looks like Mercury, the wing-footed messenger of the gods!). Then lunch and either a sight-seeing trip to a small mountain mining town or a local Indian ruin or a lazy afternoon reading, playing games in camp, or Jan and I going for long walks (one at a time of course, so the other one can stay with the kids). After dinner, maybe a family card game, a campfire, and watch the stars come out. Then into the bag for a sound night's sleep.

It's about 10:00 at night, by the campfire. What a productive day for all of us. We decided to return to Jerome tomorrow instead of today, and spent the day around camp. The girls got a great start on writing their stories for home school, really getting into descriptive detail and humor. As Jordin said, "It's hard getting started, but then my brain just starts clicking with ideas!" They both did an initial period of maybe a half hour on their stories, and I made sure they got a strong start. Then they took off and must have worked on them for three hours. What mental stamina! I genuinely enjoy the stories. They're good.

Jan worked hard today and finished up a big load of dream catchers and earrings to ship off to Anza-Borrego, for their big season starts soon. If they all sell we'll be richer by over $200. I like her art work.

And me? I finished up eight job applications that will be in the mail tomorrow.

In our baseball game today, I started pitching a little faster to match the speed that their peers would use. After a short period of adjustment, they were smoking line drives again! It's a hot time on the diamond in more ways than one. The tops of my ears are sunburned and very tender!

Tonight after supper I went for a walk down the park service road past the lagoon. As I was walking to the east, I turned around to head back and was bowled over by the sunset that had quietly snuck up behind me. The sun had just gone down over the mountains, leaving them a black silhouette highlighted by the sparkling jewelled lights of Jerome 2/3 of the way up the slope. The sky was bright red, fading into orange, purple, and then many shades of blue. What a treat! It lasted for 10 to 15 minutes as I walked back to our campsite.

To top off the show, a coyote went trucking across the road 25 or 30 yards in front of me, a beautiful healthy animal trotting at about 2/3 speed. He saw me but never slackened or increased his pace. I was just a momentary blip on his sensory screen. I had goose bumps on my legs and back.

March 17

I talked briefly to a man tonight who said he has two portable air conditioners that he plugs in and "lays in the door of his tent" to ease the muggy Texas nights when he's camping. No kidding!

I enjoy walking around the campground at dusk. People are leisurely fixing dinner or talking around a campfire. Back in "civilization" our array of electric lights and gadgets drive us just as hard after sundown as before, but here the sunset really brings a softening of the day's pace. Time for sharing and socializing, contemplation and renewal. Was this how it was in the "primitive" pueblo?

March 18

I wasn't looking for it today, but the eternal found me. Jan has been telling me about this gravel day-use road that she's been visiting on her walks. I finally tried it today. About ten minutes outside the park entrance you could see the Tuzigoot pueblo ruins on a distant hilltop. The road wound along the Verde River, gradually drawing closer to the ruins. I actually liked the distant view much better than walking through the ruins themselves. You could see the symmetry and beauty of the stone foundations, the light reddish brown of the stone, and how the design followed the natural contours of the land. It was a very powerful moment. I made my way off the gravel into the scrub, coming to a high bluff overlooking the river, probably a half mile from the ancient pueblo. With the breeze to my back I watched the cliff swallows testing the thermals and a huge heron lazily scouting the river for lunch. The wind, tickling the mesquite, actually talked to me. What a rich place to make your home. When did the cycles change from surviving and pondering your place in the universe to getting more than enough and still wanting more?

On my way back down the gravel road, my head in the ethereal, I heard a sound that I couldn't place at first. Then I saw an old beatup dusty white Camaro winding its way through the brush, radio blasting some tinny rock and roll. As they went by, I smiled from behind my sunglasses. There were two young squires in the front and three young ladies crammed into the back seat. The driver gave me a crazy grin and the middle lady kind of smiled and shrugged her shoulders. It was obviously "hot damn and carpe diem!!" Life gives us lessons on all levels.

We made whole wheat Indian fry bread today. The girls helped mix and cook it in the hot oil. We ate a ton!

Just today for school Kaitlin and I made Indian fry bread. First we helped Mom mix the dough (flour, baking powder, salt, and dry milk). Then you had to heat up an inch of oil. Then you had to flatten out how much dough you wanted and put a hole in the middle. Drop it in the oil. When it comes out dip it in cinnamon or powdered sugar. Take it out and EAT IT!! YUM!!!! (Jordin)

March 19

Since we're heading back to Andy and Laurie's tomorrow, we celebrated Kaitlin's eleventh birthday today, one day early. After pancakes for breakfast, we ate the few survivors of yesterday's fry bread pig-out, along with cheese, bologna and root beer floats for lunch. Then macaroni and cheese and more root beer for dinner, followed by a birthday cake ordered special at the local deli. Poor Jord's tummy was a casualty.

I think Kaitlin enjoyed the special attention. A family tradition has always been to decorate the house with balloons and streamers after they've gone to bed so that they wake up to a wonderland on their birthday morning. This will be a bit dicey. I'm not sure I can stay awake longer than Kait to get the job done tonight, but we'll try.

We spent much of the day at the Archaeological Fair in Cottonwood. They had many interesting hands-on activities for the kids, including clay medallions with stamps for imprinting designs, different kinds of rubbings, a wire horse, several pictures and designs with crayon and marker. The girls even tried their hand at grinding corn on a metate, using a smaller stone for grinding.

There was also a nice display of edible native plants. We spent some time talking to a very knowledgeable couple who had set it up, and we were invited to attend a two and a half hour school presentation in Flagstaff on Thursday. They'll actually cook and eat prickly pear cactus, among other desert delicacies. I asked the woman what her theory was regarding the apparently large-scale exodus around 1,400 AD. She had studied this for her thesis and felt that it was because of a lack of iron in their diet, due to the absence of large-boned game animals in their area.

There were several native artists displaying their goods as well. We bought three modern petroglyphs, or images, carved on desert basalt by David Morris, a Choctaw native from Maricopa, Arizona. He used rocks to chip off the black outer layer of "desert varnish," revealing the lighter layer beneath. He works with native images from the Anasazi culture, the "Ancient Ones" that predate the contemporary Navajo, Hopi, and Zuni cultures. My favorite is Kokopeli, the humpbacked flute player. He is a symbol of fertility, both human and plant.

We talked to another man, a silversmith from Flagstaff who also maintains a home on the Hopi reservation. In talking about Tuzigoot and Chaco ruins, he said that the natives do not consider the sites to be ruins. "These are still active, sacred shrines that are used for prayer."

We topped off our day with a visit to Sugarloaf Mountain, a pueblo site that has not been restored or stabilized and has suffered waves of looters looking for arrowheads and pottery. It was a steep climb, but well worth it. We stayed for an hour and the girls found lots of pottery fragments which were 500 years old or more. Kaitlin discovered one small fragment of a more modern type of pottery as well. It was more colorful, with a design reminiscent of reeds at the edge of a river. They also found a fair amount of obsidian chips, which the natives used for arrowheads and carving tools. A man at the Archaeological Fair said that obsidian can be honed to an edge sharper than modern surgical tools. Progress.

The girls experienced real archaeology, the thrill of discovery and the guesswork involved in trying to make sense of the specific fragment and how it fits into the larger fabric of an extinct culture. This is education you don't get from the pages of a book.

The day was rainy but we survived. The tent and all the bags are dry thanks to Big Blue and our advanced Creativity and Coping Skills.

She'll be 11 when we wake.

March 20   Scottsdale, Arizona

We saw a baseball game in pantomime today, the Cubs and Mariners. The only seats left by the time we got to the park were grass seats beyond the left field wall. The pitcher and batter were so far away we couldn't see the ball. Were they really playing with a ball?

The bullpen was out there though and we watched a couple of pitchers warm up. Boy, can they smoke it!! We were impressed.

I had to wake up Jim late last night to help do the dirty deed, but between the two of us we managed to decorate the tent with balloons and streamers. Kaitlin was all smiles as she awoke this morning.

March 22   Dead Horse Ranch State Park
Cottonwood, Arizona

I've had my first feelings that the end of the trip is coming. I've enjoyed it, but it's time to start gradually gearing up for re-entry. It's OK.

March 24   Mather Campground
Grand Canyon, Arizona

Two nights ago in Dead Horse Ranch State Park, I slept without a shirt on and was comfortable. Last night we camped 2,000 feet higher at Pine Flat Campground in Oak Creek Canyon just north Sedona. We broke camp early this morning by 7:25 and there was a good layer of sparkling frost on the hood. (We were up, loaded and on our way in 30 minutes!

> This is education you don't get
> from the pages of a book.

Tonight, as we fixed dinner in Mather campground at the Grand Canyon (an additional 2,000 feet higher) it started hailing! Well, at this point I guess hail is better than rain and besides, it only lasted 15 minutes.

We attended a Prehistoric Cooking class at Marshall Elementary School in Flagstaff today from 9:00 to 11:30 with Mrs. Wilson's fourth grade class. It was organized by staff members of the Northern Arizona Museum in Flagstaff. (We had met them at the Archaeology Fair in Cottonwood last Saturday.) It was very interesting on several levels. We learned a lot about native plants and where they fit into the nutritional needs of the local tribes, we helped cook and then we ate a variety of foods (venison stew with prickly pear cactus for one).

It was the first time in a "regular" school for quite a while. The girls did well, answering some questions, joining in with the cooking groups, and doing some socializing over "lunch." I felt at home in the school environment and saw several kids in the class that I would have enjoyed working with. Jan really helped out by circulating around the room during the sessions. I think we were all ready to breathe the Air of Freedom at 11:30, however.

This afternoon we drove to the Grand Canyon and reserved one of the last available sites in Mather campground. (Most of their campgrounds are still closed.) We drove along the Southwest Rim, which had a spectacular view of reds, browns, oranges, and greys, changing with sunlight and shadow.

There is a storm that has been approaching for three days from the Pacific Northwest. We are looking over our shoulders.

I overheard the girls playing in the tent just before dinner. Their toy people were "archaeologists digging in the Indian ruins." Their horizons of possibilities are expanding.

One interesting note. I had read previously that pueblo dwellers seldom lived past 40. Well I learned today that one reason was their method of grinding corn on a flat rock called a metate. The lady noted that the small rock chips that inevitably mixed in with the corn meal wore down their teeth so that by age 40 they were basically gumming it. They often died of starvation or gum infection. Youch!

I overheard the girls playing in the tent just before dinner. Their toy people were "archaeologists digging in the Indian ruins." Their horizons of possibilities are expanding.

March 25

Last night we went to the Shrine of Ages Auditorium by the Visitors' Center to see a one-man play based on the journal of Major John Wesley Powell's chief boatswain. It reflected on Powell's 1869 expedition down the Colorado River. Tough men and tough times. Some quit, some died, but some made it all the way through the canyon and into the Gulf of California.

Afterward there was a question and answer session. One fact that amazed me: the average length of stay for a visitor to the Grand Canyon? Six to eight hours!!!

This morning we hiked part way down the Kaibab Trail on the South Rim. It was neat to be next to and below some of the rock formations we had previously looked down on. The trail was steep and rocky in places, but the girls acquitted themselves with honor. They are real hikers and we began talking about making the hike all the way to the bottom next spring break for a stay at Phantom Ranch. (All their supplies are packed in on mules!)

That got us back in time for a short lunch of Hebrew National Kosher Hot Dogs wrapped in leftover whole wheat pancakes from breakfast, followed by a simple trail mix of peanuts and chocolate chips.

Then on to a ranger-led hike entitled "Winter Walk." Ranger Glen Yanagi, a cheerful guy, talked about plant and animal adaptations through the winter season. Appropriately enough it started snowing! Continuing through the afternoon, by dark an inch and a quarter of sparkling white, wet snow had accumulated.

We went back to our campsite to take pictures, brush off the tent so it would start drying, and then load the sleeping bags into the truck for a later rendezvous with a laundromat drier just prior to beddie-bye time. A hot shower brought us back to snuff and we stayed warm and dry in the Visitors' Center watching a video on the Canyon.

Well, no need to watch over our shoulder now. The storm got us. Now for our first night tenting in snow. Tomorrow we break camp and start heading east toward New Mexico and Chaco.

The snow covered top of the Grand Canyon created spectacular scenery.

We were deluged by snow during the night, which created endless beauty, but lots of hard work breaking camp and drying out!

March 26

Meteor Crater RV Park
Leupp Corner, Arizona

8:00 a.m. There was some premature rejoicing during the night. I had worked at re-patching my air mattress yesterday morning and it actually seemed to be holding air, but I awoke this morning to find it flat again. It sprang a leak sometime during the first month of the trip and hasn't been right since.

It snowed more during the night. We can hear the cold crystalline flakes hitting the tent. It sounds a little like soft static on a radio. The girls' bags and pillows are wet from where they touched the tent walls, but the human flesh stayed warm and dry throughout.

7:30 p.m. We did a good job of overcoming the weather today. The tent was very wet and the fly was frozen to the poles of the tent frame, so we packed it up wet. The snow was great for packing so we had a family snowball fight as we loaded the truck. Then we stopped at the Grand Canyon Village laundromat to dry our sleeping bags and pillows.

As we headed out of the park, we stopped at two or three scenic view points. The Canyon was incredible! We were at 7,000 feet at the rim and the snow extended down the canyon wall 800 feet. There were patches of mist and clouds floating in and out of the canyons, with the sun adding highlights. Of course we had run out of film, but negotiated with a young German couple for a roll of 36 shots. We're back in business.

Around noon we stopped at a little pulloff by the side of the road and took advantage of abundant wind and peekaboo sun to dry our tent.

This afternoon we viewed the Meteor Crater near Winslow, Arizona. It's something I had wanted to see for a long time. Parts of the iron-nickel meteorite, which has been estimated to be 100 feet in diameter and travelling at 12 miles per second (INCOMING!!), are buried 3,000 feet deep in the crater, which is about a mile across. It happened 49,000 years ago. There was also a space suit on display that had been worn on a lunar landing. I could imagine myself in a Tom Corbett sci-fi book from my childhood, looking at the glass case and being amazed at how "crude" the first space suits had been. Brave folks indeed.

Tonight we're camped at Meteor Crater RV Park by Interstate 40. The couple running it are very hospitable. We were short-handed on the fixings for dinner and their convenience store couldn't add much to our meager supplies. The lady offered to get a can of spaghetti sauce from her own pantry! While I was setting up the tent, the man came out to check if we'd be all right in their newly-sodded tent section. Unexpected kindness really puts a shine on the day.

March 27   **Canyon de Chelly National Monument**
Chinle, Arizona

7:45 p.m. at Canyon de Chelly. I was going to write in my journal, but it's way too cold. I'm diving into my sleeping bag and hope to get and stay warm.

I've had dry, peeling lips and can't decide if it's from the hot, scorching sun in Southern Arizona, or the extremely cold temps of Northern Arizona. Or it could be the lack of fluids. This life often ignores basic needs and instead focuses more on survival: warmth, shelter, and food. Fluid intake is obvious, a basic nutritional need, but one that is often ignored, and for us requires effort to keep water in the mugs for daily drinking. Our dinners and breakfasts lately have been quick and speedy; we're shivering, and the food is cold by the time it hits the plate. Who has time for adequate fluid intake when your hands are freezing, the wind howls and the warmth of the truck calls to us?

I've enjoyed my time on the Navajo Reservation and have relinquished my fears of them. Prejudice? Pre-conceived social stigmas? Media misconceptions? Their social problems are not isolated to their culture, but their dilemma of trying to exist in two worlds is their unique struggle.

I respect these people and their struggle to survive in what is now a white person's society. They've been treated as second class citizens, their land stolen from them, and left with untillable, barren acres for their survival. Their arts are beautiful and I wonder about supporting them by selling their arts in the Midwest.

The Native Americans were, in my opinion, the first Christians in our nation, if you define a Christian as someone who leads a spiritual life and honors all living things. What did the missionaries think they had that surpassed the native's deep respect of our earth and its people? Our white Christians have proceeded to damage the earth irreparably and create the means and ways to obliterate our society. So, just who were/are the great scholars? the good Christians? We would do well to honor and learn from the Native Americans.

March 28

Hoo hah! Was it cold last night??? Well, Jan just got back from the Visitors' Center and the official low for last night was 18 degrees! We stayed pretty warm in the tent, but the condensation from our breath made everything wet. The morning sun has dried it out pretty well by 10:30, as I'm writing this on the picnic table.

We've just finished up the morning session of school. In social studies we're talking about the social changes resulting from 17th century European world exploration and trade. We talked about how the Spaniards treated the natives when they first came to North America, which was also a part of the video on Navajo culture that we saw at the Visitors' Center yesterday.

Arriving at 4:00, we were in the Visitors' Center for only 45 minutes, but was it a full time! Jan made contact with Brian, a young Navajo National Park ranger. He told us about how the Navajo nation is considering the legalization of gambling and setting up a casino here at Canyon de Chelly, their spiritual homeland. He just quietly shook his head. It's the same everywhere. The Winnebago tribe in Wisconsin has put in bingo and slot machines and it has gone wild in the two and a half years since we moved. People that live there are concerned about crime moving in, but it's hard to say no to the "quick buck." In Alaska the debate is whether to exploit mineral and timber resources or to leave it all intact and hope for a growing tourism industry. (Ideally, the state would like to do both.) The trouble is that it's hard to turn back the clock.

We told Brian that we were embarrassed because of what our white ancestors had done to the native population. He said that he could understand. As part of his job he told visitors that his people were the children of mother earth and father sun. But then as he left the center each day he saw the garbage they had left alongside the road. It seems we're all looking for balance.

Jan and I had been looking for a Navajo rug for the past three days. At the last trading post before leaving the Grand Canyon Park we looked at a beautiful rug of dark reddish-brown, grey, black and white geometric designs, probably 5' by 7'. The price tag was nearly $6,000. Yikes!! At least we have good taste. Smaller ones went down to $100. As we made our way into the Navajo reservation we stopped at a roadside stand called Chief Yellowhorse. We looked at some rugs there, probably 3' by 4' and priced at $900, but quickly reduced to $500. Still too pricey for us.

Well, Jan was in the middle of her conversation with ranger Brian and I was browsing through the books when two teenage girls came up and quietly asked, "Have you been looking for a rug?" Trade negotiations, the oldest game in the book, began in earnest. We ended up getting a small 2' by 2 1/2' rug for $50. It's nicely done. The rug found us and the money

**The girls hard at play setting up their toys at Canyon de
Chelly. L-R, Kaitlin, Jordin.**

went directly to the natives. Do you believe in magical connections?

As I was writing this, two more Navajos came driving through the campground. We bartered with a quiet, gentle woman and purchased a slightly larger and more finished rug for $40 plus a pair of Jan's beaded earrings in barter. A man offered rugs and woven baskets, but we declined, saying that we'd bagged our limit for the day.

I have a nice feeling here. The Navajos that we've met so far are very gentle. They have a spirit of pride in themselves and they seem to have a nice energy in presenting themselves and their products.

March 29   **Red Rocks State Park**
                                                Gallup, New Mexico

Dear Shona,

Guess what? WE WENT TO THE GRAND CANYON! It was huge! The rocks were reddish brown, with some black. We hiked down about one mile and hiked up one mile. So we hiked about two miles. Once Mom said, "In about two years, when Jordin is ten, we can hike all the way to the bottom." We went up faster than we went down.

After we hiked we went back to the campsite and it snowed like crazy. Later we had a snowball fight! Kaitlin and I made snowballs and pretended that the trees were the white people, and we were Native Americans. And we would practice our target. Later mom and dad threw snowballs at us and we threw them back.

I just finished doing a book about one week ago. The story was about 18 pages long. It's about a dog, a cat, and a horse. The names are Shona (the horse), Jordin (the cat), and Justin (the dog). Justin is the enemy. When I come back (around June 1) I'll show you a copy and give a copy to you. It's great.

A few days ago I bought two rings at an Indian trading post. One is for you. The ring for you is yellow and red and pink. I have one too. Friendship rings.

Miss you tons!

Love,
Jordin

Dear Nikki,

We went to the Grand Canyon a couple days ago. When we camped there it snowed about three inches! The first night it didn't snow, but that day it hailed and rained. Then it started snowing! I think it got down to 22 degrees! In the morning when mom and dad were packing up the tent, we stopped and had a snowball fight! Jordin hit the video camera!! (good thing it still works) I hit Dad right smack on his back! It was fun!

The day we got there we hiked down the canyon

about a mile one way. The trail we hiked was South Kaibab. It is seven miles long. Next spring we are going to hike down to the bottom of the canyon by the Colorado River and stay two nights at Phantom Ranch. We might ride some mules at the ranch! I can't wait!!

I am enjoying the trip a lot!! My favorite part was the Grand Canyon. And I liked the Oregon sand dunes. In about two months we will be back in Craig to run the Sub Marina. I can't wait!!

Miss you!

Love,
Kaitlin

In the wee hours of this morning Jan and I were treated to a rare performance of the "doggie opera." I've taken in the scene from Disney's *Lady and the Tramp* where Tramp and his dog pound friends harmonize, and the famous "Twilight Bark" from *101 Dalmations* where Pongo spreads the word of lost puppies by barking to distant dogs who in turn pass it on.

Well, this performance had elements of both, but transcended them to aspects of "The Tempest" and even "Hamlet" by the Old Bard himself. The instigator, a lead baritone, was about 20 yards from our tent, max. He began with a soliloquy around 3:00 a.m. He persevered and soon had two or three canines collaborating in a riveting dialogue. His performance was uninspired as far as emotion, being rather, well, dogmatic. But what he lacked in spark he more than made up for in endurance. He was the glue that held this performance together, the one character that was always on stage with his yapper open.

At one point there were probably 12 to 15 dogs barking at the same time. It was fairly cool, so Jan and I both had our sleeping bags up over our heads. Her disembodied voice whispered, "It's a regular chorus!" I got the giggles. What else could a guy do at 3:30 a.m., short of taking an aluminum softball bat and going after that baritone? But I'm a fan, not a critic, so I snuggled deeper and listened as the tempest tossed the boat onto the rocks.

There was a basso profundo (I imagined him to be a Great Dane or

Russian Wolfhound) whose voice rolled across the valley like thunder. There was a soprano who didn't bark often but was the emotional star of the show. By the sounds of it, she was mourning a murdered lover. There was one guy whose delivery imitated a wolf crooning at the full moon. His notes would float against the more staccato singing of the canine chorus. At one point a raven even joined in. It went from the ridiculous to the sublime. The performance lasted for over an hour. From the crescendo of the massed chorus with soloists, it faded down to two or three dogs from perhaps four or five miles down the valley faintly offering news of distant lands. But always Luigi the baritone was there. I'm sure he's sleeping off his performance now as I write this critique in my sleeping bag, surrounded by my family and the soft light of early morning.

Inspiration, true art, seldom surfaces. I was there.

March 31   Santa Fe, New Mexico

The rhythm, we are in the rhythm. It feels like we have the flow of travelling. The clue: don't travel every day. We've gotten in the habit of staying in each campground at least two nights. This gives us a day in between making camp and breaking camp. This also allows the girls time to play and for Jim and I to take long walks. Visits to area highlights can also be done on the "off" day. Staying more than two nights is pure pleasure, with more added free time.

The weather has sure given us a variation recently: snow in the Grand Canyon, 18 degrees in Canyon de Chelly, and 50 mph wind gusts at Red Rock State Park outside Gallup, New Mexico. It's amazing how winds of that speed can distort the shape of a tent. But the good old tent held up like a grand champ and was none the worse for wear and wind. The wind did howl; I heard each gust barrel down the canyon seconds before I felt it hit the tent.

The night of the canine chorus did not solely belong to the dogs; in my opinion, the campers also had supporting roles in this one act play. Those intent on "doing something" about the noise were soon walking up and down the road. For what, I asked myself. Were they going to shoot them? Coerce them into silence? Find a responsible party to reprimand? Where did they think they were going at 3:00 a.m.?

The conversations began filling the airwaves as couples started waking up and discussing the noisy predicament. Did anyone sleep through the fiasco?

> **Inspiration, true art, seldom surfaces.**
> **I was there.**

I had felt a personal connection with the land and the people of the Navajo nation, the Dineh. Yesterday on our way toward Santa Fe we stopped off at Sky City, the oldest continually inhabited pueblo, home of the Acoma. The mesa-top village has been occupied since the 12th century and is currently home to 11 families.

There were probably a dozen artists offering their work for sale, with most of them being potters. One man did pencil and ink drawings, another worked with cut mattings, another etched designs on blackened pottery that his wife had done, and there was a woman from the Santo Domingo pueblo who made jewelry. Their themes and designs were native.

The work was stunning. Intricate designs that called to mind M.C. Escher. Cosmic explosions intricately symmetrical in black on white, all done by hand using yucca fibers chewed to get the desired tips. As we moved from table to table I was totally in awe. The work was of very high quality, very geometric and pure, and all done free hand!

The people impressed me even more, however. They were quiet but very outgoing, more than willing to talk about their art and their lifestyle. They seemed to have a very subtle cosmic sense of humor, with a smile always playing around their lips. They genuinely thanked you for stopping even when you didn't buy anything. I left with no pottery, but a very filling sense of calm.

Jan has been looking for a drum. In talking with the woman from Santo Domingo, she asked if she could recommend a drum maker. The woman started talking about a man in the pueblo of Cochiti. She was describing how to find his house and said, "There's usually a police car parked outside." I quickly tossed in, "Oh, he's a trouble maker, huh?" There was a space of just a nanosecond as we looked at each other and then she quietly chuckled. It was a nice moment. (P.S. The man's son-in-law is a member of the Native Police Force.)

The girls did a nice job with home school today. They were playing with their set up native village, but came willingly when I "rang the school bell" and worked hard without grumping.

April 1   Taos, New Mexico

We've stayed two nights in a Santa Fe motel since we're at a higher altitude (about 7,000) and it's a little chilly for tent camping. Yesterday we went into downtown Santa Fe, mostly to visit the New Mexico Museum of Fine Arts, but also to walk around and window shop. (We saw some incredible artwork.) It was a gorgeous sunny day and we really enjoyed ourselves. The main style of architecture is adobe and the streets right in the main square mile of town are very narrow. You can easily imagine it as a bustling cow town where several different cultures lived side by side.

Our time at the Museum of Fine Arts was nice as well. There were two paintings by Georgia O'Keefe and a video on her life and works. What a strong individual. One woman in the video, a friend of O'Keefe's, told of the time when two tourists had come to the artist's front door. When asked what they wanted, they replied that they wanted to see her. She said, "Front," turned around and said, "Back," and walked into her house.

There were some scissors, glue bottles, colored tissue and construction paper left out on a bench from a fourth grade field trip that had just passed through the museum. Kaitlin and Jordin took right to it and created some very nice art that we've kept and hope to frame. What a rich experience to soak up that environment and then create. Jordin cut out a heart shape and wrote "I love art!" and signed it. I asked her to leave it on the bench as a thank you. As we were leaving the museum, I ran into an older woman who was responsible for the materials being out. She was grinning from ear to ear and said that she had given the heart to the director of the museum, who was going to put it up on her wall. We've left our mark in Santa Fe!

April 2   Navajo Lake State Park
Turley, New Mexico

Dear Darcy,

A week ago I (with my family of course) went to the GRAND CANYON! It was huge! It was brownish red and sort of orange. We hiked two miles up and down. When we came back up it started snowing hard. In the morning when Dad was packing up the tent Kaitlin and I were making snowballs. Then dad threw a snowball at me. And mom

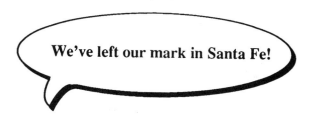

We've left our mark in Santa Fe!

threw one at Kaitlin. Pretty soon we were having a regular snowball fight. It was fun.

When we come back we'll probably spend a night in Ketchikan first. Then I could call you! The next day I could play with you and Shona! I can't wait! Can you?

Just a few minutes ago we went over a 450 foot bridge over the Rio Grande! That's like 40 of your houses! And we saw people kayaking down a huge, fast-flowing river. They must have been crazy!

Miss you a TON!

Love,
Jordin

P.S. Send your letter to my old address. Uncle Dave sends our mail to us. Now you can reply.

Dear Claire,

Right now we are in New Mexico and heading northwest. In about a month and a half we will be in Craig! I can't wait!! I think we will stay a night at Ketchikan and then take the ferry to Hollis. I could call you from Ketchikan!

And while we were going to Taos, New Mexico in the truck, I thought maybe we could start a club with just you and me in it. Do you want to? If you don't, could you tell me in your next letter, please? If you want to I will send some stuff for the club that I made. The two papers in the envelope that say stuff like: Club Name: Phantom Coyote Club are the plans. The blank sheet is for you to fill out. First you should read the one I filled out. If you like what I wrote, put an X on your sheet in the same place you like it. If you don't like it you can write what you want on your paper. After you are done, please send it back so I can make the official club paper. The other paper is a certificate for official member of the club. After you are done please send them back.

How has the weather been? Did you get any snow? I hope that when I come it is sunny so we can go bike riding and make sea-pools with tarps.

MISS YOU A LOT!!

Love,
Kaitlin

P.S. The address to send your letter to is: Kaitlin Marousis, Box 532, Craig, Alaska 99921. My Uncle Dave will pick it up and send!

P.P.S. Please write!!

April 3

Easter Sunday at Navajo Lake, New Mexico and we had an adaptable Easter egg hunt. We found some oval, rounded rocks, decorated them with markers and water color paints, and then took turns hiding them by our campsite. We each colored five "eggs," then Jan and I hid them for the girls. We videotaped the hunt, with some "hot or cold" clues. Then the girls hid ours. It was good family fun and we'll leave all but our favorite one for the next tenants of this spot to find as a treat.

After the egg hunt the girls asked me to take them to the playground, so I picked up my book and off we went. After a while six or seven native kids came along. At first they were playing on the swings and slide while Kait and

Jord played on the merry go round, taking turns pushing, but soon they were all taking turns pushing and riding the merry go round. Laughter and giggling sound the same in any language. Between the two years in Craig and the time travelling in the southwest, my girls have learned to look past the color of a friend's skin. A good foundation for further life explorations.

April 4   **Chaco Culture National Historic Park**
                                        Seven Lakes, New Mexico

Chaco. Chaco Culture National Monument. It was to be one of our highlights, like Baha. Chaco.

The wind blew relentlessly as we inched along the rutted, washboard dirt road. The dust swirled and whipped. Everything and everybody shook and bumped for one and a half hours, the time it took to travel the last 30 miles of dirt road to Chaco. The air was grainy and foggy from the dust, whipped by 35 mph winds.

Wind. Wind and dust. There was never any doubt the direction of the wind—everyone's back was turned to the wind's direction, saving their eyes from penetrating dust particles. The tent and wind were great allies, fighting to be released from my grip, tipped sideways, shape distorted, waiting for Jim to get the stakes from the back of the truck so that we could anchor things down. While I wrestled and Jim looked, the ground tarps flew. Away. I wanted to be away from the wind and dust.

The cold. By evening, the wind released its stronghold, taking a back seat to the cold. Cold. The girls scurried into the truck to get out of the cold, while Jim set up our sleeping bags, pillows and blankets. For the first time we hadn't set them up ahead of time to prevent the dust from infiltrating all our bed gear.

The dust. It already baptized every inch of us and the truck, both inside and out. While Jim was getting beds ready, and the girls were trying to stay warm, the cold took on a new dimension.

Cold rain. Pelting hail. In haste, I found the tent fly from the back of the truck. We hadn't put in on earlier because it would have behaved like a sail and caused more trouble than it prevented. But now with the wind diminishing and the hard rain threatening, the fly was needed in the hopes of keeping us dry.

Hail. Wet snow. We didn't know it was snow until much later in the evening, so we were ignorant to its adhering itself to every spot of the tent that presented itself as a shelf, the biggest on Jordin's side. We didn't know until I heard Jordin sniffle, and I was going to ask her in the wee hours of the morning if she needed a tissue. "I'm soaking," came her reply. (I guess a tissue won't do.)

Soaking. The wet snow, packed on her side of the tent, had wicked its way slowly to the warmth of her bag and camp pad, leaving her lying in a puddle with outside air below 30 degrees. She quickly stripped (she was wet to the bone) and replaced Jim in his bag as he got up, went to the truck, and returned with dry, warm clothes for her. It was at this moment when he looked outside that we found out that indeed snow had been the culprit.

Wet. To make sure the same thing didn't happen on Kaitlin's side, we had her slide closer to the middle, toward Jim. So there we lay, four bodies in three bags, all in 5 feet of space. As we attempted to settle back in, I listened to the night, and I wondered if I heard snow melting or dogs licking.

It took hours to dry out in the morning, and we had the additional problem of trying to get the tent poles apart. Dust. It infiltrated the tent poles, and they could not be dismantled. They were locked together by sand particles. Jim and I tugged, twisted, pulled, pushed, cussed and I cussed some more. To no avail. My stubbornness and determination separated the final pole sections, but not without breaking the shock cords in the process. A remembrance of Chaco. It left its mark. No sooner had we packed up, the snow started again, as a mocking departure farewell while we were leaving Chaco.

By that time, Chaco had stolen my sanity and I realized that it was all part of the witchery Leslie Silko talked about in Ceremony, published by Penguin Books. I had concerns about the spirits of other worlds, those beyond or behind, those above or below. I had heard the spirits were very alive, and that if I heard voices and noise during the night not to open my eyes. But it was not other worlds that caused chaos, it was the earth spirits of this world. Or was it? The other worlds work in this world. I found no peace at Chaco. Or did Chaco's spirits find little peace with my presence and were the creators of my internal chaos? I will not forget Chaco.

We found still another chapter in the "Is there really widespread violence in America's schools?" We talked to a 38-year-old store manager from Ruidoso, a town of 4,600 people in south central New Mexico. He spoke of the violence in that town. Recently his 11-year-old son and a friend had gotten off the school bus and gunshots were fired in their general direction. A group of four high school boys in a car had been tailing the bus and had fired the shots for no apparent reason. When picked up, they were found to have ten weapons, including shotguns, and an open bottle of whiskey in the car.

We found still another chapter in the "Is there really widespread violence in America's schools?" We talked to a 38-year-old store manager from Ruidoso, a town of 4,600 people in south central New Mexico. He spoke of the violence in that town. Recently his 11-year-old son and a friend had gotten off the school bus and gunshots were fired in their general direction. A group of four high school boys in a car had been tailing the bus and had fired the shots for no apparent reason. When picked up, they were found to have ten weapons, including shotguns, and an open bottle of whiskey in the car.

Today we came to Chaco Culture National Monument, the highest oint of Anasazi culture. The structures, dating from about 850 to 1400 A.D., re beautiful in their construction. Doorways and windows are level and lines f construction are straight. They have square and rectangular rooms for ving and storage, with different sized round kivas below ground level. These ere used for ceremonies of some sort.

The road into Chaco is a 30-mile dirt washboard which tested the nettle (and metal!) of a truck that has bested the logging roads on Prince of Vales Island, but it's worth it. I can hear voices in the wind.

Pueblo Bonito, the largest of several structures, is striking. It's a ymmetrical half moon in shape, with some parts being three stories high. There is a central plaza and several kivas of differing sizes. Standing in the laza I could imagine the flow of everyday life around me.

Some of the natives we've met have spoken of trying to live in two vorlds. Well, here I am, a rabid basketball fan (especially at NCAA ournament time!), and as Duke and Arkansas tip it up for the national hampionship tonight I'm in a tent in Chaco at the end of a long dirt road, probably the farthest away from a TV that I've been at any point in this trip. Every day we must look for balance.

April 5   Farmington, New Mexico

Our Alaska license plates have attracted conversationalists all hrough this trip and yesterday was no different. We had just endured 30 miles of vertebrae-rattling road and pulled into the Chaco campground. The wind

Chaco Canyon National Historic Park

was blowing pretty hard as we tried to set up the tent. Before I could drive the corner stakes, a gust actually picked the tent up eight feet in the air and saw it disappear around the corner of the truck. Luckily Jan hung on to on of the poles and I grabbed another and we managed to wrestle Icarus back t terra firma. While Jan held on I staked it down.

At that point Jan went to sit in the truck and put her head on her hand resting on the steering wheel. I got in the back seat, pulled the sleeping bag pillows, and blankets through the capper window and began piling them in th passenger side of the front seat. A woman popped her head in the ope window saying, "I don't want to corral you, but are you really from Alaska' She of course then proceeded to corral us for an hour, mostly complainin about the public school system, but also tossing in tidbits about how h family had been living in several countries abroad, the fact that her husban was a well-renowned artist, where she had gone to college, where she ha grown up, and her daughter's experience with school in Italy, Holland an Taos, New Mexico. I felt a little foolish sitting in the back seat with my kne halfway to my chin, but she was nonstop. I kept my eye on both Jan and th tent to make sure that neither one got blown away.

We later met Anna's husband, a tall gangly Dutchman with John Lennon glasses, a beard gone white on the sides, and a very dry sense of humor. I liked him, and asked him if he was still able to produce real art in Taos, and he said, "Oh yes, I work every day." Then he smiled and added, "But I like to be around the campfire with my family and play with my children. They are living works of art." Yes, Aat, I like that.

After dinner the lady tried to sell us a silk scarf that her husband had hand painted. She asked $40 (they'll go for $200 in New York, you know). We declined and that was pretty much the end of that story.

As we started to turn in it began to rain. Just a few drops, but fairly big ones. We quickly put on the fly (which we had taken off earlier because of the wind). Well, we were soon getting every bit of that "30% chance of rain" posted at the Visitor's Center. I dozed off to the sound of a steady rain. I awoke sometime around midnight or 1:00. It had stopped raining and was now so quiet that it was as if we were in a total vacuum. Soon, however, I started hearing a periodic dry rasping sound on the outside of the tent. My only guess (after a very short flirt with the thought of spirits) was that the rain had splashed sand up on the tent walls. As it dried it slid off.

Wrong-O! The rain had turned to wet snow some time during the night. Just then Jord woke up, soaked to the skin. We took her wet clothes off and I took her shivering body into my sleeping bag. As soon as she was warm enough, I went out to the truck to get dry clothes for her and to shake the snow and ice off the tent fly. Her sleeping bag was soaked so we both used my bag for the rest of that long, long night. She dropped off to sleep again pretty quickly, but I couldn't get the zipper past my waist. I kept my hooded sweatshirt on, Kaitlin's stuffed lion kept my nose warm with his paw, and I covered myself with the blanket that Jordin had crocheted.

This morning, in between snow squalls and hail, we climbed up on top of Alta Mesa which overlooks Pueblo Bonito. We couldn't stay long because of gusting wind and limited visibility, but the view from above was haunting. An exhibit in the Visitors' Center said that because it was such an all-pervasive part of their daily lives, there was no separate Anasazi word for religion. From the symmetry and grace of the Pueblo Bonito construction plan I would say the same for art.

> Then he smiled and added, "But I like to be around the campfire with my family and play with my children. They are living works of art."

April 6

As I write this from the warmth and comfort of our motel room, remember Anna, the first American born citizen I've met who did not kno about the plight of our Natives. She thought they chose this beautiful barr land where they live and cannot farm nor subsist. She had never heard abo "Trail of Tears," the forced relocation from their homelands, nor any oth indecency imposed upon them. She was born and raised in one of our fi eastern finishing schools where they seem to perpetrate the lie regarding t early history of our country, and just who this land belonged to.

April 8   Slickrock Campgroun
                                                              Moab, Uta

My veins are singing tonight. We hiked on a ranger-led expeditic through the labyrinth of Fiery Furnace in Arches National Park toda Beautiful spires, fins, and arches of reddish brown Entrada sandstone. Kaitl and Jordin spent most of the walk glued to the ranger's tail at the very he of the line of hikers. It was a pretty demanding trail and they did more th keep up, with barely a glance over their shoulders for mom and dad. Anoth milestone on the path to independence.

We were in a group of 18 people. One couple was from the Olymp Peninsula, near Chimacum, one of the areas that we have looked at for possible job next year. They gave us lots of encouraging background info a gave us their names, addresses, and invitations to look them up if we mo there. Another lady was American-born but presently living in New Zealan and she gave us some tips on other nice spots for hiking in southern Utah. really enjoyed talking with them, more outside-the-family socialization th I've had for a while. It felt good.

Moab is just crawling with college-age kids, heavily into hikin jeeping, and especially mountain biking. What a gung-ho, carefree attitud Everybody's cruising, trading stories. Lots of laughter. It's a strange bree from my past. I like where I'm at and wouldn't trade my family for anythin but I sure enjoyed my Marco Polo years. Friendships from those years are st strong, and although meetings are far less frequent as the years go by, I st enjoy trading stories and observations on milestone experiences a changing viewpoints.

> **Would I recommend this life? Yes,**
> **the gains far outweigh the losses.**

Would I recommend this life? Yes, the gains far outweigh the losses. I hope. Financial losses could yet come if Jim or I do not secure a job for the fall. We've started "charging" lots of items, so we will have bills (probably in excess of $2,000) by the time we reach Craig.

April 9

I'm tired today and a little discouraged. After getting snowed on at Chaco, we've had three fairly rainy, windy days in Moab. We did get a decent afternoon yesterday and made the most of it with that out-of-this-world hike through Fiery Furnace. Last night and this morning were very wet, with heavy rains. All four corners of the tent had small puddles of standing water and three out of four sleeping bags were wet to varying degrees. We combined dry-out time with clean clothes-patrol, and spent two hours at the laundromat this afternoon.

There was a huge 28-mile mountain bike race today and we saw some of the stragglers coming in as we watched the driers spin at the laundromat. A couple of bikers rode right up to the car wash behind the laundry and just hosed themselves and their bikes down. Red mud from head to toe, frames encrusted like the Carlsbad Caverns.

We spent some time at a local horse show today. It was a nice low-key production, no admission charge. Some of the same riders participated in five or six different events. Most of them seemed to know each other and the competition was friendly. There was one little girl who competed in the ten and under age division. She looked like a fairy on top of her horse, but boy could she ride! It was obvious that she and her horse spent a lot of time together. They were like two parts of a whole, beautiful to watch. She won at least two blue ribbons and was a very gracious winner. Kaitlin and Jordin have been devouring horse books lately (*Saddle Club* and *Black Stallion* series, mainly), so they thoroughly enjoyed themselves today.

April 11

Being in a campground is one way of keeping track of the Monday Friday/weekend time split. It's like the ebb and flow of the tides. Slickroc Campground was rockin' all weekend, full of tents and RV's, campers in th shower, music blaring, hot tubs full. Now it's Monday morning, th campground is like a ghost town, and we're back to quiet country living.

April 12

Weather is one of the biggest factors in this trip. Weather affects ou sleeping, eating, leisure and exercise time.

Just the other day the tent zipper started misbehaving; it wouldn close except with lots of coaxing, cussing (I'm positive that this helps), an alternately, patience. If this were a home, and it is for us, that would be lik having most of one entire side of a house exposed to the elements. Wide ope No screen. Nothing except lots of outside. Would you live like that?

Or, how about waking up with wet floors and mattresses each time rained or snowed, with not another dry room?

Or, how about cooking and eating on your bed when the weather ge snotty?

Yes, we are weather effected. Our tent is 8' x 8', just enough room fo us to sleep comfortably. (But that's my opinion, and the girls' opinions var greatly from mine.)

Well, the tent zipper proved to be another successful, cost efficier repair on our part. After searching unsuccessfully for someone to repair th zipper pull (like we had done early on near Portland), we heeded local advic and attempted to "squeeze" the puller, forcing it tightly onto the zippe Success!! Another no cost repair.

The frayed shock cord, ah Chaco, we repaired by re-knotting one enc and gaining most of the needed length we lost, refeeding it through the pole and then placed a final knot at the other end. Simple enough.

It feels good to not be so dependent on others. I wish I were more sel sufficient in regards to the truck. I'm still in awe at every noise and quirk "Bucky."

Jim reads aloud most nights, by lantern light, to the girls (and me!) a we lay in our sleeping bags. We used to depend heavily on flashlights an batteries (very costly) for reading, but have learned that the lantern is mor efficient and adds needed warmth to the tent. (But for adequate ventilatior we keep all four windows opened for fresh air.) But I'm still not used to it, as each morning I hit my head on the lantern as I stand up to get dressed. How many knocks on the head will it take me to remember the hanging obstacle dead center in the tent. If I miss it, it's only luck.

We've been here at Arches for a week now, and have explored lots of the park, but the area surrounding Moab swells with more recreational opportunities than we will experience.

Karma has proved itself to me (us) again. While at the Painted Desert, we stopped to help a couple who had sunk their vehicle knee deep into soft sand on the shoulder of the road. We pushed and rocked, changed drivers, pushed and rocked some more until we freed that Chevy mini van from its sandy grip. The couple was from England.

A few days prior to that, we had lost a letter with an enclosed $200 check. It was addressed, sealed and stamped, waiting for a post office deposit box. Before it found its way to a post office, it jumped ship. But, safely did it arrive to its destination, with a note on the back that Chris and Teresa had found it at one of the viewpoints of the Grand Canyon. They "posted it on" (their terms, written on the back of the envelope) from Las Vegas. Chris and Teresa were from England. Karma goes full circle.

I am grateful to that couple for mailing that envelope, which caused great duress and anxiety. Should I stop payment on the check? Was it lost globally (outside the truck) or locally, inside the mayhem of the truck? What oh what should I do? Patience and karma came out the winners. I wish patience was more active in my life.

Wait? You want me to WAIT? EEEEK!! Just let me do, act, change, fix, worry, mope and wonder. Let it go? Then who? These are some of the many reasons that AA will always be a part of my life. Like Bill H. says, "AA has taught me how to live life on life's terms." AA has brought me more than sobriety. It gives me a healthy way of living, a guide to life's everyday problems. But, I don't always pay attention to subtleties.

This morning we went on a brief journey to pick some sage. 12.4 miles up the road toward Castle View, along the muddy Colorado River just outside Moab with majestic, high reddish-brown cliffs on both sides. We stopped in a couple of places, but didn't find the Wise One. Then we hit paydirt in a small flat and gently sloping hill across the road from the river. We spent 30 minutes respectfully gathering sage from several plants in the area. Then we sprinkled corn meal to give thanks to the plants for sharing. We picked up trash, mostly beer cans and bottles, to help the area feel clean and honored. Right now, as I write this back at our campsite, the sage is spread out on an old sleeping bag, drying in the bright sunshine while a Western Meadowlark serenades us in the background.

The sage will be burned to purify the space of our new home and probably the homes of some of our friends as well.

April 13

We planned to leave Moab today and head southwest towards Canyonlands National Park, but my Minnesota teaching license didn't arrive in the mail today, so we'll be here another day. It's our third beautiful, warm, sunny day after quite a stretch of rain and cool weather. The wheel goes around. We'll make the most of it. The girls have been enjoying playing with their Barbie™ dolls around the campsite, Jan and I will go for long walks, we'll probably do another hike in Arches, and finish off the day with a hot tub and shower here at Slickrock Campground.

School will be over five weeks from today. I enjoy the rhythm of the teaching year: a burst of initial energy that usually lasts until Thanksgiving, then ride the excitement of Christmas and a nice vacation. The period after Christmas break until mid-February is often the most productive. The kids are energized from vacation, happy to see their friends, and used to your expectations, so they can crank out some good work. From then to the end of March is like walking through waist-deep mud for me psychologically, so I usually plan fun projects like paper mache, plays, or videotaping during that time. It helps me get excited about school. By the end of that time the daylight hours are getting noticeably longer and that gives me a surge of energy. I'm like a racehorse heading for the finish line and my oats. By the time we get down to five weeks, I feel like I've taught the bulk of my main objectives and it's time to relax the rules and really enjoy the kids.

Well, we're there!

April 14   Needles Outpost Campground
Canyonlands, Utah

Dear Gay,

Right now we are leaving Arches National Park by Moab, Utah. There's one called Broken Arch. And Window Arch, North Arch, Double Arch, South Arch, Landscape

Arch, etc. They're HUGE! Have you been there? If you have been, did you like it? I did.

When we were at Arches Park I got a bow, three arrows, and a knife (all fake). Another time when we went into Moab, Kaitlin got a set exactly like mine, but instead of a knife there was a spear with a fake flute at the end. (It could come off). And we would put up dish cloths and towels and shoot at them. It was fun.

Love, your friend,
Jordin

Dear Gay,

A few days ago we went to a horse show at Moab, Utah. Most of the people in the show were kids six to sixteen. Some were adults. In the jumping round only one person jumped! Of course, she won the blue ribbon. My favorite part was the barrel race. The people in the race rode around the three barrels as fast as possible. A girl about three years older than me won.

When mom went to a Health Food store (it also had tons of books) to try and sell her necklaces, the guy wouldn't buy them. Then they started talking and mom told him about Plan Z and that Jordin and I love to read!! He gave mom a book for each of us. Free! Jordin got one called *Giant, or Waiting for the Thursday Boat* (by Robert Munsch, Annick Press). The book's thin but I still like it. Mine is *The Forbidden Door* (by Marilee Heyer, Puffin Books). It is a story about an elf girl named Reena. She and her parents live in an underground cave in the valley of the Bao-Bickle tree, on a star. Her parents told a story of the Outside world, one that is forbidden. Reena is determined to find a way to Outside and does. There she meets the Okira, an evil monster that trapped her ancestors. Reena and Nimar, a good person that helps, go to the Okira's lair in the Tangled Forest to get the Ruby Crystal, one of the sources of the Okira's power, the other being beauty. Finally the Okira's power is broken with help from an ugly mask.

The pictures are beautiful. I can't wait to show it to you.

Miss you!

Love,
Kaitlin

April 17   **Devil's Canyon Campground**
Blanding, Utah

Today is our third day in Manti-La Sal National Forest, between Monticello and Blanding, Utah. The campground doesn't officially open for another month so there is no water, but that means camping is free. It's a gorgeous spot, somewhat reminiscent of the Midwest, except for some sage bushes. There is a pitted sandstone bluff 8-10 feet high running along the north side of our site, a grass meadow to the west, and high pines all around us that echo the wind. We have lots of room and rarely see other campers.

The first night was very cold, but last night was better. The days have been sunny and warm. We've all enjoyed the leisure time to sun, read, and have the Barbies™ do some rapelling and tree climbing.

We had a family ceremony honoring Kaitlin and Jordin at our campfire last night. We set up the kids' tent our first night here and they've slept in there the last two nights. They helped put it up and have taken real pride in fixing up the area and keeping the inside of the tent neatly arranged and cozy. It marked another very tangible example of their growth in responsibility. Some native cultures used ceremony to mark and honor the passage of juveniles of both sexes into the adult world. We smudged with sage to purify ourselves and then talked to the girls of our pride in their growth.

April 18

Paradise at Devil's Canyon north of Monticello, Utah. Not an appropriate name for this piece of heaven. No water, no people, no cost. Quiet. A white, crystal-like, snow capped mountain in the distance. Time. Space. The girls have lots of places to play and explore, room to set up their tent, and time here to enjoy it.

We had a family ceremony honoring Kaitlin and Jordin at our campfire last night. We set up the kids' tent our first night here and they've slept in there the last two nights. They helped put it up and have taken real pride in fixing up the area and keeping the inside of the tent neatly arranged and cozy. It marked another very tangible example of their growth in responsibility. Some native cultures used ceremony to mark and honor the passage of juveniles of both sexes into the adult world.

They've slept in their tent the last few nights and from the bottom of my heart, I miss them. I'm proud of their autonomy and responsibility in keeping it picked up each day. But, our tent has grown quiet and cold without their warm bodies to fill all the empty space. The girls' warm bodies, tucked inside their down bags right next to us, kept us all warm and cozy. Now, there's empty, cold space that suck our blankets off us. The first night we froze, but last night we sided our bags with boxes and coolers to keep the blankets on. Also, we used the extra, light-weight sleeping bags and slipped them up around us. Finally, we were warm, even if we couldn't move!!

The cool nights find me layering clothes on my sleeping bag at my feet. First, I take my jacket and lay it over my feet, then my hooded sweatshirt, and finally my shirt. These are all in addition to the two blankets I already have on top of my sleeping bag. It becomes obvious, then, doesn't it how our sleeping bags lack insulative quality? But with the added pounds of clothes perched precariously over me, I sleep in comfort most nights as do the girls in their down bags, with much less weight.

I pay strict attention, though, during the night to my "pile" and continuously need to pamper the layers, tugging and pulling them back up and onto my bag. Yes, warmth sustenance.

Adjacent to the campground is a dirt (hard, dried mud) road that meanders for miles through this high country (7,000-8,000). Criss-crossing this road are tracks of many animals including deer, elk, caribou, raccoon, wild turkey, coyote, wolf, and possibly some type of wild feline. We've all had a great time using crayons and paper to make rubbings of the tracks. Some turned out well, some not so good, but the exploration and adventure were the highlights of this excursion.

This campsite, in its relative isolation, has brought me peace, happiness, and serenity. I wonder if I will ever live in a spot like this? I could, but I know that I would eventually lose my appreciation and take it for granted. (A common human ailment and curse.) Day to day life of work and home leave little time to really enjoy those things we long for, seldom appreciate, and then eventually take for granted. Our family members? The beauty around us? Our jobs? Food on the table? Health? A flush toilet? A couch? A bed? A sink in the kitchen and bathroom? Carpet for barefoot pleasure? A roof over our heads? How long will it be before I take all these things for granted again?

Later...Newness and excitement gave way to security and belonging, and the girls came back to the home tent last night as they neared bedtime. Ah, but one step forward and one step back is the story of life. Make sure the footing is still okay behind in case of a mandatory, quick, retreat.

Another sign of Kaitlin and Jordin's growth in taking responsibility: I had asked them to clean out the back seat of the truck, which is their exclusive domain. It's kind of like the ebb and flow of the tides, only in this case it leaves tide pools of books, Barbies™, art supplies, autographed baseballs, rock samples, ropes, horses, etc. This time it had really gotten out of hand, the tide having not ebbed for at least three days.

Without a single grumble or knitted brow, they dove in right after breakfast. They dug everything out of the small compartments next to their seat and out from under their seats and began sorting. Some toys went back into storage in the back of the truck, I helped corral two plastic grocery bags chock full of books to be stored in the back for future consumption, and we collected a large bag of leftover paper, pamphlets (including the state tourism book for Texas, which burned forever, emitting strange vapors and green flames), and bits of rope for the campfire that night.

About three hours later they were finished and proud of the results! This was no shortcut or superficial effort, folks. This was war. At the apex, the back seat was completely cleared! A job well done!

April 19   **Goblin Valley State Park**
                                      Hanksville, Utah

Dear Grandma,

The day before yesterday dad and I started building my model boat. It is made of balsa wood. For the masts

I wonder if I will ever live in a spot like this? I could, but I know that I would eventually lose my appreciation and take it for granted. (A common human ailment and curse.) Day to day life of work and home leave little time to really enjoy those things we long for, seldom appreciate, and then eventually take for granted. Our family members? The beauty around us? Our jobs? Food on the table? Health? A flush toilet? A couch? A bed? A sink in the kitchen and bathroom? Carpet for barefoot pleasure? A roof over our heads? How long will it be before I take all these things for granted again?

we will use dowels. The name I picked out is Sea Star. Yesterday we got the shape with the saw, and today we might work on the keel. A keel is the part of the boat that keeps it from tipping over.

It is usually a chunk of lead put on the bottom of the boat. It helps the boat stay upright in big waves. I am having fun doing it, and so is dad.

When we went to the Moab library they had a sale with old books, each book 25 cents. Dad, Jordin, and I got about 14 books! My favorite books were five books in a Bronc Burnett series. They are baseball stories. Bronc is the Sonora, New Mexico's team pitcher. Daddy used to read them when he was a kid.

How is the weather up in Minnesota? Still any snow? We wear shorts and shortsleeve shirts down here in New Mexico. We are heading up to Alaska now!

Miss you!

Love,
Kaitlin

P.S. Thanks for the $10 for my birthday.

Dear Grandma,

How are your jobs going? School's going good.

Right now I'm into Black Stallion books. It's about a boy and his stallion (a wild stallion), and the boy (Alec) saves his horse from a bad death and the horse learns to trust him and stay wild at the same time.

At the last campground Kaitlin and I set up the kids' tent. And we slept in it. Then we brought in all of our stuff. It was like a sleepover. It was great fun!

Love,
Jordin

P.S. Is it getting warmer up there?

P.P.S. Miss you a ton.

April 20   **Capitol Reef National Park**
Utah

Well, the Plan Z odyssey now has a definite endpoint. Jan called the Alaska Marine Highway ferry system yesterday for information. After mulling our choices, we've decided to drive through British Columbia, a distance of just under 1,000 miles (from Seattle), capped off with a possible stay in the Terrace Hot Springs, then take the ferry direct from Prince Rupert, B.C. to Hollis, Prince of Wales Island, Alaska, U.S.A. The alternative, taking the ferry all the way from Bellingham, Washington to Hollis, was an attractive idea but just too expensive.

So in the end, Jan made reservations to leave Prince Rupert on our old friend the Aurora, Monday, May 23. We'll be in Hollis later that same evening and the circle will be complete. That will give us four or five days to do any necessary clean up, repairs, and painting at the Sub Marina, stow away meat, cheese, and produce and open the doors for business, probably on Friday the 27th or Saturday the 28th.

How does it feel? A little strange. I think we've pulled the trip off successfully and the girls have definitely done well socially, physically, and academically, but it has put a strain on Jan's and my relationship.

> **To do it over again? Yes, I would. I think the trip has made us more resilient and resourceful, both individually and as a family unit. I think that we know each other very well now, which will be a valuable asset in surviving the bumps of adolescence.**

To do it over again? Yes, I would. I think the trip has made us more resilient and resourceful, both individually and as a family unit. I think that we know each other very well now, which will be a valuable asset in surviving the bumps of adolescence. Academically the girls are on very solid footing as they head into upper elementary and middle school.

It will be interesting to resolve some of the uncertainties of the near future, job and housing being the two biggies.

We met some people in the campground we are staying at. It is a writer with her husband and kid.

At the campground they had sprinklers. The kid, Kaitlin and I all got our bathing suits on and ran through the sprinklers by her campsite. The girl, Hanae, was fun to play with.

Her mom's name was Trish and her dad's name was David. He was Japanese. They were nice! (Jordin)

April 22

Capitol Reef National Park is proving to be an unexpected surprise. Lots of color, great hiking, a river for greenery and, BUGS. Yes, the water brings pleasure to all the senses and bug bites to the skin. Personally, I enjoy seeing and hearing the Fremont River next to our campsite and also from the high overlooks we've reached by hiking.

The kids' tent was set up again, but I was uncomfortable with them sleeping so far away (four feet) because the noise of the river drowns out their sleepy sounds that bring me the comfort of knowing they're okay. So, the next night, Kaitlin and Jim slept in one tent, Jordin and I in the other. Tonight we'll switch. I have strong fears of my children being taken away/kidnapped/ stolen, and at times I can't overcome that fear of losing them, and therefore I keep them close to me. Will I ever be able to let them go? I think I will once they become black belts in karate.

(I just took a break to film the 20 or more deer that quietly arrived in our campsite while Kaitlin and I were writing (me) and coloring (her) here in the cab of the truck.)

The trip will be over in one month as we catch the Aurora at Prince Rupert, British Columbia. Many mixed emotions. Yes, I'm sick of living out of the truck, but the trip has had many wonderful highlights, the best ones the most unexpected. (i.e. McDonald Observatory, Anza-Borrego, Capitol Reef, and Trish.) Yes, I met a woman here at the campground. I didn't hesitate like I often do, wanting to avoid the responsibility of another relationship. Instead it was like the convergence of two mountain creeks, greeting, joining, blending, continuing the journey. Separate sources, separate identities, but parallel journeys beyond. It happened so quickly and painlessly, and then we quickly said our first goodbyes after a short 24 hours of intimately sharing our thoughts and emotions that live in the bottom of our hearts. A thing that women do so well. See you again, Trish.

April 23

Why is it that I feel the urge to pee only when in the horizontal position? I always pee immediately before climbing into the tent, but soon thereafter I feel that tinge, that quiet little bell reminding me that the bathroom is a multitude of steps away. It's like a two year old beginning the early stages of a tantrum. I ignore the signs, trying to remind myself of the very recent trip down the road to the restroom. Unconvincing. The bladder whimpers and whines harder, I continue to be deaf, until I can no longer ignore the pleas. It's all in my mind, watch, I'll press on my bladder and show you....yikes, it's full. (It's also very cold outside, and I'm dressed in my "nighttime" clothes of boxer shorts, sweatshirt and socks that even a rugged mountain man would deem worthless.) So, I get dressed, put on shoes, tie them or tuck in the laces, put on a jacket, unzip the tent, re-zip the tent after I crawl out, walk (quickly) to the room that spells relief, walk back and repeat the above procedures backwards. I can go ALL day and not have the urge, but the cool night times provoke and stimulate this old bladder relentlessly.

Tonight will be our fourth in Capitol Reef National Park, which has turned out to be a real jewel. The Fremont River runs down through the main canyon, making it an oasis in dry, southern Utah. The Park Service uses sprinklers to maintain acres of green grass and irrigation to water more than 25,000 fruit trees in the valley. Cottonwoods give lots of shade from the sun which has been very hot from 10:00 in the morning until 6:00 in the evening.

We've had some exhilarating hikes here. The night before last we meandered along the Fremont River trail, which follows the flat land along the singing river for most of its course. The last half mile or so it climbs 800 vertical feet to a mesa top. We didn't really have the top as a goal when we started, but enjoyed the setting sun from 6,100 feet. At the time it seemed like the top of the world.

Yesterday morning we did the Cohab Trail, which does its vertical climb right off the bat and then does a 90 degree turn into a huge split in the rock face, down into the "hidden valley." We continued through a dry wash and then chose another branch trail that did some switchbacks up a gradual rock face out onto a higher mesa that overlooked the river valley. I'm not fond of heights and the overlook was enough to give me the heebie jeebies. Twenty feet back from the rim was a rock that I dubbed the Kings' and Queens' Throne where we all took turns sitting and regally looking down our noses, surveying the vastness of our dominions.

Today was the topper though. We set off after breakfast, intending to do the moderate two-mile round trip trail to Hickman Arch. On our way we stopped to feed carrots to Toby, Rio, and Sti, the three friendly horses just over the fence from our camp. There was a Park Service volunteer, a white-haired gent, feeding them. We talked with him for awhile and he suggested we take a side trail that went to a higher overlook. He quietly smiled and said it was worth the hike. It proved to be longer (four and a half miles round trip) than our other hikes, but a more gradual ascent. It was really windy at times, but we persevered. The girls grumbled a little, but didn't quit and we were all mighty proud when we gained the summit at 6,400 feet (a vertical of 1,100 feet). The view was incredible, as we overlooked the two previous days' viewpoints. We came back down the trail 100 yards to a sheltered spot and had a feast of crackers with peanut butter, cinnamon raisin bagels, one apple shared four ways, and water. With renewed energy and a sense of accomplishment we bounced back down the mountain.

April 25   Zion National Park
                                                            Utah

We capped our string of hikes with a five and a half mile round tripper along the sandy banks of Calf Creek. At the end of the trail lay a waterfall, about 100 feet high, spilling over a rock lip into a basin 15 feet below the crest and then cascading down a steep rock face to a small emerald and turquoise pool that would have been a good anchorage for Captain Hook's ship. The path of the falls was accented with moss and algae in infinite shades of green.

On the return trip the girls broke off long stalks of dry grass with tufts at the end. They used these as paint brushes, twirling down the path in an elvish dance as they painted wild flowers. We stopped to look at small fish in pools where the creek slowed down.

It drizzled lightly on and off during the hike, but falling temps and a forecast of rain and snow persuaded us to get a room at Ruby's Best Western in Bryce Canyon. The "heated" pool was a bit chilly and holes in the roof let in the cold evening air, but the girls and I made the most of the opportunity for a night swim before bedtime, and then another in the morning before checkout time. Jan joined us in the hot tub, which was outside, but covered by a gazebo. It was a freezing run from the pool building to the hot tub! YIKES!!!

Today we headed 80 miles southwest to Zion National Park, arriving about 4:00. It was raining, but somewhat warmer, as we're at 4,000 feet compared with 8,000 at Bryce.

I'm writing this by lantern light in the tent. Everyone else is either asleep or on their way. It's really pouring now, testing our lines of defense. Jan and I spent an hour and a half testing the wind direction, hitching Big Blue to trees on one end and the truck on the other to act as a watershed (the Maginot Line?), then setting up the tent underneath the shelter and digging small trenches to divert runoff that threatened the integrity of our sleeping space. It's cold enough to see your breath, but nowhere near as cold as some nights we've endured. The ranger said low 30's for tonight. Piece of cake, amigo! In less than a month we plan to be in Gay's house in Craig, under a roof again.

For a half hour just after supper tonight the rain stopped. It was gorgeous. Heavy mist drifted around the mountains and a few patches of hazy blue sky tried to break through. Then the rains came back with a vengeance.

Just before she drifted off Jordin said, "I hope I don't have to crawl into your sleeping bag again tonight." She said the other time she awoke from a dream that she was drowning.

> **It's cold enough to see your breath, but nowhere near as cold as some nights we've endured. The ranger said low 30's for tonight. Piece of cake, amigo!**

April 26   Callville Bay Campground
                              Lake Mead, Nevada

Dear Papou,

When we were at Capitol Reef National Park in Utah we saw some horses in a pasture near our campsite. When we went over to pet them they came right over. I think they expected a carrot. Anyway they let us pet them for a little while and then they walked away and started grazing. The next day we all got some carrots and went over to the barn. After we called a little and waved the carrots they came out. We fed them and petted them and then they went back to eating hay in the barn. The day before we left we went over there and a guy was there. He told us their names: Rio, Toby, and Sti. My favorite was Toby. I miss them, but dad got some pictures of us and the horses. It was fun!!

When we were at Calf Creek we went on a hike to a BIG waterfall. It was also a big hike! It was five and a half miles round trip. The whole hike was near the creek all the time. At one point we stopped and saw some trout. At the end was a big pool with the 80 foot waterfall. Mom said, "If it was hot we could go swimming!" I thought that was a good idea! But it was cold! On the way back Jordin and I got some reeds and pretended that they were paint brushes. It was fun!

Love,
Kaitlin

P.S. Thanks for the card!

Dean's fiftieth birthday. For days I've been mentally jotting down things I wanted to write in my journal. Now I have the time and my memory rings up ZERO.

There is no rain tonight, first time in, let's see, three days. Our haven (heaven) at Capitol Reef ended with heavy winds on Saturday and rain the next morning as we departed. The rain turned to snow as we climbed (in altitude) on Hwy 12 going south out of Torrey, Utah. It's marked as one of the first and finest scenic highways and the views are supposed to be fabulous as you descend from the summit at 9,400 feet. The views? What views? The clouds were puffy, hung low, and obstructed any view over a half of a mile. Darn. I like a good view.

We stopped at the Calf Creek Recreation Area for a beautiful, slightly rainy, hike to the falls by the same name. It was a vigorous 5.5 mile hike for which the girls rose to dignified "hiker" status. The falls were camera quality, and of course we did not have ours.

That hike was the fourth consecutive in so many days, starting with a 2.5 mile, 1,000 foot ascent up the Fremont River Trail, the Cohab Canyon 3 mile hike with another 1,000 foot ascent, the Rim Overlook, a TOUGH, strenuous 4.5 mile hike, 1,200 feet to an overview of Capitol Reef, and then this Calf Creek hike.

Having the girls old enough and strong enough for longer hikes adds another family activity. They are excited about hiking the Grand Canyon in the future.

The recent stint of rain and cold weather has again reminded me (although I didn't need reminding) that I am a fair weather camper. Call me a cheap date, but being inside a tent for 13 hours does things to me mentally, emotionally, spiritually and physically. None of them pretty.

I eat too fast at dinner time because it's either too wet or too cold (or both) and then have gas all night as a result of speed eating (an assault on my digestion system). We don't eat very healthy, nutritious meals because "cooking" is either impossible (at worst) or a pain in the neck (at best). We spend an equally enormous amount of time in the truck killing time. Now that's great fun. Try it some time. Go get in your vehicle, (you don't need the keys unless it's locked), and just sit. Sure, bring a book or a magazine so that you don't look totally stupid to your neighbors, and you could add a sign indicating that this is not a suicide attempt. (If you are the mother or father of an infant, you might find this activity both rewarding and addicting. But we don't and we didn't.) No fair driving to the store or the ice cream shop; we're pretending, remember, and there isn't one around.

During snotty weather you can easily categorize the tourists at the Visitors' Centers. The tent campers are hanging out, drying out, and making the most of the warm, dry Visitors' Center for the ten hours (or less) that it's open. They look disheveled, muddy, damp, and in many stages of disarray. The RVers are slightly disgruntled; they wear an extra layer of clothing, have slight mud spots on the shoes, a few cross words, but are not in too bad of shape.

The motelers are in great spirit. Their meals are being and have been cooked by someone else and served to them, keeping their tummies full and satisfied (compared to the tenters who are looking slightly ravenous for not having had a hot meal in days). They seldom need an extra jacket as they go only from their warm room to their vehicle to the restaurant to the car and into the Visitor Center dry as a cactus in a desert. They smile and have pearly white shoes, no spots. Their clothes (you can see them because they are not layered in warmth and rain gear) are neatly pressed, no wrinkles, and life seems incredibly fine to them.

I think I'd like to move down/up (however you look at the travel experience) a notch to a semi-quasi RVer. A pull along, pop-up camper (sounds like a toy) would prove adequate and on days like today would feel like heaven. But then, I don't think we'll be taking this long of a trip again until an RV becomes mandatory: too old and gimpy to bend over and climb through a tent door, lay on the ground, and be able to get back up. The coldness would send flags up on all arthritic joints and my bladder wouldn't hold enough to make it through dressing, unzipping, zipping, and high stepping to the bathroom. I'd have to sleep fully clothed to cut down on the emergency response time (ERT). Or is it port-a-potty time (PPT)?

Note to add in while at Zion: regarding the storm, wind and falling tree—the few seconds in between the time the tree snapped and the time it hit the ground were very frightening. I prayed quickly, exuberantly and with fervor, asking God to spare us of that falling branch. She did.

It rained hard throughout most of the night and at one point in the deep dark hours Jan and I heard a tree go down, but Azul Grande did its job and we stayed dry till morning light. As it was gray, cold, and still raining, nobody was really in a hurry to get out of the sack. Since I was the first to be driven out by Nature's Call (I get up early in the morning to shake the dew off the lily!) I brought back bagels (Bay-Gulls, not Bag-Gulls, Kait) and bananas so we all had breakfast in bed. I had written out a cursive writing exercise and some math problems in the girls' school notebooks the night before and they were still in the tent tucked under my sleeping bag, so the girls did their home school from their sleeping bags as well. They wrote some newsy letters to my dad about our stay in Capitol Reef National Park.

Eventually we did get up. The rainy weather had driven us to a 13-hour stint inside the tent, and it showed little sign of letting up. We spent a little time in the Visitors' Center, then drove up through part of the park. We had planned to take a short two-mile hike to the Emerald Pools, but by the time we had driven from the Visitors Center to the trailhead, fleeting patches of blue sky had given way to wind and rain again. It promised to be a long day followed by another early bed time. We decided to blow this pop stand.

We took advantage of a letup in the showers to quickly pack up. Then we drove to the southwest toward Las Vegas, telling the girls stories of legal gambling and 24-hour neon. The *USA Today* weather map looked a little more promising in that direction. The rain became more intermittent, but heavy clouds still hugged the horizon.

As we made our way down the northwest shore of Lake Mead, we drove under a huge thunderhead. There was ominous lightning and about ten minutes of fairly heavy rain punctuated by small hailstones. Ah, the Promised Land!

We finally made our way to Callville Bay campground (it boasted showers in the National Park Brochure) and began setting up camp as Mr. Thunderhead ominously and silently drifted up behind us. As a basketball coach I've always felt that early season games gave you a chance to work for the team chemistry and efficiency that will hopefully peak at tournament time. Well, today was tournament time for our team. At Zion, under threat of rain, we broke down camp and had it packed up in ten minutes. Jan took down the tent fly and loosened the ropes on Big Blue while I got in the tent and put sleeping bags and pillows in stuff sacks. I passed them to Jordin at the tent door and she relayed them to Kaitlin in Buckie's back seat. She put them through the capper window and stowed them in the back.

At Callville Bay, Jan and I cooked tacos, we all ate dinner, did the dishes and packed them up, set up the tent, transferred all the air mattresses, blankets, pillows, and bags into the tent and set up Big Blue again, all in just under one hour. We are lean and mean!

Tonight we went for a leisurely stroll at the marina and looked through some magnificent houseboats that rent for $2795 per week in the peak season. Sleeps 12 and has a slide off the roof, shooting into the water! Now I'm writing this by campfire light, almost ready to turn in. The sky has cleared and stars have come out, just in the last 15 minutes.

Dear Papou,

Two days ago we were at Capitol Reef National Park. It was by a river and they had tons of sprinklers so they had dark/light grass. There were tons of deer, fawns, bucks, and does. Once mom and dad saw a fox. They said it was greyish brown. It was chasing a deer.

At Capitol Reef there were also horses. The horses were all chestnuts. One was darker than the others. His name was Rio. That means river in Spanish. Maybe because he was fast or smooth. And the other horses' names were Toby and Sti. Sti was kind of shy. He was light brown with a blaze and one sock (the blaze and sock were white). Toby was (I think) older than the others. They were nice horses.

We also did a hike while we were at Capitol Reef. It was called Cohab Canyon. It was two and a half mile long, the trail. It was very pretty.

Love,
Jordin

April 28

Las Vegas, another city of extremes. It's obvious that the casinos are making money because of all the freebies they offer to lure the gamblers (the free parking and the many freebie shows). As usual, the city sucked our energy bone dry, but for once it left our pocketbook intact. I spent 50 cents on Nevada Nickles and other than that, came out unscathed. Tomorrow will be a different story—our anniversary. We hope to find a good Chinese restaurant (but how do you know it's good until you've eaten there?), a used book store for the girls, and then an evening view of the lights on the strip. We're all looking forward to a night on the town. Jordin said she's going to wear a dress (we'll see) and Jim even pressed his best shirt (no, we don't have an iron, we soaked it in the campground sink, hung it out without wringing it to avoid additional wrinkles, and then let the sun dry it crisp and pressed). Amazing what luxurious camping exists if you have sun, time, water, and a hanger (found by Kaitlin down at the phone booth).

Originally I called it the 5 o'clock wind, I've now renamed it the dinner wind. It's the temporary evening wind that picks up when we start dinner and usually doesn't end until after the campfire. I understand that it's probably caused by changes in air temps, and I like the fact that it eventually settles down, but it sure can raise a ruckus during dinner time. Oh, and the oxygen it adds to the campfires can cause a REAL blaze. I remember the night at the Needles Outpost Campground near Canyonlands. Well, that was not actually a dinner time wind, it was an all day sucker. But what a fire it nourished that night. I thought we were going to burn down the tent, the picnic table, our neighbors, and the entire state of Utah. What a show. It reminded me of a bon-fire Jim started once in our backyard in Reedsburg. I'm still unsure why the fire marshall didn't show up on the scene. All the neighbors did.

We have 25 days until we catch the ferry in Prince Rupert, and we're at a loss of where to spend those days. Not a loss, so much, but lack of desire to "see" anything else. Tourist burn-out, I guess. Is that what Las Vegas did to us? Or was it this weather front that continues to haunt us and keeps us on guard and Big Blue hovering over our tent?

We've discussed going back to Bryce and possibly Zion, seeing as our stays there were brief because of inclement weather, but I'm not sure I want to reclimb 9,000 feet, the same 9,000 feet we just descended. I'm not sure truckie is up to it either.

We'd like to spend time on the Olympic Peninsula, but are gun-shy due to (what else) the weather. Storms have been socking that area right and left, and I don't want to be stuck in the middle of one for days at a time.

So, where to go? We'll see if Gay is going to meet us in Seattle. If not, we may make another trip to L.A. to see Mary, Larry, and the kids. It's slightly out of the way, but friends are always a comfort, as is a bed to sleep in, a toilet to flush, and an inside shower.

In this journal I've written about touching the eternal. Well, whatever the karmic opposite of that is, perhaps instant gratification that turns to vapor just as it touches the very tips of your nerve endings, has to be centered in Las Vegas, Nevada. We spent two hours there yesterday afternoon and my psychic gas tank was sucked dry by the endless stimulation. We parked by the Mirage (Seigfried and Roy's white tigers!) and took the tram to Treasure Island (featuring a live 20-minute sea battle between a 60-foot pirate ship and Her Majesty's frigate, which sank after taking several cannon balls amidships and erupting in flames whose heat we could feel from 40 feet away! Wow!!) Then we spent half an hour cruising the Treasure Island casino. The girls were totally amazed. We spent a few minutes explaining the "logic" of gambling. They saw several slot machines noisily spewing their payoffs, but still just kind of shook their heads. Why would anybody choose to do that? Not only choose to do it, but sit on a stool and mechanically insert a coin and pull the arm over and over until the memory of the sun fades away. Ah, the intricacies of the adult mind.

Well, today the rain clouds broke up and we were outside after another 13-hour evening of taking shelter in the tent. We saw Hoover Dam and then went to tour the Ethel M. Chocolate Factory on the outskirts of Las Vegas. I'll tell you what, the City of Lady Luck outdid itself today. In the lobby of Ethel M. we met Bettina Best, a real live Marilyn Monroe impersonator. She autographed 8 X 10 glossies of herself for the girls, chatted for a minute, and shook our hands. She had it down, folks. The vulnerable, venerable sex kitten of our dreams lives on. And guess what? She told us that she had recently married an Elvis impersonator on Good Morning America. A match made in heaven, eh?

April 30   **Zion National Park**
                                                               Utah

Yesterday was our 16th wedding anniversary. Kait and Jord had been plotting and whispering for several days and they started our day off right. Our campground at Callville Bay on Lake Mead was surrounded by bushes thick with huge red, white, and pink flowers. The girls took some of these blossoms and made us corsages. They had made bolo ties for themselves and the guests, their stuffed animals Lion, Snuggles, Buffie, and of course, Sidewalk. We each opened hand made cards with poems. Kaitlin had also made a cart pulled by a horse and Jordin had made a heart-shaped face with yarn hair, both very well done. Love freely given is the sweetest gift of all. Thank you, girls!

We spent a couple of leisurely hours at the camp after breakfast and then headed into Las Vegas. We found two used book stores side by side and replenished our reading stock, then headed for Las Vegas Boulevard, the "Strip." We went to Circus Circus and fed the girls at an indoor burger stand within the building while we watched a high wire act. Jan and I donated some nickels and quarters ($3 total) to the one-armed bandits just to test our luck. Our luck is in the things that count, like family and health. We have very little in gambling. (My favorite line from a song is Greg Brown singing, "I'm a man who's rich in daughters...")

Then we went to China First, a low-key Oriental restaurant. The waiter was friendly and the food was great, with enough left over for dinner tonight.

After dinner we went back to Las Vegas Boulevard to tour the sights. Our first stop was MGM, the largest hotel in the world. It had a reproduction of the Emerald City of Oz inside and a huge statue of a lion guarding the main entrance. Next up was Luxor. The creators had really outdone themselves here, both inside and out. There was a tremendous laser and water fountain

Happy Anniversary decorations made by Kaitlin and Jordin.

show outside the entrance, in front of a reproduction of the Sphinx that must have been 100 feet high. At one point green laser beams shot out of the eyes of the Sphinx. The hotel itself was in the shape of a gigantic pyramid topped by a 315,000 watt light, supposedly visible from outer space. The last place we visited, Excalibur, was a bit anticlimactic. It seems that each wave of newly created hotel-casinos outclasses the previous establishments. The Sahara and Flamingo, a couple of the originals, were shabby country cousins by comparison.

We got back to our 8' by 8' tent around 11:00, tired but happy.

May 2   **Bryce Canyon National Park**
                                                        Utah
Dear Travis,

A few days ago we visited Las Vegas, Nevada. The first time we went we visited Treasure Island. It is a big hotel with fake pirate ships and palm trees and fake skeletons. At 1:30 the people that own the hotel put on a show. Two real pirate ships fought with cannons and one ship sank! It was really neat! The next day we went at about 2:00 and stayed to 11:30 at night! We saw lots of lights and went to more hotels and a circus.

My favorite hotel was Luxor. The hotel is shaped like a pyramid, and all the rooms are on the outside of the pyramid so everybody in the hotel rooms gets a good view. The inside has river rides on a fake Nile River, restaurants, shows, and a casino. At the entrance is a ten-story statue of the Great Sphinx of Giza. The sphinx has the body of a lion and head of a person. It was neat!

When we were in Utah we went to Coral Pink Sand Dunes State Park. I didn't think it was pink. More like orangish yellow. Dad and Jordin and I walked and climbed in our bare feet to the top of the biggest sand dune. Then we ran down the side (it was steep!) and halfway down we would twist our bodies and slide on our sides like in baseball. We would also roll down it laying on our sides. We got very sandy!

After we leave Bryce Canyon National Park in Utah we will start heading north. After Bryce Canyon we will get to Manti-LaSal National Forest. We think it has hot springs. After that we will head into Idaho, a corner of Oregon, and through Washington to Seattle. Going through those three states I think will take about three days. Then we will stay in Seattle for about a week. Then up to Alaska! We will drive through British Columbia and stay in hotels. Miss you!

                                              Love,
                                              Kaitlin

Bryce National Park
Hardy hikers, healthy campers, pleasant companions.

Zion remains a disappointment—we saw it with clouds and rain and it was gorgeous; we saw it clear and not so gorgeous. The clouds hid some peaks, softened others, and made for an overall good effect. The tent caterpillars made the biggest impression and stayed with us the longest. For days after leaving Zion we continue to flick off these transient/uprooted caterpillars still clinging to our tent. (And this is after a great family crusade of "find all caterpillars and leave them here.")

We did one hike at Zion to the Emerald Pools. A memorable hike as we still are trying to figure out how the name "emerald" was tagged to these pools. Another hiker we spoke with also questioned the naming process.

After hiking, we left for Coral Pink Sand Dunes State Park, north of Kanab, Utah. Upon seeing the orangish, rust colors of the dunes, Kaitlin said, "I think the park rangers in this state are color blind." Yes, emerald was not greenish blue, and coral pink left much to the imagination.

While hiking in Zion, I found myself simultaneously at greeting distance to an approaching hiker, and at the same time felt a sneeze working its way out. Lest I sneeze on the hikers while saying "hi," I thought I'd sneeze first, then greet. At that moment my foot became stubbornly wedged (lodged) between two boulders and I could not free myself. So there I stood, trapped, not being able to talk, walk or sneeze. After the hikers passed, I dislodged my foot, no longer had to sneeze, and was able to throw a "hello" back over my shoulder to the passing hikers who were giggling with me about my predicament.

But now we are back, once again, in Bryce. The weather is cool and the low temps remain in the 20s. We did a beautiful hike this afternoon in 60 degree, sunny, weather, so we will gut out the cool evening here and then head north tomorrow to lower altitudes. I'm beginning to wonder if the rest of the trip, as we head north, will continue to be on the cool side. I sure have enjoyed the warmer weather.

I am definitely a morning person. I woke up this morning around 6:00. The air was cool and sweet, and there were areas of dappled shadow and sunlight on the side of the tent. At this point the day is in its "becoming" stage, a clean slate waiting for the course of that day's events.

We drove back into Bryce Canyon. The weather was much better this time around, and we did a beautiful hike of more than three miles through the Queen's Garden, a series of orange-yellow-gold-cream colored turrets rising from the canyon floor. The sky was a deep blue, the temperature was perfect for a hike. We had a great time.

The girls were champs!

Dear Travis,

Three days ago we were at Las Vegas! We went to MGM Grand Hotel and Casino. A casino is a place where you go to gamble. MGM has the shape of a lion. It was huge!

We also went to Circus Circus. The only thing we saw was tightrope walkers. But their show was for free and it was good.

A few hours ago we were at Coral Pink Sand Dunes. They looked yellow orange to me. Oh well. Anyways we got to go on the most bushy one and the most high one. They were two different ones. Kaitlin and I rolled down the sand dunes. It was really fun.

Before we were at Las Vegas we were at a campground. It was called Lake Mead. And they had a gift shop. It had toys and other grownup stuff too. There were toy lizards for 45 cents. One was orange, two were green, and one was purple. At first I got the orange one. (He had a frilled neck). Then I got the rest. I named the orange one Phil, rhymes with frill. I named one Green Poy Boy, Poisons. The other one is Elvis, got him by Las Vegas. And the purple one is Marilyn.

Love,
Jordin

May 3   **Palisade State Park**
                                              Manti, Utah

Kaitlin has really been helping out lately. Three days ago, out of the blue, she offered to help dry the breakfast dishes, and the last three days she has taken charge of setting up air mattresses and sleeping bags in the tent. What a joy! She's taking pride in doing a good job and it relieves some of the load off Jan and I. She's growing right now in so many ways. It's a rare treat for us to be spending so much family time with her as she goes through these changes.

I woke up to the early-morning birdsong chorus before sunrise
day. It was peaceful with the sounds of my family's soft breathing in the
r around me. As Kait and Jord wake up, they blink a couple of times and
en reach for the book tucked under their pillow. I will miss that slow start
) our days when the tenting is done. We should have a family sleepover
nce in a while after we're settled in a house. It's a special time.

We have been lucky in the weather department lately. We had a
ve-day soaking in Moab, and then another 6-day stretch of rain and snow
rough Calf Creek, Bryce, and Zion. The Salt Lake City newspaper
redicted showers Saturday and Sunday and the Bryce rangers predicted
in Monday, but we've enjoyed lots of blue through partly cloudy skies
nd no precipitation. Thanks for the break, Lord. We needed it.

Tonight we're camped on the shores of a pretty, man-made lake in
alisades State Park just outside of Sterling, Utah. The sun is 45 minutes
om setting and the redwing blackbirds are trilling in the reeds and
ottonwoods that line the shore ten feet from our tent.

Iay 4

)ear Kaitlin and Jordin,

I watched you today while you used your plastic buckets to catch
mall fish in Palisades Lake. You were joyous and proud of your
ccomplishments and yet aware of the needs of the fish too. You were
areful to maintain the temperature of the water in their "aquarium bucket"
nd put in plants and rocks to create a diversified habitat for the captives.

As I watched you playing in the sun, how can I tell you about the
mes when being a good person may not be enough, when the adult world
oesn't make sense, isn't fair? Those times are in your future as sure as fish
re in Palisades Lake. In the end, your character will pull you through
mes of pain and confusion.

Take pride in your accomplishments. They are real. Be aware of
he needs of others as well as your own. They are real too.

Love,
Your dad

May 5   Bear Lake Campground
St. Charles, Idaho

As the trip begins to wind down I find myself weighing the pros and
ons. As far as the big question, yes I would do it again. There have been

As I watched you playing in the sun, how can I tell you about the times when being a good person may not be enough, when the adult world doesn't make sense, isn't fair? Those times are in your future as sure as fish are in Palisades Lake. In the end your character will pull you through times of pain and confusion. Take pride in your accomplishments. They are real. Be aware of the needs of others as well as your own. They are real too.

rough spots when the weather or our moods made life uncomfortable, but we have pulled off a great family accomplishment here. Going beyond the comfort zone can provide you with opportunities for growth. We've explored new environments both physically and socially, and have spent a year of close family time. We've done what social experts espouse, namely, imparting our values to our children firsthand through family discussions as we travelled down the road or sat around the campfire, but also in a more concrete sense as our children saw us in high times as well as low, and as we saw our children interacting with themselves and others. Do as I do or do as I say? We've seen it all.

Our children have learned from us much as pioneer children did, not only with the home schooling in academic skills, but also how to read a map, scrounge kindling, build a fire to warm your bones, how to set up a tent, balance (sometimes very precariously!) a delicate budget, resolve interpersonal disagreements, and weigh options and consequences in order to make and evaluate decisions.

I'm proud of what we've done.

May 6   Pocatello, Idaho

We all had a scare early today. We hadn't found a camping spot until 8:00 last night. We set up the tent, enjoyed a nice family campfire and turned in.

We got up at 8:00 this morning and went into the owners' double wide trailer to use the bathroom since John hadn't yet finished the campground john. As we were talking with them, Jan began to feel light headed. We had started walking back to the tent so that she could lie down—we didn't make it. She went down on all fours, feeling that she was going to pass out. After a minute she got up, but only went another five o

> **Yes, I would do it again.**
> **I'm proud of what we've done.**

six steps before going down again. This time she did pass out and went into convulsions. Her head began rocking and her breathing became ragged. I was scared. The girls were very upset, but I sent them back to the trailer for help. JoAnn came out, but then went back in to call 911 for the EMT's. John brought out a blanket and JoAnn brought a pillow. The girls put their hands on Jan to give her some Reiki energy, and I kept talking to her, feeling that I needed to keep contact. After about 20 seconds she came around, although still weak. Don, a local EMT, was there within two minutes and gave Jan oxygen, which improved her color and seemed to help her feel better. Within 15 minutes the ambulance had arrived to take her to the hospital in Montpelier, Idaho. JoAnn offered to watch Kaitlin and Jordin, but I knew they'd want to be there with their mom, so we quickly got in the truck and followed the ambulance.

I wasn't looking at the speedometer, but the girls said we were doing 85 mph as we zoooomed through three or four small towns on our way to Montpelier. I reassured the girls that their mom was going to be OK, and after about five minutes they began to enjoy the rocket ride. Not having eaten breakfast, we wolfed down some dry granola and whole wheat bagels on the way.

The Emergency Room folks took her vitals and talked to us about what had happened. They drew some blood and ran it through the lab. In the end, all signs appeared normal. The doctor gave her a prescription for some antibiotics as a safeguard against the longshot possibility of toxic shock syndrome, but seemed to feel that maybe it had been a small seizure after all, since there didn't seem to be any other readily available theory.

Everyone was very concerned and helpful from beginning to end. Jan and I talked about the advantages of small town life. There are some glittery things in life that you miss, but the real substance of life seems to survive better in the more rural environment.

I think Jan is feeling her mortality. It can be unsettling.

May 7   **Three Island Crossing State Park**
                             Glenn's Ferry, Idaho

On Friday morning I had what has been diagnosed as a seizure. It was preceded by a few minutes of dizziness which, hard as I tried, I could not alleviate. (Going outside for fresh air, head down, body down.) Once I passed out, Jim said I jerked some and that my breathing was noisy and labored.

I spent the rest of the day feeling very weak and lightheaded, trying to recuperate. It was all frustrating, and in the darkness of the tent the thought of dying loomed heavy over me. I've dreamt of Jordin having falling accidents and John Owens dying on July 11. Are these dreams really of my death? I've also dreamt of owls and numerous other dreams I don't remember. Why am I spending so much time in the dream world? Do I have a long term or short term future? Is my death imminent?

What caused my dizziness? My fainting? My presumed seizure? Lack of answers are unnerving, unsettling. I'm not sick, and have no symptoms that would trigger an episode such as I had. Unless, of course, it was a seizure, solely. The chances of another one within two years are one in three; leaving a two in three chance that I won't.

Am I grateful that with my presumed seizure I had a warning? Most people don't. Will I again? Did I? If not, what? Am I physically okay? Was this just a fluke? If so, why? More and more questions. Not enough answers to calm my taunting fears.

Am I grateful that it's not something serious or life-threatening? Is it?

May 8

Tonight is our second night camping at Three Island Crossing State Park on the Snake River near Glenn's Ferry, Idaho. Jan seems to be doing okay, but her energy level is low. She is worried about the possibility of a recurring seizure. We've talked about it, and she also called Gay, her best buddy back in Craig. Two weeks from tomorrow night we'll be at her house. Gay's company will be good medicine for Jan.

Yesterday afternoon we visited the camp of a black powder enthusiasts' rendezvous here at the park, the site where the Oregon Trail crossed the Snake River. Many of them wore buckskins and full beards.

d camped in tipis along the river. We saw a hatchet and knife throwing
mpetition where they tried to stick the blade in an upended cross section
log from 12 feet away.

We talked for a while with one man who had been doing this since
75. He said that at times they've been joined by Native American
oups. He felt the part of the weekend rendezvous that seemed the most
thentic was the story-telling around the campfires at night.

Tonight after supper we walked down to the river. Most of the tipis
d been taken down and the frontiersmen and women had gone back to
eir "real" lives. We looked at the river where the wagoneers made the
cision to ford the river and take the shorter, more fertile northern route to
oise and on to Oregon or stick to the southern route, which was longer and
d less forage for the oxen. The land looks much the same as it must have
oked then: rolling hills and grasslands, with the river stretching 140 yards
ide. There was a modern reproduction of the pioneer covered wagon
arby, 11 feet long and 2 feet wide. It was easy to visualize the scene.

The girls have played the computer simulation game of the Oregon
rail passage. They said there was a part that actually showed the crossing
this point. You could go by ferry for $5 (Glenn's ferry no doubt), hire a
tive guide to help you ford the river in trade for sets of clothing, or calk
e wagon and try to float it across. Sometimes you made it and sometimes
u didn't.

*Fear overwhelmed me as I left the safety net of my family and went,
sitantly, on a walk. What if I have another seizure somewhere out in a
mote area? Who will find me? Will I be okay?*

*The walk was a short, slow stroll, a far cry from my most recent
eks of 5-6 miles at a very quick pace. When I returned, Jim said I looked
hite. I felt white. I had legs of rubber and was worn out after just one
ile. Tired. Depressed. So I sat. Rested. Is that what happens with age?
ut that was a hurdle, the first one, and each one since has been easier. We
ent for a family walk tonight, and I had more stamina than earlier in the
ay.*

My strength (emotionally and physically) is returning.

> Jan and I talked about the advantages of small town life.
> There are some glittery things in life that you miss, but
> the real substance of life seems to survive better in the
> more rural environment.

May 10   **Elks' Flat Campgroun**
                                              Featherville, Idah

Part of a family lesson on complimenting each other:

Jan,

1. Today you complimented Kaitlin for bringing your Berkies back to th
truck.
2. You wrote a really nice love letter to her. It will bolster her self image
3. You've done a nice job on your health concepts with them for hom
schooling.
4. I appreciate how you enjoy wild places like the spot where we'r
camping now.
5. You take care of yourself physically and that's a good role model for th
rest of our family.
6. Your views of the future are flexible and creative. That's fun for me t
share.
7. I respect you for your resourcefulness, gutsiness, creativity, an
strength.

I've begun to repeat myself on adjectives, but we are in anoth
gorgeous spot. While checking with National Forest rangers we hear
about undeveloped hot springs near Deer Creek, 45 minutes northeast c
Mountain Home, Idaho. We searched them out and ended up in Elk Fl
National Forest Campground on the banks of the boisterous Boise Rive
The hot springs seep and flow out of the bank on the far side of the bridg
and they are HOT!
After a breakfast of whole wheat scratch pancakes with real mapl
syrup, and some home schooling, we headed over to test out the water.
People had obviously enjoyed the area before because there were some lo
rock barriers thrown together to enclose small areas where the hot spring
intersected the cold river water. Engineers Jordin and Kaitlin had bee
drawing up plans to work on the walls and set right to work excavatin
improved hot water channels and shoring up the existing stone walls.
It was a sunny day with a few high-floating majestic white clouds t
accent the green pine forests and sparkling river water. We spent an hou
working on the main pool, but in the end the erratic flow of hot and col
ruled out any heavy-duty horizontal lounging. However, we moved to

Elks Flat Campground
Relaxing in our bedroom—an 8' x 8' tent!

Elks Flat Campground
Where hot springs meet the Boise River, we find a naturally temperate soaking tub.

small creek bed 25 yards downstream and found paradise. The creek, which effectively mixed hot and cold water 12 yards from the its mouth, was lukewarm but pretty constant in temperature. We quickly built a 12-inch stone barrier and reclined in the pool. After setting the camera on its 10-second automatic timer, we took a family portrait with the river and piney woods as a backdrop. Next year's Christmas photo?

Afterwards we dried off and played some family baseball in the meadow above our campsite. The girls' batting is getting smooth and powerful. It's fun watching them grow and develop. We can play a pretty mean game of catch now.

Tomorrow is Jordin's ninth birthday. She's really excited and very confident that we will indeed decorate the tent after she's asleep and will also have surprises for her tomorrow. Of course she's right. It's a family tradition that goes back to their early years. She even asked if I could sleep next to her so she'd have somebody to talk to when she wakes up early. (She and I tend to catch the early worm in this family). In the afternoon we'll head to Mountain Home and pick up the chocolate birthday cake with horses on top that we ordered two days ago. Then we'll eat some Little Caesar's pizza pizza, Jordin's birthday meal request.

Jan took her last antibiotic tablet tonight. She's been feeling a little stronger each day, but has experienced dizziness at times, which may be due to the medication. We'll see. She's still concerned and wondering about future developments. Me too.

Another spot of heaven here at Elks Flat. (Coincidentally, another forest service campground, like Devil's Canyon, that is not officially open yet so the services are minimal and the privacy is maximized.) The South Boise River borders most of our campsite, there are pine trees and birds at every turn, mountains loom in the south and west, and just over the bridge are mineral hot springs. Undisturbed, uncommercialized, unpopulated mineral hot springs. We've seen only a few people there during our two day stay, but mostly the springs are vacant. Maybe it's their heat—they are too hot to stand or wade in, so they need the cold mixture of the river water to temper them. But temperature control is difficult with only rocks for enclosing the pools, and the result is too much cold river or too much hot spring. But the "process" of trying to control both factions was an afternoon, delightful project that the girls and I enjoyed and jumped in with both feet, literally.

So in an attempt to alleviate the temperature problems, the girls and I spent an enormous amount of time rebuilding rock pools on the bank of the river where it was joined by the hot springs. Hours of time brought minimal results, so we moved down to the creek that had a constant, comfortable temperature, and there we sat (laid) for well over an hour while the kids further upgraded the rock dam at the mouth of the creek. The water was perfect, and I let it flow over me as I laid there with only my face exposed to the air.

I'm glad we've had the time here at the shore of the South Boise. This will be remembered as one of the highlights, not because of conveniences (no running water and a smelly out house), but because of luxuries: privacy, the river, mountains, hot springs, solitude, sunny weather for warm days, high altitude for cool nights, fresh pine mountain air, back roads for walking, lush green colors and no neighbors. I'm surprised, though, at how little wildlife we've seen.

I'm feeling stronger, but not yet 100 percent. I hope it's the medication (antibiotic) that is making me lightheaded; if that's the case, things should drastically improve tomorrow because today I finished taking 750 mg. twice daily.

We are all waiting patiently for Jordin to fall asleep so that we can decorate the tent. This will be our last birthday on the road. Tomorrow we'll pick up her cake in Mountain Home, Idaho, and on to pizza!!

The girls have changed so much this year, and Jim and I were with them to witness it. What a rare event. Most parents normally see their kids just a few hours each day—at the end of the day when everyone is tired, chores need doing, stomachs need feeding, phone calls are intruding, etc. etc.

I'll miss being so close to the girls all the time, especially our tent time, falling asleep, and waking up together. I wonder if the girls will miss the closeness too. I bet they'll have many mixed emotions—being glad to have their own room but feeling far away from us either down the hall or on the next floor. Distance is relative and it won't take much after having all of us in an 8 x 8 foot tent for months at a time.

How many more nights of camping? Few, very few.

This day will not end until we decorate the tent for yet another birthday girl. Kaitlin and I will be able to stay up, but I bet we'll need to wake Jim up to help join in the fun.

May 11   Givins Hot Springs, Idaho

Jord enjoyed her day. "Hey, hey, read this sign. Jordin Marousis just turned nine!"

We ate delicious and reasonably priced pizza in the park in the

> The girls have changed so much this year, and Jim and I were with them to witness it. What a rare event.

shadow of a large air force jet mounted on a pedestal. A nice family celebration.

May 12   Emigrant Springs State Park
                                                        Pendleton, Oregon

Last night we stayed at Givins Hot Springs and Campground, in the "town" of the same name. (It was quite small, and we could have missed it if we blinked.) The pool was large and warm, true delight for a cold blooded person such as myself.

We decided, upon arriving at 7:30 p.m. to celebrate, sing, and eat Jordin's birthday cake, set up the tent, and then hit the pool to relax, followed by a shower (first one in three days), and then to bed, all in that order.

While eating cake, Jordin's thirst took hold of her, so she got her mug from the truck—it was empty—and went to the faucet at our campsite to replenish the water. "It's hot," she said. Well, I figured everything was, (as we were) seeing it had been over 90 degrees all day. "Let it run, it will cool off." She did, it didn't. Free hot water? Sounds deliciously luxurious, but not very thirst quenching. I told her we'd get some inside the pool building.

We got ready for a dip, paid the $9 (Total!) fee to use the pool and asked where we could get some cold water to drink and use at the campsite. Three young females behind the counter all looked blankly at each other, pondering the obvious rarity of cold ground water, and finally shrugged their shoulders and one said, "We can give you a glass of ice water here."

I, in all my travels, had not chanced upon such a predicament. (Were they sprinkling the grass with hot water also? I found out later, the answer was yes.)

So we took the glass of ice water, found a spot for our towels, clothes, sandals, etc. and went to use the restroom before jumping into the pool.

As I said earlier, it had been a hot, hot day, compounded by driving through the hottest part of the day, a radiant sun cooking the cab of the truck, (no A/C because of previous problems), so the heat of the locker room was not comfortable nor pleasant. But, hotter I became as I sat down to use the toilet.

Have you ever noticed that the space between your gluteus and the water of a toilet is just that, space? Not notable, not in the least. Basically, the same temp as the air outside the toilet.

As I sat there, cooked from the day, over-cooked temporarily from the heat of the locker room with a wall of windows that don't open facing west, I began to get even warmer. "Warmer?" I asked myself. And as I questioned this sensation, my gluteus maximums continued its barrage of messages to my brain, shouting, "Hey, check out this hot air down here, hey, it's warm in here, hey, can you feel this? Hey, where are we?"

Yes, as you might have guessed, the toilet ALSO used hot water. I would have given an eye tooth for a warm toilet on most ANY night of this trip. But it just so happened on our HOTTEST day in nine months.

What a rare feeling as you pee to have steam emanating from the waters of a toilet.

I had another death dream last night—a friend died of breast cancer. I haven't thought of her since leaving Reedsburg, I wonder why she and death occupied the same dream. Getting to her funeral posed many obstacles including climbing dirt hills, crossing traffic at the intersection where John and Helen Owens live. How is this related to the dream I had of John Owens dying? There was an incredible number of cars lined up, many couldn't even get into the church parking lot. I expect that would be more like John's funeral.

So whose funeral was this? Mine? (Note: A few weeks after this dream a classmate of mine died of cancer. Her funeral did indeed go by Owens' house.)

I ask myself again and again, why am I having all these death dreams?

The girls are anxious to be on the move, knowing that the ferry trip is only 11 days away. They're excited about seeing friends again and being in a house.

Today marks the first "good" day since the seizure—I went for two walks and felt minimal lightheadedness (isn't that a doozy of a word?). It feels wonderful to have strength, clarity, and balance, all things I took for granted and probably will again.

Jan finished up her medication yesterday and feels stronger today. She mentioned that at times she still feels like she's "in a fog," but she did go for two walks and appears more sure of herself again.

As we passed through Baker City, Oregon this afternoon we visited the Book Man, a used book store. Keeping the girls supplied with reading material has turned out to be a very enjoyable part of Plan Z. We spent 40 minutes talking with Mark Alderman, the owner of the store, about the business end of the operation: buying, selling, markup, staffing, marketing, ambience of the store itself, public relations, hours, what kinds of books to stock and what not to stock, and of course the bottom line, net profit. It was very interesting.

The girls just love to read. They've had their noses buried in their "new" books since we left the store!

Tonight we are camping at Emigrant Springs State Park in Oregon. We are definitely back in big pine country and I like it. It's getting toward dusk as I write this and the sunlight is filtering down through the treetops. Each succeeding row gets a little more grey with tinges of gold in the distance. It makes me feel like I'm in a cathedral. (I am.)

I went for a nice walk after dinner. Since we're basically right on the interstate here, I started out just walking around the campground loop, but quickly headed off on an unmarked trail that I spotted leading out the back of one of the campsites. It led to a two-track dirt road that followed a fence line along the back edge of the park. The sound of the freeway, although still audible, faded and I could now hear birdsong and the sigh of wind in the pinetops, one of my very favorite auditory stimuli.

May 14   Dosewallips State Park
Brinnin, Washington

A few weeks ago, I told Jim about a dream in which Betsy (one of our partners in Sub Marina) didn't teach next year, a rare thought as far as we were concerned.

Last night, after talking to Betsy, Jim told me that she wasn't going to be teaching next year. A rare coincidence? I hope, for the dreams I've had lately would create monumental sadness among friends and family if they (the dreams) played out in real life.

While at the horse show (auction) in Hermiston, Oregon, yesterday, I had yet another dizzy spell. It was minimal and I was able to subdue its impact by sitting down and putting my head between my knees. Shortly thereafter I ate, which also helped. But the rest of the day found me in that foggy/grey area with a slight headache.

Jim and I talked about possible diagnosis—(1) loss of weight (he thinks me too thin); (2) hypoglycemia (I've always needed to eat often to

> It makes me feel like I'm in a cathedral.

prevent getting lightheaded and nauseous). I usually crave sugars and sometimes proteins, and know that the nights prior to those episodes I did not have sugar (per se), nor the morning before the dizzy spell and seizure.

Today I've been conscientious about eating both natural (fruit and fruit juice) and processed sugars. I've had a good day and feel strong.

Is any of this connected? Does any of it matter?

My reaction to Washington (and the NW in general) has been less than positive, as it is cloudy, damp, cool and interspersed with showers. My first view of the ocean after an eight month absence did not stir a longing I had anticipated. I really expected it to be "in my blood and soul," and that I would warmly and fondly gaze upon it as an old friend. I haven't, and I'm surprised. Has the weather affected my response, have I not seen the big expanse of ocean but only just this small canal, or was it not as important as I thought?

Camping, once again, in this weather is not appealing, and has dampened my spirits and I'm crabby.

Kaitlin is deeply saddened by my response, for as far as she knows, she wants to live in this area. I've asked why, but so far have not been clued in. I know she connects this area to horses, but I try to assure her that horses live most anywhere.

Jim reminded us that when we first arrived in the Midwest, namely while driving across the horrendously flat state of Iowa, she said "Isn't it great to be back in the Midwest? It feels like home." (Or something very similar to this.) Where does her allegiance lie, and why?

Breathe easy, railroad buffs. When the Santa Fe, Milwaukee Road, and Northern Pacific have all gone the way of the dinosaur, there will be one railroad, here in the Columbia River valley, that will still be blasting that whistle and humming down those endless parallel tracks. This particular railroad is apparently so flush with business that it sends a double-engined set of cars blowing past Viento State Park every 45 minutes or so, including those crucial middle-of-the-night freight deliveries. In a way this is a sign of closure on our trip, gathering two ends of a loop separated by dry desert days, howling Midwestern winter winds, thundershowers, cliff dwellings, Las Vegas neon, Mark Twain, and countless starry nights. I remember trains roaring into my nocturnal consciousness in a Washington state park back in September. Maybe I have grown in the intervening days and weeks. I see it not as evidence of injustice or insanity now, but merely another sample of the systematic chaos that underlies our lives. Of course someone would put a state park campground twenty yards from a railroad and of course someone else would schedule nightime trips past those tents and RVs. Why not? I just look at the dazed campers the morning after and chuckle. They just haven't seen the pattern yet.

May 15   **Fort Worden State Park**
                                        Port Townsend, Washington

We're definitely back in the Northwest now. Towering pines, green everywhere, the smell of the sea and of course, overcast skies with a forecast of "chances of showers today and tomorrow." We camped last night in Dosewallips State Park. You know, just past the Duckabush River... Anyway, we woke up dry this morning. Only four or five more nights of tent camping and then we'll store our camping gear in our Seattle storage shed, lightening our load for the last leg up to Prince Rupert, British Columbia and then Craig. (Our camping will cease in Seattle, and we'll stay in motels through British Columbia.) Today we'll drive 30 miles up to Port Townsend on the very northeast corner of the Olympic Peninsula. We'll camp there and use the next two days to scout out the area. I've applied to six different schools in the vicinity and we'll try them on in our imagination to see if they could be home for the next decade or so. There's an Art Fair of sorts today in Port Townsend. We'll spend some time there, looking around, talking to folks about schools, art and dance classes, basketball, job opportunities and the general lay of the land.

By golly, as I write this I begin to see the shadow of my hand moving across the page. I believe it's clearing up.

Evening of the same day—not much need to get the lay of the land. Stopping at a realtor was the first and last stop. Real estate prices in this area are waaaay ahead of the salary I would draw as a teacher! 'Nuff said.

I was pretty discouraged for a few hours, but maybe this just makes our choice easier. I think we were leaning toward the Midwest anyway (proximity of family, four seasons, more reasonable housing prices, better job opportunities for Jan, and better community-organized activities for K and J). We got out our winter coats around supper time. The Northwest is cloudy and cooler.

May 16

After ten days or so of weather forecasts predicting rain and ten or so mornings waking up dry, our sentinels slept right through all the obvious signs and we paid for it. We didn't post Big Blue last night and starting in the middle of the night it rained fairly hard for about seven hours. We stuffed wet sleeping bags and pillows in the truck, went to eat breakfast and now we're heading to the laundromat to wash and dry out. The sky is typical Northwest overcast.

We woke up with a pool of water in the tent. We failed to put up big blue last night; why, I don't know—had we forgotten that we were camping in a rain forest? The rain started sometime during the night and was relentless.

Tonight we have big blue in position and an obnoxious party two sites down. Am I grateful that it's not one site down? No. They're making so much noise that they could be on top of us. It costs $5.00 for extra cars, so all the extra riffraff left their vehicles outside the park, and walked in, each person carrying a 12-pack of beer. I fear it will be a noisy night here at campsite number 48.

We're all a little edgy, no, we're all very edgy. The girls act out with too much energy, and it's wearing on their parents' nerves. I really think this climate has a lot to do with it. We've had a lot less exercise, we're cold, they're excited about getting to Craig, Jim and I are worried about interviews, jobs and our future. It all makes for some tense times.

We ate dinner in a bitterly cold north wind, shivering, and complaining in between bites about how miserable we all were. It brings back memories of the first month of the trip, when every day was like this.

To break the monotony, Jordin and I had our hair cut today. Mine's shorter than it's ever been, probably since birth. Jordin now has bangs and the rest is slightly longer than chin length. She also has a "box" braid underneath and behind her left ear. We'll see how long it lasts; it's the length her hair was prior to cutting.

We're both pleasantly satisfied (I had many doubts about getting 12 or more inches cut off), and I'm having a great time looking at myself in the mirror, making sure my opinion doesn't change. So far, so good.

I felt a rush of blood to my scalp as the beautician sliced off my ponytail with just four quick clips. The weight was gone and my head felt free of a heavy burden. It still feels very light and the blood continues rushing all around my scalp.

Dear Michael and Keely,

Yesterday we went to a town in Washington called Port Townsend. There were three hair cutting places and mom went into one (I wanted my hair cut) and saw some ladies that had their hair all wackey. So mom came out and said, "No way." (She wanted to get her hair cut too). Then she went into another one and came out and said, "2:30." I wanted my hair cut higher than shoulder length and with bangs. When 2:30 came around mom and I went into the hair place. We started flipping through the books that they had. When it was my turn mom asked the lady if she could leave a long piece of hair for a small braid. First the lady box-braided it so when it was done I had a little braid. It's weird.

A few days ago we went to a horse sale. It had saddles, halters, bits, bridles, and boots. EVERYthing and EVERY kind of horse for sale! Kaitlin and I bought toy horses.

My favorite thing of the trip was the horse sale. It was nice.

Love,
Jordin

Dear Michael and Keely,

Right now we are camping at Fort Worden State Park in Washington. The campground is right by the

My favorite thing on the trip was the horse show.

Kaitlin

My favorite thing of the trip was the horse sale. It was nice.

Jordin

beach. The campsite we stayed at had a hiking trail right next to it, and after dinner we decided to go for a hike. It was all uphill, but at the top we saw lots of old army buildings, about 50 years old! It had old ladders and big metal doors and basements. My favorite were the basements because there were lots of hallways and it was like a maze! All of the hall was dark because there were no windows. I also liked the gun holes and the places where cannons sat. It was awesome!!

While we are here we went to the beach and looked for shells and played. Jordin and I found lots of snail shells and rocks and clam shells. About halfway down the beach we saw a bunch of logs that were tied together. The logs were HUGE! Jordin and I climbed on them. It was fun!!

My favorite thing on the trip was the horse show. Jordin wrote about it in her letter.

Love,
Kaitlin

May 17 **Salt Water State Park**
Seattle, Washington

Jim informed Bob tonight that he won't accept a job next year in Craig. So, here we are without a job for the upcoming school year, and no interview prospects. It was a hard decision to cut our financial throats by declining to exercise the leave of absence option, but remembering our family goals and possible opportunities for our soon to be adolescent daughters, it was the decision we needed to make.

My Mom continues to ask,"What will we do if Jim (nor I) doesn't get a job." We ask ourselves the same question. What will we do? In lighter moments we chuckle and say we'll be house guests of friends and family; stay a few weeks here, a few weeks there, and plan on staying with Andy and Laurie in Phoenix during the snow bird months of winter.

That is the plan during our lighter moments, when humor suffices. But in all seriousness, our plans are few and not promising. I wonder if this will be a time of change in our lives, leading us onto paths and through doors we would not have opted for if everything else had worked out as we wanted, planned, and thought we had desired.

The bottom line is that we both could probably get jobs in Mesa, Arizona. They continue to open new schools there each year. It would be the ideal climate; having a business in Alaska during the summer would chase us out of AZ during the hot summer months. I bet we'd have lots of visitors during the winter.

Well, the big news today is that this is our last night in the tent!! Tomorrow we stay at Trish and David's and the next night we'll either stay there again or in a motel. It's time to empty the truck of camping gear, making room for all the things that will make the exodus with us from Craig. We'll travel as light as possible up to Alaska, staying in motels and (God forbid) eating out for four days. EEEEEEKKK!!! I can't imagine. . hope Canada has lots of delis. Otherwise we'll do fresh fruit, crackers and cheese from grocery stores.

So many mixed emotions surrounding the end of the trip and declining our only job offer for next year.

May 19 **Bellingham, Washington**

Where to start? So many things to write about today. Foremost guess would be the job status. Two days ago I called Bob in Craig. There was a specific job offer, a 5/6 split teaching assignment. I declined. Jan and I talked about it quite a bit and decided that even though it felt like jumping off the high dive with no water in the pool (we expect it to be filled by the time we land) it was the right decision for our family.

Calling Marge tonight from a motel room in Bellingham, Washington, we got word of the first nibble from the Midwest. I made the first cut into a preliminary pool of 60 applicants for the North St. Paul district. I'll call them tomorrow to follow up on that. It feels good to finally have a tangible contact!

We spent last night at the home of David, Trish, and their five-year-old daughter Hanae in Seattle. We had met them in Capitol Reef National Park. It was a fun stay. Hanae is a very energetic, articulate child and our girls enjoyed her company. They played horses, logged lots of time swinging in the huge frontyard hammock, and practiced guerilla attacks on the adults as we sat on the porch talking over the remains of a great vegetarian lasagna. David is a filmmaker (one of his many and varied artistic endeavors) and we watched one of his early films, a very powerful documentary on Taiko, a traditional form of Japanese drum music. We enjoyed the evening very much.

The next morning, after waffles from scratch, we headed out for a full day of running around Seattle. The first and major task was cleaning out truckie and leaving as much stuff as possible in our Seattle storage unit. It took three hours, but Buck the Silver Truck rediscovered the spring in his step (it only lasted 25 minutes—we picked up 400 pounds of dog and cat food for our animal friends Magic and Toots, Tawanda and Bikini Man back in Craig). The girls did a great job of sorting through books, stuffed animals and toys.

Tomorrow we'll drive into Canada and begin the three-day, 1,000-mile push to the ferry in Prince Rupert. We stopped at a big, used book store today, so Kait and Jord are stocked with lots of books to read. Heeeeere we go!

May 22   Prince Rupert, British Columbia

Prince Rupert....we board the ferry tomorrow. I must be looking forward to the trip's end, as my spirits are high. Physically I'm feeling better, and I wonder if the seizure and ensuing dizzy spells were due to weight loss. I've lost 10 pounds since the middle of January and remembered, recently, a time years ago when I tried to lose weight and had a severe attack of nausea and dizziness.

I'm eating more often and I'm sure I've gained back a few of those pounds. I think that has helped me physically, but mentally I hope I don't put anymore back on.

The first whiff of sea air today enlivened my sense of smell, and I sniffed and sniffed until I remembered that kelpy, salty smell that was the ocean. The breeze was coming in from the water, so the air was thick with the smell that only the ocean can produce. I don't remember experiencing this while in the Port Townsend and Hood Canal area, but here in Prince Rupert we are less protected from the expanse of the Pacific. And still I didn't have that "oh, it's great being back" reaction. It's beautiful, I love the ocean, but I don't think it's right for us at this time. (And maybe I'm in denial of my feelings, holding them back, knowing that I won't be living here so I might as well not like it.) Not only is it not right for us, it's also unaffordable: you couldn't pay me to live in California, we can't pay what's needed to live in Washington or probably even Oregon. The Alaskan shorelines are remote enough and to our liking, but the housing is too high and the opportunities for the girls are too limited.

I'm not one to live "near" the ocean, I'd rather live on its shores or have its view out select windows. Why else bother? Of course, I can't afford to live on coastal shores. Others suggest to live in a place like Juneau or Ketchikan, where there ARE opportunities for the girls. But if I'm going to live in a city, it won't be where there is 160 inches or more rain annually. I'll live in a city where the sun shines and there are roads that lead away when I feel the need to go.

So maybe I do have the desire to live on the ocean and know I can't afford it financially and parentally, so I dampen (deny) and deaden my reaction when I smell that sea smell, and view the trees and water that are seldom separate sights here in the Northwest. For this part of the country is just that, oceans of forests, and an ocean of ever changing tides, waves, currents, and colors.

We've had two days of relatively hard driving, 450 miles to Quesnel, B.C. the first day and another 350 miles to Smithers yesterday. Since the night at Trish and David's in Seattle we've spent three nights in motels. We're on the road now, about 180 miles from Prince Rupert and the ferry that will take us back to Craig tomorrow.

I guess in some ways then this is the last day of Plan Z, our year on the road. It has been an extraordinary experience, a strong family time, a break from the expected and common.

There are several major themes that have run through this nine-month stretch since we closed the window at the Sub Marina last mid-September and stepped on the ferry heading south.

The first and foremost would have to be the quality of our family time. In "normal" circumstances, we would have seen each other only at the end of the work/school day and on weekends. This year the bulk of our "prime time" has been spent interacting with each other. We know each other very well, and the girls have strengthened their sibling bond, one that will last a lifetime. I think the time spent with our extended family around Christmas was especially warm. Jan and I have grown to appreciate family ties more than we did before.

The road school experience has been a high point for me. I've really enjoyed working with two bright and highly motivated students. We've accomplished a lot and I've been lucky enough as a parent to directly invest myself in my children's future. Their academic skills are very sound as they head into their upper elementary and middle school years, and the wide range of their firsthand experiences adds invaluable seasoning to their knowledge base and self-confidence.

Because of our limited budget we spent the majority of our nights in a tent and that meant that we had an intimate relationship with the forces and moods of Mother Nature. At times we struggled with wet or cold weather, especially in the fall as we headed down the west coast. Although we weathered two or three extended stretches of rain and snow in the spring phase of Z, we generally had better weather and more daylight.

As we travelled, I talked to lots of people about the violence in our society, in general, and specifically, in our schools. I have to admit that I was mistaken in my assumption that schools were holding their own and able to provide a safe environment for learning. Urban and rural areas across our travels appeared to be struggling with rising levels of violence. I saw towns and school systems that were able to establish safe zones, but it takes a concerted community effort and hands on involvement by parents.

Well, we're heading down Highway 16 in the beautiful Skeena River valley. Jerry Lee Lewis is rocking out and I'm checking out.

May 25   **Craig, Alaska**

We've arrived and my emotions are many and varied. It's great to see the people I love and care about, but the weather leaves a lot to be desired, for instance, the sun. I think we've made the right decision about not coming back here, but once again, we'll need to say goodbyes.

Gay has welcomed us with open arms, well as much as she could without being here. Our bedrooms were ready and freshly painted, our furniture (including Jim's and my bed) were strategically placed so that it looked like "home" to us, and there was milk in the frig for breakfast in the morning. The dogs, cats, and girls have become immediate friends and look forward each day to play time. It's great having a bathtub again, and all the amenities only a home provides, and Gay has done that for us.

I'm excited about opening the sub shop; it's such a fun place to be, making sandwiches, serving ice cream. The rhythm is driving and upbeat, when we are busy, and the clientele are always smiling. Being open only 13 weeks (11 this year) makes anything tolerable, doesn't it?

The first few days back, I played a game of hide and seek. I tried to go for walks, but could not avoid the people who wanted to stop and talk. (Not much exercise in doing that.) So, then I tried walking the logging road on cemetery island, and but still ran into people who wanted to hear about the trip.

My solution? Today I didn't walk. But throughout the day, running errands in an attempt to get the sub shop ready, I saw lots of people and am finally "here." Enough people have seen us and the rest will see us Saturday—opening day of the shop.

We've arrived, and in six weeks we'll leave, destination unknown.

June 4

Updates from Craig:

Portions of the ferry ride were a little rough, but we arrived in Hollis on time and drove to Craig. It felt good to be back. The first person we saw was Joni Kuntz. That was a good beginning I think.

The Sub Marina has been open for business for a week now. The weather has been cool, windy, and wet, and that has slowed things down, but we have money coming in for a change. The night before we were scheduled to open, the switch on the slicer shorted out and we had flames spouting, and the belts on the ice cream machine gave up the ghost. We were there until 10:00 jerry-rigging things to work. Jerry for sure. Jerry Carter gave us a switch that he had taken out of his airplane and that got the slicer back in the game, gimpy, but moving. Some belts, (not exactly the right size), got Taylor reluctantly turning out ice cream for us.

Gay has been great in welcoming us and sharing her living space. Jan and the girls have been doing clay art and having a ball. I'm going to clean the moss off Gay's shake roof and maybe split some wood. I like helping out when we're staying somewhere, and these are things that Gay would have difficulty doing for herself.

The job situation is puzzling. The first interview for North St. Paul was the only action I've had so far, but there was not a second interview, and no first interview anywhere else. I know I'm a good teacher and my letters of recommendation are excellent, so what is the problem? Age? Who knows? Maybe my teaching days are done. I'm ready for that, I think, but what comes afterwards? At this point the front runner appears to be a used book store. Again, time will tell.

Leaving Craig, Alaska one final time. Photo includes Dave Fischer, Brother.

July 16, 1994   Craig, Alaska
The big king salmon caught by Dave, netted by Janet and Mike
(Dave's son).

REFLECTIONS

Jordin:

Last year we went on a long trip where my mom and dad home schooled me; we called it Plan Z.

A few of my favorite places were the Grand Canyon, White Sands National Park, Carlsbad Caverns, the redwoods, and Bryce Canyon.

My most liked place was Carlsbad Caverns. To get to where the stuff was you had to go down half a mile. It was really scary. Luckily we went down an elevator.

When we got there, our tour guide took us all around. At one end of the cave was a bottomless pit. Really, it was at least 250 feet down. By that there were little puffs of rock droppings, they looked like popcorn balls. That is exactly what they're called.

Right now we live in a town called St. Peter. It's kind of small but it's nice. We live in an apartment.

I go to North School which has grades K, 4, 5, and 6. I'm in fourth grade, my sister is in sixth grade. I have lots of friends, so school is okay. My favorite part of school is science. My science teacher is Mrs. Nelson, she is really nice.

I'm also in gymnastics. We're working on handstands. It's really fun. I have eight kids in my class, including me. There are two teachers, Ann and Faith. Their gymnastics equipment stays up all the time.

Kaitlin:

I think Plan Z was fun. I enjoyed having mom and dad for my teachers. Some of my favorite spots were the San Diego Zoo, Sea World, Seattle, Anza-Borrego Desert, the cliff dwellings, and the Grand Canyon. In the spring we are going to hike down to the bottom and stay at a lodge. To get to the lodge you have to cross a suspension bridge over the Colorado River.

I like camping, but got kind of tired of it after nine months, especially when it rained or snowed. One night we got drenched. Not my idea of fun. The bugs were sometimes bad also.

We saw some pretty things like waterfalls, glaciers, and lots of wildlife. I enjoyed going to used book stores.

I like St. Peter very much. My teacher is Ms. Johnson. We have 24 kids in my class, and I have lots of friends; Kaitlin (spelled the same as me!), Amanda, Sarah, Alice, Marit, and Monica. I'm in choir and band; I play the clarinet and guitar. Dad is helping me with both. School is between 8:05 and 2:30.

At the apartment we live in, there is a basketball court, and I practice a lot. I'm also in Tae Kwon Do with mom, dad, and Jordin. It is fun.

I like watching the Gustavus Girl's Soccer team. I like St. Peter very much.

Janet:

Thirteen years ago I made a conscious decision to have children, and every day I make decisions that will benefit my daughters. Our move to St. Peter was one of those decisions, as was "Road School."

The year of Road School created a family bond that I don't think is possible within the structure of our society as it exists today. The family unit is together for a limited time daily, if at all. During our travels, we transcended the norm.

I'm content with the results of the journey, and know in my heart that we did it during ideal ages of the girls.

Our daughters now have a history that is unlike most children today. Their background is broad, they are very adaptable, and they know that "life" is much larger than their school or their town. Their concept of geography was developed in the best hands-on approach available, their student/teacher ratio could not have been better, and the skills they are bringing into the classroom this year enhance their chance for success.

I have no regrets.

Jim:

St. Peter, Minnesota, has now become home. The school system seems to be very strong, and Kaitlin (sixth grade), and Jordin (fourth grade) are both excelling. Kaitlin is taking clarinet lessons, and is a member of the choir. She can't wait for basketball to start and hopes to go out for softball. Jordin is taking Spanish and gymnastics. They are both involved in the Gifted and Talented Program.

I'm proud of the work we did while road schooling last year. Both girls are at or near the top of their class, and successfully meeting both academic and social challenges. They are making friendships that will last through their senior high school years.

This is still a period of transition for us. At present we're in an apartment and looking for the right home. Jan is working part time at Gustavus Adolphus College, while I'm working two part time jobs, one at the local photography studio, and the other as a factory laborer. The wages are all fairly low, but it pays the rent. We sold the Sub Marina just before leaving Alaska in July, and that has eased some of the financial pressure.

I was unable to find a teaching job. It seems that a 20 year veteran with a Master's Degree is an overpriced commodity. I'm ready to go onto something else, however, and continue to look through the want ads.

We're back in the Midwest, but we are definitely different people. The time in Alaska, and our nine months on the road presented many new vistas, challenges, and opportunities for growth. I feel good about the way we've met those challenges, and I'm optimistic about our future.

APPENDIX A

Proposed Road School Curriculum

I'm a licensed teacher in both Wisconsin and Alaska. This coming year will be my 20th year of teaching. Jan was previously licensed in Wisconsin and is current in Alaska. She has three years as a P.E. and health instructor, one year as an all-around substitute teacher, and a year as an adult racquetball instructor.

We are following a set curriculum in addition to the learning that will take place "on the road" to make sure that our girls will have no problems re-entering the public school system if we so wish.

We've filed a "school calendar" and proof of immunization with the State of Alaska Department of Education. I guess that makes us official.

1. Reading:

All four of us enjoy reading. We'll explore lending libraries, paperback exchanges, used book stores, and any other means of keeping us all supplied with reading material as the year goes on.

I would like to have a time to read out loud every night. We could explore the classics: *Tom Sawyer, Kidnapped, Treasure Island, Around the World in 80 Days*, etc.

I'm not sure what kind of reading log I want the girls to keep. At a minimum we should have them keep track of what books they read, with title and author. I'd like them to write a short summary of the plot, with maybe main characters and setting as well. The trick is to keep the emphasis on the joy of reading, and not let accountability get in the way.

We'll also be doing a lot of reading with newspapers, magazines, and brochures or exhibits for points of interest during our travels.

2. Math:

For a text, we'll use Scott Foresman's *Invitation to Mathematics*, both grades 3 and 5. I'll use it mainly as a course outline, however, and most of our math lessons will be one on one discussions with practice problems for them to do as a followup.

A priority will be for both Kaitlin and Jordin to be proficient with addition and multiplication flash cards. I feel the best way to do that is 5 minutes a day at least 5 days a week.

There will be math in a lot of our daily routines as well. Keeping track of mileage on the map, converting scale mileage, keeping track of mileage hiked on various trails, shopping totals as we fill the grocery cart, converting fractions in recipes as we cook, looking at daytime and night time temperature differences, and ratios as we sort accumulated treasures (black rocks to speckled rocks, shells to feathers, etc.).

3. English:

For a text, we'll use *World of Language* by Silver Burdett and Ginn. Again, this will be used as an outline of topics.

We'll use daily oral language exercises to give small daily doses of capitalization, punctuation and usage. Letter writing will be at least a weekly exercise in communication, with an emphasis on learning to use paragraphs.

We'll be learning a lot from the people we meet and the different environments that we explore. I plan to use these sources in conjunction with the reference sections of different public libraries to periodically have the girls (and us!) produce polished research reports highlighting a certain topic. This will provide a framework for using writing skills (brainstorming, seeking additional sources, organizing information, writing maps, rough draft, editing, and final draft.)

I'd like the girls to write journal entries giving their impressions of noteworthy places, people, or events. This will be another context for using paragraph and punctuation skills.

Spelling will need to be a weekly unit too. I think the best way to do this is to pull words from their writing. There should be a master word list that we keep on the computer for review. This should be made as fun as possible! We'll need to do cursive handwriting practice for both girls as well.

4. Science:

Science will be around us constantly as we travel. There will be organized themes such as classification of animals into vertebrates and invertebrates and then sub-classes. A looseleaf notebook would be good for this. We could do a short write-up on any new animals we encounter. Name, classification, size, diet, environment, means of protection, etc. We can also study different environments and how the parts of an environment (animals, plants, rocks, moisture, soil or sand) are all interdependent. I think there's a large telescope and observatory in Arizona. That would be a good focal point for a study of the universe.

We'll keep a log of questions that come up and try to answer them. That would be an ongoing folder that we can always update with additional questions or information.

The text will be Scott Foresman's *Science*. The world will be the laboratory.

5. Social Studies:

For a text we will use Heath's *The World Past to Present* and *The United States*. I think it would be fun to read parts of these books out loud and talk about them, maybe 15 minutes a day. We could keep a time line to visualize the progress of civilization and the development of the United States. We could put important dates on there (such as the dinosaur age, the land bridge, the ice ages, the civilizations of Mesopotamia, Egypt, Rome and Greece, the Middle Ages, the industrial revolution, the founding of the U.S., the invention of the airplane, the car, TV, and computers) to give an overall view of the scope of development of our history.

We'll visit factories, airports, trucking firms, etc. to get an idea how various goods are manufactured and shipped around our country. Why does a factory locate in a certain area (availability of raw goods, a dependable labor force, and shipping)? How do people make a living by specializing? How does it all hook together to keep our country running? It will be fun to tour Sysco Foods in Seattle, the supplier for Sub Marina.

I'd like to have us study and compare various Indian cultures as well. We are now living in the Northwest area. Wisconsin was the Woodland Indians' territory. On our way to Alaska we travelled through the Plains, and we will be heading to the land of the Southwest and maybe even Central American Indians. We would want to explore and compare housing, food, methods of protection, art, religion, transportation, etc.

6. Others:

Art should be an ongoing area of study. We'll be running into all kinds of artists along the way. The girls love producing their own art and Jan and I will be exploring beading and painting too.

We will continue our music, using this time together to reignite the energy we had going in Wisconsin. The girls will be more and more a part of this too with singing and rhythm instruments. Again, we should encounter musicians along the way. We'll share and learn. I think our music will open doors as we travel.

We've bought a set of Spanish language tapes and hope to learn some Spanish that we can use in our travels in the southwest or Mexico.

We plan to take our Macintosh™ computer along. Jan learned a lot last year. We'll all continue to explore and become more computer literate. It remains to be seen how easy this will be to carry along and set up on a daily basis.

For Physical Education we'll continue to develop skills in baseball, basketball, and swimming. Hiking will be a daily activity I would imagine. We should all be in great shape after a couple of months.

The real challenge for me as a teacher is to make this "school without walls" a vital, flexible and interesting venture for all. I've been in search of a meaningful teaching experience. The school district where I taught in Wisconsin had capable students and for the most part supportive parents, but choked me with paperwork. Alaska had a very innovative and human administration, but some real behavior problems in the group I worked with for two years. At this point I'm professionally numbed.

However, I have two interesting and interested students for next year and an open, mobile classroom. This is an optimal opportunity (O.O.!!!) I need to really clear my head of the past as far as both my experiences with kids and administrators, and also to approach this year of teaching in a new and fresh way. I would love to rediscover the joy of learning and teaching.

APPENDIX B
ROAD SCHOOL EXPENSES

Month	Income Art	Income Misc.	Food	Lodging Camping	Truck Repairs, Gas	Clothes Misc.	Medical	Laundry	Entertainment	Art Supplies	Camping	Books	Ferry Tolls
Sept		119.00	210.54	173.62	R297.93 G93.75	21.60	168.00	6.25	25.00	8.58	59.59		580.90
Oct			568.05	370.09	R134.45 G206.15	64.05	198.00	21.50	149.00		41.78	29.48	
Nov	16.00		406.29	223.44	R6.50 G186.75	148.17	168.00	10.50	69.94	151.77	5.04	41.61	1.50
Dec		87.00	266.57		R110.00 G123.70	336.36	248.00		47.25	32.09	53.24	11.40	
Jan			190.77		G170.05	152.45	338.00		130.90	11.00	8.00		11.60
Feb	85.60		382.16	330.10	R84.92 G141.51	54.07	168.00	9.50	70.77	73.90	68.71	6.20	
Mar	98.00		471.01	240.79	R110.71 G142.22	214.45	168.00	18.00	369.48	247.82	44.41	55.00	
Apr	125.00		502.67	456.75	R42.50 G182.89	13.45	168.00	14.75	42.07		21.56	30.67	
May	92.40		483.25	319.18	G175.00	362.12	224.46	10.00	24.81	28.35	12.15	31.16	7.00
Totals	417.00	501.00	3481.31	2113.97	R787.01 G1422.02	1366.72	1848.46	90.50	929.22	553.51	314.48	205.52	601.00

APPENDIX C

Lesson Plans

The next five pages are examples of Daily Lesson Plans that we actually used.

August 30, 1994—Day 1

Reading—20 minutes of reading on Grandma's bed. Kaitlin read *Jessie's Gold Medal*, a Baby Sitter's Club book. Jordin read *The Baby Sitter's Little Sister (Karen's Doll Hospital)*. At the end of the day we talked about them, stressing which character they felt was most like them and why.

Math—5 general math problems for each.

Language Arts (LA)/Writing—They each wrote about what it felt like to be staying at home when all the other kids were going back to school. I assigned Jordin to write at least 5 sentences and she wrote 6. I asked Kaitlin to write at least 8 and she wrote 12. We talked about the rough copy and changing or adding words to get it right. I read over their work and we talked about it.

August 31—Day 2

Reading—Each girl read for about 1 1/2 hours at the Sub Marina while I worked. Kaitlin read *Ready, Aim, Fire, the Adventures of Annie Oakley*. Jordin read *The Baby Sitter's Club (Kristy's Great Idea)*. Jordin and I talked about the characters and plot of her book.

Math—Some general problems for both. Kaitlin and I worked on multiplying a two-digit number by a one-digit, with carrying. Jordin and I worked on some one-digit dividing, with remainders. We mapped it out too. For instance in 7 divided by 3, we made 7 marks and circled groups of 3. That showed the answer of 2 groups with one left over. We also worked on estimating and graphing by counting the different colors in a Reese's Pieces™ package.

L.A./Writing—There was a dragline excavating next door to the Sub Shop. I had both girls write about it. Jordin used some of the rough copy/rewrite techniques that we talked about yesterday. Kaitlin did an excellent job of describing the dragline operator.

Science—We looked at the power lines coming from the pole into the Sub Marina building and looked at how the city would read the meter so they would know how much to charge us. The girls got a little bit of it, but we'll need to go over that again. This could be a nice lead into power usage in homes and businesses, where the power is generated, and the environmental impact of different methods.

Spelling—Kait asked about a spelling list. I told her that we'd start on that in a few days. I want to take each week's words from their writing. The trick is to do it in a way that won't make them self conscious about using new or uncertain words in their writing.

Penmanship—Both girls practiced capital letters in cursive today.

The girls and I are really excited about home schooling so far. I am enjoying teaching bright, motivated kids!! Kaitlin asked how we were able to do so much in such a short time and why it was so much FUN. Well, as I was walking home from the Sub Marina yesterday, I ran into two girls from my LAST class. They talked about how they only did about an hour's work (probably less productive than our first day), and how the teacher spent so much time talking about the rules. Home schooling one on one is so much more productive and humane.

September 1—Day 3

Reading—Both girls read this morning at home and this afternoon at the Sub Marina. They totalled about 2 hours of reading each. Jordin finished *If Wishes Were Horses*. We talked about it for a while this afternoon. She is really on a reading tear right now. She reads out loud with such expression. Kaitlin is reading in the journal that the Wuests sent us from Wisconsin.

Math—I gave the girls each 20 problems to copy and work out in their notebooks. I gave them each some problems that I thought would stretch them, and they both handled them with ease! Jordin worked on showing division with "stick pictures." That's the concept that we worked on yesterday. It should make math a more concrete concept. She also worked on multiplying two numbers by one, with some carrying. Kaitlin worked on adding with carrying more than once, subtracting with borrowing, and multiplying three numbers by one. Their computation skills are very accurate. They rarely miss one. Yesterday Kaitlin helped Jordin with division with remainders. That's a good experience for both of them.

LA—We went over story maps and brainstorming. I'm going to have them write about their time in Craig. We'll use this as a vehicle for talking about main ideas, details, and paragraphs. We didn't get to this until after dinner tonight because of our work schedule. School definitely goes better in the morning. This project is turning out to be about 4 or 5 days worth of work instead of the original 2 that I planned, but I think it will be a nice way for them to put a wrap on Craig and set down some memories while they're fresh.

Cursive—Jordin practiced her capital P's, R's, and Z's, problem letters from yesterday's practice. She is doing well.

An idea: do a comparative grocery price list in different cities. For example, the cost of a dozen eggs or a gallon of milk or a head of lettuce in Craig, Seattle, Salt Lake City or Tucumcari, New Mexico.

September 2—Day 4

Math—Jordin did 17 problems, dividing with stick pictures, borrowing, carrying twice, and multiplying 2 numbers by one, with no carrying. She also helped Jan for about an hour at COHO, checking figures in two manuals that required matching and sequencing. Kaitlin also did 17 problems, borrowing twice, multiplying two and even three numbers by one. She is also doing some pre-algebra, figuring out missing numbers. They are both doing some work on the times tables, one number by one number. We also did another Reese's Pieces™ check today. Although the number of different colors vary, the total has been 61 in a pack three days in a row!

LA—We did some excellent work on our story maps about our time in Craig. The paragraphs are school, ocean, friends, and home. They each listed details. Tomorrow we'll start talking about paragraphs.

Reading—Jordin read for about 2 hours today from *The Boxcar Children*. Kaitlin read for about 3 hours from *If Wishes Were Horses* and the Journal book. I started reading *If Wishes Were Horses* last night and Jordin and I started talking about that today.

September 3—Day 5

Reading—Each girl read for about two hours today.

Science—We started working on an experiment on bread mold today. This will be a vehicle for exploring the 5-step scientific method (question, hypothesis, experiment description, observations, conclusion) and the concepts of control and variable.

Math—Each girl did 15-20 problems continuing yesterday's concepts.

Penmanship—They did a row of each lower case. I went through the alphabet with Jordin to make sure that she was making the letters right. I remember several kids in my last class that made letters in very bizarre ways. The finished product looked right, but the method of making the letter looked really contorted. She only needed help on "f". We did it together about 5 times and she got it.

Extra—A man came to the Sub Marina looking for donations to help deaf and blind people. His calling card had a braille alphabet on the back. I had the girls write their names in braille code. I think I have a reading book that has a neat story on Louis Braille's life, a great story to read aloud and discuss on Monday.

Tomorrow is the last day of business for Sub Marina. That will swing home school into a different gear!

September 7—Day 6

Spelling—We started spelling today. I took 8 words for each girl from the writing they did last week. Today we broke the words into syllables (a new concept for Jordin but not for Kaitlin) and wrote each one 3 times.

Reading—I started reading aloud from *Black Gold*. We read one chapter. Kaitlin is reading *Canyons* by Gary Paulsen (a favorite author that we discovered during our time in AK.) Jordin is reading *James and the Giant Peach* by Roald Dahl, another favorite author. I'm reading a book about travel in Baja.

Science—We reviewed the questions from the experiment we started last week. Then we looked at the bread and updated our observations. I got hand magnifying glasses for the girls to see the mold up close and personal. They wrote down their observations and then we shared them. Good Job! They both noted the blue-green color and the "hairy" texture.

Language—We started our story of our time in Craig. We talked about the concept of a paragraph and indenting to mark the beginning of a new paragraph. We brainstormed our ideas on each subtopic, such as friends or ocean and borrowed a few ideas from each other. Then we started writing. Today we wrote an introductory paragraph about what we thought was the single most important aspect of our time here. We each picked the subtopic that we'll write about tomorrow. Jordin and I picked friends and Kaitlin picked home. This is going to be a major piece of work, but it should turn out real nice.

We also did Daily Oral Language (DOL from here on). I put one sentence with mistakes and omissions in their notebook and they recopy it with corrections in cursive. Math—This was not a major focus today. We spent a lot of energy in Language and Science. I gave each girl 15 problems reviewing concepts that we covered last week. I am going to need to continue to make this more individualized and flexible. I still tend to be the focus of the lesson (too much talking from me and not as much from them.) This will be a good learning tool for me as a teacher.

September 8—Day 7

Reading—I read aloud 2 chapters from *Black Gold*. As we're reading we talk about vocabulary and concepts, such as why characters do certain things and how the physical environment affects both the plot and the characters.

Art—While I was reading aloud the girls were drawing. This is something that they spontaneously started last night after the music concert at the City Gym, and wanted to continue this morning. Jordin is doing a drawing of three race horses and Kaitlin is drawing a dragon with three or four people fighting against it.

Spelling—We studied the words and I gave each girl a practice test orally. We are stressing syllables to break bigger words into shorter parts.

Language—We continued on the story map development today. After yesterday's introductory paragraph, Jordin wrote about friends and Kaitlin wrote about home. She really has the concept of paragraphs down. I had planned to have all the home activities as one paragraph, but after writing about Tricker, Kaitlin started on Plan Z and looked at me and said, "That sounds like a different idea, Dad. Shouldn't that be another paragraph?" So we fluidly skipped up to the next level and wrote several paragraphs out of one section of the story map. This part of the lesson worked well because I could do less talking and the girls were really working independently. I could give lots of individual attention and guidance.

We also did some D.O.L. What a great way to practice punctuation and capitalization in small bites. We wrote a short description of the musician, Paul Ruboff, who played last night's concert here in Craig.

I planned to read aloud the story of Louis Braille and do some work with the Braille cards that the girls have, but postponed that until tomorrow in favor of more beach time for the girls, as the sun broke through the clouds after yesterday's rain. We have so few days left here.

September 9—Day 8

Reading—I continued reading *Black Gold* out loud to the girls. We're really enjoying this. It's an excellent vehicle for developing vocabulary. I also read the story about Louis Braille today. We talked about the code and how it stood for the letters we read. I had them each pick one of their spelling words and write it in Braille, then I decoded it.

Language—We continued the story map about our time in Craig. They're doing a nice job, each writing their stories in their own way. Jordin needed to work on having the lines other than the first line of each paragraph start out at the margin line so that the indentation showed up. I worked on mine today too. It's a good idea to do some of these assignments with the kids. I felt like it was taking too long (same as the girls this morning!!!) and had to force myself to slow down and be thorough. We also did DOL today. We studied their spelling words too.

Math—Continued work on dividing with remainders, multiplication tables, multiplying 2 or more numbers by 1, missing addends, borrowing and carrying. Tomorrow we plan to go to Thompson House grocery and price some staple items. We'll then do the same in Seattle and maybe Phoenix as comparisons.

Science—We wrote observations for the mold experiment today. By skipping a day, the growth was visibly evident and really caught the girls' attention! We circled one patch of mold with a magic marker and measured it, using millimeters. We'll then have a method of tracking the rate of growth.

September 10—Day 9

Reading—We read out loud two chapters from *Black Gold*. It's getting to be a more complex plot than most kid's books. The main character really feels this impending sense of doom all the time. His personality contrasts with the personality of his horse, a real overachiever who has overcome physical limitations to become a winner.

LA—I decided to take a break from the story map today. I think it's best to be aware of pace and limitations when doing a longer writing assignment. If you want it to turn out to be better than average, you have to avoid making it drudgery. Instead we did the old alphabet shopping trip (I went shopping and bought an apple; I went shopping and bought a blue banana and an apple; etc). At first I wasn't sure that Jordin was up to it, and I almost bagged it rather than embarrass her, but she got the hang of it pretty quickly. As the rounds went on, the things we named got fancier and it led to a discussion of alliteration. What fun!!! We did DOL today. It is always written in cursive now. We went through our spelling words too.

Math—We did a few problems of review today. In addition we went on a consumer shopping trip to the grocery store. We're going to note the prices of some food items and then do the same activity in other towns to compare prices. This will lead to a discussion of shipping costs and the effects of monopoly and competition.

September 13—Day 10

Reading—Kaitlin was reading from the *Reader's Digest* and *Best Horse Stories*.

Math—Some review problems and began our time on the "punch board," practicing the times tables.

LA—DOL and some further work on the story map. The girls are really getting the concept of paragraphs, one of the main writing concepts we will be working with this year. They also gave each other spelling tests and both scored 100.

Science—Finished up our mold experiment today! Wow!! Furry green buns, totally covered with mold!!!! Fun!

ORDER FORM

Now you can hear their music!!!

Jim and Janet, the **ROAD SCHOOL** parents,
are also the Sunset Highway Band,
and have recorded ten original songs
on cassette entitled:

"Dreaming' Again"

Send this order form today to receive your copy of
"Dreamin' Again" for just $10.00 (includes shipping)

Name:_____

Street:_____

City, State, Zip:_____

Phone:_____

Please enclosed $10.00 in check or money order and
send to:

Marousis/ DeMars
PO Box 383
St. Peter MN 56082

Please allow 4-6 weeks for delivery.

ORDER FORM

To order more books from Blue Bird Publishing, use this handy order form. To receive a free catalog of all of the current titles, please send business size SASE to address below.

_____ *Road School*	$12.95
_____ *The O.J. Syndrome*	$11.95
_____ *Parent's Solution to a Problem Child*	$11.95
_____ *Home Schools: An Alternative* (3rd Edition)	$11.95
_____ *Home Education Resource Guide* (3rd Ed.)	$11.95
_____ *Home Business Resource Guide*	$11.95
_____ *Dr. Christman's Learn-to-Read Book*	$15.95
_____ *Expanding Your Child's Horizons*	$12.95
_____ *They Reached for the Stars!*	$11.95
_____ *Parents' Guide to Helping Kids Become "A" Students*	$11.95
_____ *The Survival Guide to Step-Parenting*	$11.95
_____ *Under Two Heavens*	$14.95

Shipping Charges: $2.50 for first book.
Add 50 cents for each additional book.
Total charges for books:_____
Total shipping charges:_____
TOTAL ENCLOSED:_____
NAME:_____
ADDRESS:_____
CITY, STATE, ZIP:_____
Telephone #: _____
For credit card order,
        card#:_____
Expiration date:_____

Send mail order to:
BLUE BIRD PUBLISHING
1739 East Broadway #306
Tempe AZ 85282
(602) 968-4088 (602) 831-6063